Not That Anyone Asked

Not That Anyone Asked

An Autobiography and Essays by a Child of the 60s and 70s

Steven E. Yates

Copyright © 2017 Steven Yates

Published by Kingston House Publishing

All rights reserved. No part of this publication may be reproduced, stored in a retrieval system or transmitted, in any form, or by any means, electronic, mechanical, recorded, photocopied, or otherwise, without the prior written permission of both the copyright owner and the above publisher of this book, except by a reviewer who may quote brief passages in a review.

The scanning, uploading, and distribution of this book via the Internet or via any other means without the permission of the publisher is illegal and punishable by law. Please purchase only authorized electronic editions and do not participate in or encourage electronic piracy of copyrightable materials. Your support of the author's rights is appreciated.

Designed by Vince Pannullo
Printed in the United States of America
by RJ Communications.

ISBN: 978-0-578-19866-8

Contents

Acknowledgments 9
Preface 11
Introduction 13

PART ONE: TALL COTTON

Chapter 1: Escobas 21
Chapter 2: West Columbia 25
Chapter 3: Bellaire 31
Chapter 4: El Campo 39
Chapter 5: Corpus Christi 45
Chapter 6: Houston 51
Chapter 7: New Canaan (first time) 55
Chapter 8: London 59
Chapter 9: New Canaan (second time) 71
Chapter 10: UConn - Terra Incognita 77
Chapter 11: Dog Lake 93
Chapter 12: Paradis 101

PART TWO: MY BRILLIANT "CAREER" OR LESSONS FROM THE "GOTCHAS"

Chapter 13: Comtech (December 1983 -
    April 1985) 111
Chapter 14: Simutronics (May 1985 -
    September 1988) 117

Chapter 15: Continental E&C
　(September 1988 - December 1990) 133
Chapter 16: Ajax (January 1991 - July 1994) 141
Chapter 17: Tri-Town WWTP
　(August 1994 - December 1994) 155
Chapter 18: SYNTECH
　(January 1995 - March 1999) 165
Chapter 19: The SWA
　(March 1999 - June 30, 2011)............................197
Chapter 20: "Career" Epilog....................................207

PART THREE: ESSAYS

Ghosts of Slidell..215
　Meemaw..215
　Pawpaw 223
　Nona..230
　Pops 234
　Mom and Dad..242
　They're Right Here 242
　Boy Scout..244
　The Last Lesson...248
　Lost and Found..253
　Eulogy 259

And the Rest..263
　Odd Job...263
　The Far-Out Club and Mr. Ruszczyk 275
　Different and the Same.......................................282

Luigi 300
Finding the Abbey 303
A Miracle at St. Barbara 311
Scary Stories 313
Walter Schalk School of the Dance 318
Happy Birthday to Me 326
Memory and the Blessing of Forgetting 332
Why I Hate Bob Guccione 338
The End of Gone Forever 342
A Natural Supply of Things to Use 349
The Honeymooners 359
Less Is More 370
Pseudoscience 378
Fighting the Last War 385
Man About Church 393
Go Out and Play 404
Getting My First Hug Update 420

Acknowledgments

I dedicate this book to my wife. Your love humbles and inspires me. And to my heroes, my dad and my son. The more I can emulate their best attributes, the more I'll be the man I want to be. And to my wonderful daughter, a fine writer herself, for the edits, suggestions, support, and love.

To drop a few names, thanks to Tig Notaro, Kyle Dunnigan and David Huntsberger for having me on the *Professor Blastoff* podcast three times. Thanks to Jason Sklar and Randy Sklar for the friendship, kindness, laughs, and encouragement you have given me. Thanks to Daniel Van Kirk for your friendship, insight and encouragement. Thanks to Larry Miller for featuring my first book on his podcast and saying such nice things about it. Thanks to Frank Conniff for being so funny and unique. Thanks to my musical muses, Eddie Arjun Peters and Matt Backer. Every time I shake your hand, I hope some of your extraordinary talent will rub off on me.

And special thanks to Stephen Tobolowsky for the wonderful feedback, friendship, and respect. I hope my emulation of your style is always more *homage* than plagiarism.

These and other talented performers have given me a taste of the show-biz life I've dreamed of, but wasn't cut out for. Their friendship and generosity have made me feel part of it and I am forever grateful.

Preface

I have these stories in my head. From my earliest memory, I have played episodes of my life over and over in my mind. I find myself telling certain stories of those episodes again and again. My wife and close friends have heard some of my stories often enough that they can probably tell them better than I can. These stories tell, at least in part, the story of my life, why I think the way I do, and why I believe in some things but not others. So, wanting to get these stories out of my head, not that anyone asked, I began the project that resulted in this book.

Since many of the stories formed my autobiography, I arranged them chronologically to tell that larger tale in the first two parts of the book. But I found there were stories about my parents and grandparents, for instance, that didn't fit into the chronology. I wanted to tell you about them all at once, not a little bit at a time. So I put those in the third part of the book with several other essays.

Mostly absent from this book are stories about my two wonderful sisters, my amazing wife and our son and daughter. I choose to let them tell or not tell their own stories. My wife is the most important person in my life. She is also a very private person. Likewise my in-laws are lovely, special people whose stories are not really mine to tell. I have omitted lots of friends who are very important to me. I hope their feelings are not hurt by this. The editor in me is a heartless, cold-blooded tyrant.

I have tried not to grind old axes in the telling of my stories because those people are not able to present their side of the stories. The first drafts of some stories were filled with unresolved anger and resentment. It was an unexpected, beneficial side-effect that I developed a more balanced and understanding view of myself and others as I revised and rewrote. Nonetheless, to be on the safe side, I have changed the names of the companies I worked for and any people who might take offense.

Why should anyone who doesn't know me read this book? For one thing, I hope it is entertaining. There are some funny, touching, human stories you may relate to. For another, it may present some insight into the mind of the middle-aged, white, American male (MAWAM). MAWAMs are often portrayed as misogynistic, racist, out-of-touch idiots who are responsible for all the world's ills. I hope that's not who I am. I don't think I have any hate in my heart, but I know I'm not perfect. Judge for yourself after you read what follows.

Introduction

WHEN I published my first book, "Getting My First Hug", in 2013 my self-publisher's rep told me that it could find a large readership as autism was a topic of growing public interest. I have been gratified by the book's reception and the impact that readers have told me it had on them. That book was easy to write. I was brimming over with the story of our son and his remarkable rise and triumphs following his diagnosis. I continue to spend significant time and effort publicizing that book in order to get it into the hands of people who may benefit from its message of hope.

Shortly after that book was published, I started writing other stories that had been rattling around in my head. With my retirement from engineering in 2011, I had time to look back at my life and think about many events that I had simply lived through. I tried to account for how I had spent over a half-century. I found I needed to forgive myself as much or more than I had to forgive others in my life story. Everyone, including me, was just trying to live life. We all make mistakes.

I thought about the times I had escorted my mother to her high school class reunions. Sitting at the table with the Slidell High School Class of 1951, it struck me that they all seemed to like each other. In spite of all the years that had passed, I could still tell which ones had been the nerds, the jocks, the popular kids, the brains, and so on. I imagined them sitting at separate tables back then, divided by cliques. And yet here, sixty years later, they were all friends. All the old grudges were long forgiven and the labels forgotten. I wanted that for myself.

Forgiving others was easier, it turned out, than forgiving myself. But eventually, I began to make progress on both. And so I hope that is reflected in what follows.

Part One

Tall Cotton

I had just arrived at the Paradis Gas Processing Plant in Louisiana, south of New Orleans. My dad had set up a summer job for me there between semesters of college. He was an executive at Texaco. When I arrived for my first day there, I was greeted by the plant manager who was a friendly fellow, younger than I thought he would be.

He leaned back in his big chair and said, " I understand that you come from some tall cotton."

The blank look on my face told him I was unfamiliar with the expression.

"Your daddy is a big wheel," he said. I smiled sheepishly and nodded. "I've been told you want to make your own way. That's very admirable." He paused and added, "But it would be OK if you put in a good word for me with him."

I guess I do come from "tall cotton". And I'm not just referring to my dad, who worked his way up from his own summer job as a field roustabout to Senior Vice President of a major multi-national oil company. As easy and charmed a life as I have had, my story starts with two families who had it a good bit harder.

*****

Slidell, Louisiana is a suburb of New Orleans located across the northern part of Lake Ponchartrain from the Big Easy. Both my parents were brought up there. Those were tough times for the Yates and Levy families. But, like the rest of the country, mired in the depths of The Great Depression, they did what they could to get by.

My mom's early life was especially hard. Her father died when she was five and she was shipped off to live with relatives. Her mother made what living she could playing piano in bars and restaurants, eventually remarrying and having another daughter. I don't think my mother ever really felt she fit in with that new family, as much as she loved her younger sister and as friendly a relationship as she had with her step-father. Mom focused on her studies and graduated *cum laude* from Slidell High. Her life really began when she fell in love with my dad in those high school years.

Dad was born in his family's home in Slidell. In addition to my dad and his parents, his mother's parents were part of the picture. Grandma Sollberger lived with them. Grandpa Sollberger split his time between Slidell and his "artist's apartment" in the heart of New Orlean's French Quarter at the corner of Toulouse and Royal. Oh, and he had a mistress who was part of the family too somehow. I've never gotten a lot of details about how that all worked. I guess when it's your family and it's just the world you grew up in, maybe you assumed everyone's family was like that.

Dad was, by all accounts, the apple of everyone's eye. He was "the golden child" and although they were not wealthy, he was spoiled as much as they could afford to spoil him. He had a dog and a goat (named Billy, of course) and lived a Huck Finn boyhood playing in the woods, fishing with his dad, being a Boy Scout and the All-American boy. When he was ten, he got a baby sister. She and a half-dozen female cousins her age idolized my dad, who would entertain them on long summer days flying kites higher than they thought possible and buying them ice cream.

And I wouldn't be here, wouldn't be writing any of this, if it weren't for a pair of surplus trombones. The band director at Slidell High had two extra trombones that ended up being assigned to Jo Ellen Levy and Elton Yates. And the rest was, as they say, history. Love blossomed for the two budding trombonists as they learned to play and marched at the football games and town parades. They were each other's one and only. A love like theirs is usually found only in movies, songs, and fairy tales.

*****

Digression - Years later, as I was about to become engaged to my wife, she and I went out to lunch with my parents. We ate at a little sandwich place and afterward, as we were walking to the car, she grabbed my arm and said, "Oh my God, your parents are amazing!"

"They are? What are you talking about?" I responded, bewildered.

"You didn't notice? You didn't see? They were holding hands the whole time! Your dad hugged her while we were waiting for a table and he kissed her while we were waiting for our food!" She was truly impressed.

"Yeah, so what? They do that all the time. It's not like they're making out. It's just a little affection. Don't your parents do that?" I asked.

"Oh, no! I mean, not like that. Not just all the time, for no reason. It's so cute!" she gushed.

It had never impressed me because I had seen it every day of my life. My parents were in love with each other. I thought everybody's parents were in love with each other. I had never given it a thought.

And maybe I should apologize to my readers. I grew up in a *Leave It to Beaver* household with *Ozzie and Harriett* parents who rarely disagreed, never fought, and who taught their kids, by their example, how married people behaved. I've since learned that what I grew up with was not universal and is becoming, sadly, increasingly rare. It's no wonder I look back on my childhood with such nostalgia. - End of digression

*****

Mom was two years older than Dad. She went off to

college and got a teaching degree and was working to help support the family while he finished his petroleum engineering degree at LSU. They were each the first in their families to go to college. My older sister was born in Baton Rouge before Dad had even graduated.

But graduate he did and he was soon employed in the booming oil business of the mid-1950s. The family was assigned to what was euphemistically referred to as the "oil patch" in Texas. Family lore includes the story of my dad crying on the phone to his parents about the God-forsaken place to which he had moved his young family. They told him to persevere in that way that people who had lived through two World Wars and the Great Depression did. In time, Mom and Dad found a way to get by. My second sister came along shortly thereafter.

Dad's career had already advanced from the field "roustabout" and "roughneck" jobs he had worked during summers in college. Each bump up the company ladder meant moving the family to another little oil town.

1

Escobas

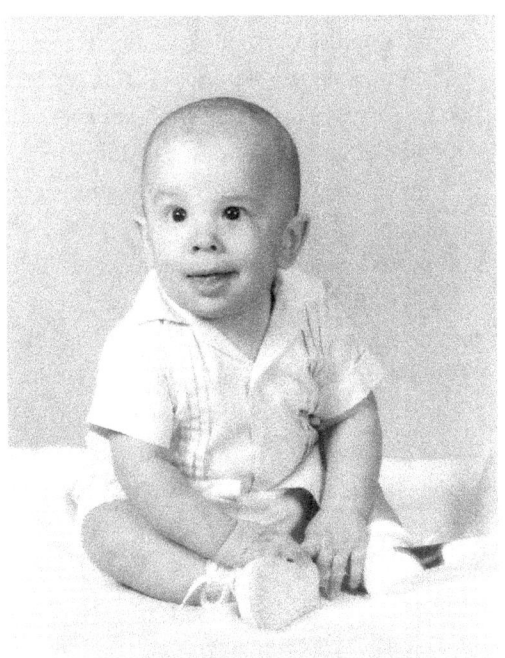

ESCOBAS, Texas is a little oil town about twenty miles from the Mexican border. I understand the population today is about 25. The land around Escobas looks a lot like where the Road Runner and Wile E. Coyote live. Outside of "downtown Escobas" is a collection of a half-dozen bare-bone houses that were built in the 1940s to house employees of the Texas Company, later to be known as Texaco. One of these little houses was where I was born. Well, in truth, I was born sixty miles away in Brooks County Hospital in Falfurias, Texas on December 30, 1959. My mother made the trip on that day because the one OB/GYN in the area was leaving for a vacation on New Year's Day.

That little house was already home to my mom and dad and two sisters. Dad was a Field Engineer whose job involved ranging over miles of desert to oil wells and pumping stations to increase and maintain the flow of oil and gas to the pipelines that fed the upstate refineries and gas processing plants. It was difficult work in tough conditions. Midday temperatures above 100 degrees are common in the summer. Scorpions and rattlesnakes were ever-present. Dad would often find numerous rattlers draped over the pipes at wells where he needed to take readings. He carried a piece of pipe with a large nut on one end to club the snakes so he could get to the meters to log the production data. He would toss the dead snakes in the back of the company pickup as he made his rounds. He was twenty-four then.

Digression - I have an old Q-Tip box with a half-dozen rattles in it that he kept as a souvenir of one night's work. Also in the box are two photographs showing over a dozen dead rattlesnakes laid out in neat rows. No lie. - End of digression.

My mom's life in those days was just as tough. Raising a four year old, a two year old and a newborn in lonely, primitive conditions far from anything resembling civilization probably made the backwater Louisiana towns she grew up in look glamorous. Family lore tells of the time Mom found that a blue indigo snake (non-poisonous) had taken up residence in our washing shed. A crew of oil field hands was called and removed the snake that measured just short of nine feet long.

Mom was totally devoted to Dad and would have followed him to Hades if Texaco had oil operations there. So it was a combination of Dad's intelligence, work ethic, motivation to improve his family's situation, good timing, and luck that allowed him to quickly rise through Texaco's ranks in the early 1960s.

This was a time when the American dream was alive and kicking for young families like ours. The Interstate Highway System was still under construction, Detroit was churning out new models of giant land-yacht cars each year, and American oil companies were pumping the fuel to make it all go. Oil men were folk heroes in Texas and beyond. Some "wildcatters" were legends for their risk-taking and go-for-broke gambling to bring in wells. The Texas prairie, ranch land, and farms were dotted with little fenced-in enclosures housing wells and pumping stations. Many a Texas landowner was enriched by speculators who bought the mineral rights to their otherwise marginally profitable scrubland.

This was a time of endless optimism in America. Kennedy's Camelot was in full swing, the space race was on and, color TV was all but unknown. Most Americans respected and trusted their elected officials, believed in their system of justice, and thought that our hard work and technology would keep us on top forever. There was prayer in school and it seemed that Norman Rockwell and Walt Disney were accurately portraying how America was and would always be.

True, the civil rights movement was grinding against widespread segregation. Women's rights weren't even spoken about in the mainstream. Vietnam was festering and the Cold

War was well under way. But much of America was insulated from these things. And for a child growing up in a loving family in little Texas oil towns, these were the golden times.

In the front yard of our little house was a "rocking horse" oil pumping rig that I'm told I used to watch endlessly between naps. I have a photo of it. I can still picture its endless, slow up and down. I was too young to remember when Dad was promoted and transferred from Escobas to Liberty, Texas for a year and then promoted and transferred again to West Columbia, Texas.

2

West Columbia

MY earliest memory is from June 1963. I took a car trip with my dad from West Columbia, Texas to Slidell, Louisiana to see my aunt Linda's high school graduation. My grandfather was Superintendent of Schools. He gave the commencement speech and handed Linda her diploma. Dad and I sat in the rickety high school football field grandstands and I watched the bugs flit around the stadium lights. It seems odd that he would have made such a long car trip with so young a child, but it was a chance to show off the "little man" who would carry on the family name.

The next memory I have is of being inside the little house we rented at 212 South Ringold Street in West Columbia. I remember a mood of sadness and the TV being on. There was a lot of talking and I remember being told that the president had been killed. That must have been November 22.

I remember the toys I got for Christmas a month later. They were mostly "war toys" for playing soldier. This was not at all unusual and was considered perfectly appropriate in those days. I also got a coonskin cap, a Golden Book about Davey Crockett and toy replica of "Old Betsy", Davey's musket. I have vivid memories of my fourth birthday a week later. I got a flashlight and a helicopter that really flew. It was tethered to the control unit that held two or three D-cell batteries. I wasn't supposed to fly it in the house, but I did.

I cherish the little snippets of memories I have from those days. It was another epoch in American life. I remember my mom was always in the kitchen cooking for us when she wasn't driving me or my sisters to various activities. My dad worked in the oil field and drove a company car. He was never too tired to play with me and never lost patience as he tried to teach me to throw and catch a baseball. My sisters shared a room and went to school. They were Brownies, and then Girl Scouts.

I attended a nursery school down the block run by Mrs. McCain. She was pretty and kind and had a million activities to occupy our time and teach us skills like cutting, pasting, and drawing. She had a playground in her backyard that provided us a place to burn off the sugar from the Moon Pies and Hi-C she fed us.

Mrs. McCain had a son and two daughters who were older. Her daughters' room was papered with pictures cut out from Beatles fan magazines. They played "Twist and Shout" and "I Wanna Hold Your Hand" 45s on a record player in their room. My sisters spent hours listening to those songs with them. They had Beatle trading cards that smelled like the bubble gum that came in the packs with them. I didn't like the smell and so I would drift away from the Beatles shrine and watch "The Adventures of Superman" live-action TV show with the McCain's son.

That year, the West Columbia Labor Day parade featured four boys from the high school on a float. They wore "mop-top" fright wigs and lip-synced to Beatles' tunes. I remember getting haircuts at the barber shop, using the booster seat. I would look down and see my dad proudly watching as the barber shellacked down my cowlick with Brylcreem, or was it Vitalis? I usually got a lollipop afterward. And I remember the ice cream truck that used to appear out of nowhere on hot summer afternoons and come down our street with its bell ringing.

One day I missed the ice cream truck for some reason and I remember crying uncontrollably as my dad arrived home from work. He scooped me up and plopped me beside him in his dusty company car. Off we went to find the ice cream truck. I can see my dad now with his black, thick-framed glasses and black, flat-top crewcut. We drove for what seemed like a long time and finally caught up with the ice cream truck on a dirt road way out of town. I have no idea how Dad knew where it would be. He flagged down the truck and got us each an ice cream and we sat on the hood of his car and ate them as the big Texas sun sank in the late afternoon sky. We were in the middle of an enormous farm with fields stretching out to the horizon in every direction. It seemed like we were the only two people on earth, but that was OK by me. I loved my dad and felt so safe and so happy. I knew that he could do anything. He could make anything right. And he would always be there for me.

Mom used to wake up early to make him bacon and eggs for breakfast every morning. I didn't know it then but we were on a tight budget. The few luxuries we had were almost all to benefit the children. Mom taught English and math at the local high school. I guess that's why I was at the nursery school. It was my daycare. We went to church every Sunday. And I thought everyone lived just the same way we did. It was a cozy, safe little world.

One afternoon I was playing in our front yard. I was not allowed to cross the street. There was a little boy my age playing in his front yard across the street. Eventually, we noticed each other. We stood staring at each other until one of us shouted a hello at the other. I remember we each walked to the curb on our respective sides of the street. We each sat, elbows on knees, chin in hands and shouted back and forth to each other across Ringold Street. His name was Kyle Matthews. His dad was the new high school football coach. He wasn't allowed to cross the street either. So there we were. Eventually, our mothers noticed us out there and we were granted the privilege of crossing the street to actually become friends. Kyle joined the nursery school and we would walk down the block to the McCain's house together each morning.

As I said, Dad got bacon and eggs for breakfast. My sisters and I got cold cereal. That was fine with me until one day. I had eaten my Cheerios and walked across the street to get Kyle but he wasn't ready yet. As I sat watching Captain Kangaroo in the Matthews' den, Kyle's mother asked me if I would like sausage and fried eggs. I told her I had never had sausage and fried eggs. She directed me to a place at their table. And they were delicious! So, from that day until my mom figured out what I was doing, about six months later, I got two breakfasts every morning!

Kyle and I were best friends. We played cowboys and army and just ran around. He was an only child and I had two sisters, so we bonded over guy stuff like football and catching bugs and avoiding girl-germs and cooties. It was nice to have a friend. As a little boy, our neighborhood was a fun place to explore. There were long stretches of sidewalk for riding my tricycle. We had a big swingset that my dad had made out of salvaged oilfield pipes. I had plenty of toys and some neighborhood friends to play with. Endless days that all seemed like summer to me stretched as far as I could see into the future. I heard talk of "grade school" from my sisters. But mostly there was just running around and playing, drinking water from neighbors' garden hoses, and staying out until Mom or Dad called us home to eat, wash up and go to bed.

One day, Dad came home from work and announced that he had been promoted and that we would be moving. I came to understand that "being promoted" was a good thing and I had no conception of what "moving" entailed. So I was all for it! My sisters cried for some reason. They were upset about moving away from friends and having to go to a different school. This sequence of events would become a recurring pattern in our family life for the next decade and beyond.

3

Bellaire

THE big moving van pulled into our driveway and we were moving to Bellaire, Texas, a city completely surrounded by the city of Houston. My folks rented a little house there. It was near the elementary school and around the block from the brand new Texaco building where Dad worked. In fact, it was possible to cross the street and walk (or ride a tricycle) on the sidewalk all the way around to the parking lot of that ten-story "skyscraper". And I remember doing just that a number of times. Mom would tell me when to take off on the sojourn and I would make my way around the block. The cement sidewalk was smooth and new and seemed to stretch for miles before me. I left my trike at the door and walked into the steel and glass palace and up to the receptionist's desk. I asked for Mr. Yates and was sent up to the eighth floor. There my dad was waiting as the elevator doors opened. He would greet me and take me around to say hello to his co-workers. Then he would sit me in the customer chair beside his desk as he tidied up and packed his briefcase. We took the elevator back down to the street, or rather the sidewalk, and he walked beside me as I pedaled home. He would ask what I had done that day. He was interested to know the progress of the highway I was building in our garden with my Tonka trucks and road grader.

I had my first day of school in Bellaire. I remember

packing a cigar box with crayons, scissors and pencils. I carried it along the same route I took to Dad's office, crossing a busy street with my sisters to get to the school. Miss Rheinhart was a kindly, grandmotherly lady who supervised my class. We did finger-painting, drawing, practiced an "air raid drill", and had nap time on plastic foam mats on the floor of the austere, concrete building.

The only other thing I remember about kindergarten was the little dance we did for parents' night. Each of us boys was matched up with a female classmate and taught a little dance that used a decorated bushel basket as a prop. The theme was "Peter, Peter, Pumpkin-Eater" and the dance ended with the boys stuffing the girls down into the bushel basket.

The other strong memory I have about that time was the debut of a certain television show - *Batman*. I had just turned six years old when the series debuted on January 12, 1966. It made a huge impression on me. Color TV was still relatively new and this series was all about color. I remember the promos that aired before the series debut. The hype and build-up were huge, especially for those days. The show came on twice a week, Wednesday and Thursday nights at 6:30 CST.

It's hard to explain to a young person today how different this TV series was from everything that came before it. Although, like Bugs Bunny cartoons, it can be appreciated on a higher level by adults, it really seemed to be aimed at kids in a way that prime time TV series really hadn't been up until then. Yes, there were family shows like the *The Wonderful World of Disney*, but *Batman* was for kids who maybe still believed in Santa, who wanted to cheer for a hero, who dreamed of a world filled with amazing gadgets, of good guys who struggled, but always beat the bad guys and the gorgeous ladies who admired them. I guess today's Disney movies with their merchandising and video releases that allow endless viewing over and over provide the same kind of immersive experience, but to me this was life-changing.

I remember literally dreaming about visiting the Bat-cave and seeing all the crime-fighting tools, the Batmobile, and even areas not shown in the show, like where the heroes' costumes would be instantly donned, as if by magic. I saw a toy Batman utility belt on sale at a department store but was unable to persuade my mom to buy it for me. I so wanted to be part of Batman's TV world. I bought my first comic books in hopes of having that world available to me whenever I opened them. Even though I was not yet learning to read, the artwork was captivating. Miss Rheinhart warned us against the show as being too violent. I can only wonder what she would say about today's fare.

The other thing I remember about our two years in Bellaire was our church. Saint Andrew's Presbyterian Church was a big part of our family's life. I was too young to understand much of the theology, but my sisters and I were in the youth choir. Mrs. Warren was the director. She used to put a dot of red lipstick on the tip of her nose and tell the children to keep their eyes on the spot. That was her way of keeping our limited attention focused on her as she directed us. And it worked. Our family was close friends with the pastor and his young family. We spent a lot of time there attending not only services, but also "covered dish suppers", and just playing. The church building seemed enormous with interconnecting rooms that seemed like "secret passageways".

I attended a summer "Vacation Bible School" at the church, the sole remaining product of which is a ceramic cast of my right handprint. It survives to this day and seems to me to hold an almost mystical power. A sense of stepping out of the timestream comes over me when I look at the small, shallow indentation that I remember making so long ago. I don't have huge hands now, but when I unconsciously hold my hand up to the tiny, white disc, I'm strangely troubled by the ease with which so many years, more than fifty, have slipped away transforming that little hand into the hands that write these words. I wonder why that is? There just aren't that many tangible artifacts that illustrate the metamorphosis of a little boy turning into a man. The handprint is a haunting impression that testifies that I was once a little boy. My memories, though dreamlike after all these years, are not dreams.

Right across the street from the church was television station KTRK, Houston's ABC affiliate. The pastor's kids, my sisters, and I all watched a taping or two of the local afternoon kiddie show, *Kiterick's Carousel*. The titular Kiterick was a woman dressed in a black leotard and black hood with ears, wearing cat's whiskers. She introduced cartoons and little puppet shows and would interview lucky studio audience members who were chosen to ride a small carousel. Although we never made it onto the carousel, we actually got to see ourselves, albeit for an instant, on TV! Oh, it was a modern marvel, but not the most amazing one I recall from those days. That distinction goes to another indelible memory.

One Saturday night the pastor and my dad loaded all us kids into a station wagon and hauled us to the newly completed Domed Stadium. Over what seemed like many years we had watched construction on a vacant expanse adjacent to old Colts Park, where the Houston Colt .45s major league baseball team played, slowly rise to become what they called the Eighth Wonder of the World, the Domed Stadium, later known as the Astrodome. The first-of-its-kind indoor ballpark addressed the two major problems associated with watching major league baseball in Houston in the summer: the insane heat and the swarming mosquitos. The Colts were renamed the Astros in recognition of NASA's Mission Control Space Center located nearby. And it was in this spirit that a stunt was conceived that is the stuff of Houston legend. And I was there. The vast Astrodome outfield was a pitcher's dream. It was where base hits went to die and yielded many low scoring games that bored a six-year-old like me to sleep, especially during night games like the one the pastor's family and ours were at.

Then, at the seventh-inning stretch something amazing happened. My dad made sure we were all awake to see it. A lone man walked from the Astros dugout to the pitcher's mound. The crowd fell into a hushed silence. Then there was a deafening roar like I had never heard and the man jetted up to almost the tip-top of the Astrodome's ceiling. He swayed to one side and circled high above the crowd, his jetpack roaring the whole time. He completed one circuit of the capacious stadium and gently lowered himself right back onto the pitcher's mound, shutting off the jetpack. There was a second of silence, then the crowd exploded in cheers. It was as if there was an unspoken promise of a jetpack for each of us, we were so excited.

The game resumed and before long the kids were dozing again and I believe we left before the game itself ended. That night I dreamt of the places I would go and the things I would explore with my jetpack.

The last thing I remember about Bellaire was my Little

League tryout. Since I had been able to wear a glove I remember my dad and me tossing a ball back and forth. I remember missing most of my catches and making Dad run a lot to field my errant throws. Suddenly, one day he loaded me in the car and we went to a baseball diamond that was a beehive of activity. There were crowds of parents here, bunches of boys there. I heard the crack of bats hitting balls, saw pop flies soaring into the high Texas sky, and watched grounders being scooped up effortlessly by big kids and rifled over to first base. I think I was among the younger boys, at five and a half, trying out. It was the first time I was ever on a real baseball diamond. My name was called and I was told to go out to shortstop. I didn't know where shortstop was. One of the coaches positioned me. Another coach hit a few balls to me, grounders and pop flies. I don't remember catching any of them. It was a little frightening, very confusing, and over in just a few minutes.

I remember the silent ride home with Dad. Even at that young age, I think I knew he was disappointed in me for not making a team. Looking back, he was probably more disappointed in himself for misjudging my readiness. Maybe he might have blamed himself for having not taught me well enough more than he blamed me for my abject performance. Dad had been a frustrated athlete himself and I know nothing would have pleased him more than to have his son be a star jock. But that was never to be. That night Dad, not Mom, tucked me in. I think it was his way of saying that he loved me, win or lose.

Not many weeks later, Dad came home from work with the news that he had been promoted and we would be moving, this time to a town called El Campo, Texas. My sisters cried again and again I was excited. A new adventure awaited.

4

El Campo

I did make a Little League team in El Campo. The Mustangs were coached by our next-door neighbor, realtor Jim Tuttle and another fellow. They taught us basic skills that we practiced for hours under the cloudless Texas skies. We weren't a bad little team. Our star player was an out-sized pitcher and slugger named Humphries. (We were all called by our last names.) Humphries provided almost all of our offense and kept us in most games by dominating opposing hitters. I think we finished third out of five teams, not good enough for the playoffs, which was fine by me as I had had enough by the time the season ended.

I was not a bad hitter. For a first grader I had some pop in my bat. My fielding in the nether reaches of the outfield left much to be desired. I had an erratic arm and an inconsistent glove. But it was fun to be on a team. And gamedays were filled with energy and excitement. There was a "press box" above each field where a PA announcer would broadcast each batter's name to the crowd as he approached the plate. My dad told me one of his proudest moments was announcing my name. Maybe it was a bit of redemption for my failure in Bellaire. I hadn't even realized it was him at the mike!

The other great thing about the ballpark was the concession stand. Thirty-five cents would buy a buy a bag of Fritos, slit down the side and topped with a scoop of chili. Eaten with a plastic fork, this was about the best thing I had ever eaten as a kid. I may have missed a number of pop flies and grounders, but I never missed the chance to buy a "Frito pie".

The Mustangs had a player who never participated in a "live" game. Billy attended every practice and was friendly and chatty to everyone. I remember liking him. But Billy had some sort of brain abnormality. It caused him to walk unsteadily and affected his vision. At every practice, Billy would take batting practice last. Coach Tuttle would position all the fielders very deep. Humphries would take laps as the Coach Tuttle pitched to Billy from in front of the mound. The other coach would stand behind Billy and help him swing the bat. Together they slapped the ball around the infield pretty well. From my spot in distant right field, I remember fighting back a tear or two (as I do now, nearly fifty years later). Finally, the Coach Tuttle would call "last raps", which meant the batter would run out his next hit as if it was a real game. I don't know if the guys had been told to let Billy's hits through, but he always made it to first safely and everyone always shook his hand and patted him on the back.

One practice, Billy didn't show up. The coaches wouldn't answer any questions about him until the end of the practice. They assembled us around them in a semi-circle and they told us that Billy was having an operation and that we would have a moment of silence to pray for him. Each of us took off his cap and bowed his head. You could hear more than a couple of us sniffling and fighting back tears. Synes, our first baseman, asked quietly if Billy was going to die. Coach Tuttle said that he didn't know. We wandered back to the cars of our parents, waiting to take us home. I assume that they knew about Billy because my mom didn't ask why I was so quiet.

A few weeks later Billy showed up at practice! He wore a grey hard hat. Each of us shook his hand and welcomed him back. He was happy, but subdued. He didn't take batting practice or get off the bench that day or for the rest of the season. One practice I sat next to Billy on the bench as he removed his helmet for a moment. His head had been shaved and there were scars on his head. Once again I found myself fighting back tears. Billy was such a sweet kid. It seemed so unfair that he should have to suffer like this. When I was called out to shag flies, I was happy to go. I felt guilty to be sitting next to Billy, me so healthy and well and him so weakened and dazed. What had either of us done to deserve our fates?

Somewhere, lost among my childhood memorabilia, I think I still have the terribly over-exposed team picture of the '66 Mustangs. I remember being able to pick myself out of the group. And Humphries, the biggest of us. And Billy in his helmet.

It's strange how you never know when you're going to be taught life's lessons or by whom. Our coaches taught us the lesson of inclusion. Helping someone to experience all they can of an activity lifts that person up, but it also elevates those who help. I imagine Billy's parents were grateful that our coaches included Billy as they did. And I look back and feel proud that all the guys treated Billy as much like one of the guys as they could. Not bad for a bunch of little kids. And the more I think about it the more I feel like none of us was so different from Billy. The coach didn't ask me to pitch just like he didn't ask Billy to field. Every one of us was special and got positioned according to our abilities, or lack thereof. Some of us were just little more special.

I attended Louise Hutchins Elementary School for first and second grade in El Campo from autumn 1966 through spring 1968. I was a good student and liked school. It was here I discovered I was a good singer. As Christmas approached each year I was singled out to lead certain carols in the Christmas Concert. Since I was missing my two front teeth, in a stroke of type casting it was decided I would sing "All I Want For Christmas Is My Two Front Teeth". We rehearsed and rehearsed. I added a little whistle when I spoke one line. The kids would laugh and seemed to enjoy listening to me. Wouldn't you know that I got tonsillitis the day before the concert and couldn't sing? Next year, the same thing happened. In fact, I got tonsillitis right around Christmas so many times it became a family tradition.

I joined Cub Scouts in El Campo too. It was fun to wear the uniform to school on days when we had "den meetings". I mostly remember eating sugary snacks and drinking soda pop at the meetings. It was really just a sort of daycare with merit badges. I got a swimming badge for demonstrating that I already knew how to swim, a religion badge because my family went to church, and a geology badge because I brought in a geode from my dad's rock collection.

My scouting highlight was the Pinewood Derby. The Pinewood Derby is supposed to be a model car race where each scout makes his own racecar. My dad made mine. I suspect many of our dads made our cars. I remember being made to watch as he carefully cut out the car's body shape and sanded it endlessly. I did get to suggest the paint scheme for the two prototypes, red and gold. Dad drilled holes into the underside of the car into which he put fishing weights to maximize the car's weight and thus its speed down the track. He even lubricated the wheels with powdered graphite. "I" won second place. I can only imagine that the kid who won first place must have had a dad who designed racecars for a living.

One day, Dad came home and made the inevitable announcement that he had been promoted and that we were moving, this time to Corpus Christi, Texas. Again my sisters cried and again I cheered.

5

Corpus Christi

YOU never miss what you've never had. I had grown up in areas that were inland. I guess we had made one or two trips to beaches in Galveston or Lake Ponchartrain. But when we made our first drive down to Corpus Christi, it was a revelation. While our new house was being finished, we lived for a month or so in a high-rise apartment on Shoreline Drive with an amazing view of the bay, Padre Island and the Gulf beyond. Better than the view, of course, was the elevator we got to ride up to our apartment. My older sister learned to sail in the bay and we made regular trips to a pristine Padre Island to play in the sand and the surf and marvel at the jellyfish and Portuguese men-of-war that had washed up on the beach.

Dad and I became regular weekend fishermen. He had access to "oil leases", areas that Texaco owned, that were off-limits to the general public and had excellent fishing. I grew closer to my dad on the early morning drives when I would tell him about school and he would tell me about his childhood, geology, and how he wanted to get a boat. Sometimes we would fish all day. We almost always caught several fish that we'd bring home for Mom to fry up. But even when we didn't have any luck it was a good time for me. My dad was patient, careful, funny, smart, and never forgot what it was like to be a kid. He wanted my childhood to be as wonderful as his had been. And it was.

I saw a "Discover Texas" tourism ad on TV and got the idea that Dad and I should take a trip to see some of the sights that weren't too far away. I know he must have been working hard and probably would have preferred to have some downtime, but when I presented him with a collection of brochures and maps and ideas, he just couldn't say no.

We spent the most wonderful day driving around south-central Texas visiting limestone caverns and other tourist traps. He had always had a keen interest in geology and used the day to try to pass some of that on to me. As interesting as the caverns were and as much fun we had at the various stops, the best part was just being with my dad. I always felt so safe and so comfortable when I was with him. Stopping for a burger and a malt at a drive-in with him was better than any fancy meal at a four-star restaurant I have ever had.

He had to wake me up when we finally got home late that night. He thanked me for planning out our special day. He said he'd always remember it. I know I treasure this memory more than most. I truly wish every kid could have a day like that one and could have a dad like mine.

I had third and fourth grade in Corpus from autumn 1968 through spring 1970. I went to Yeager Elementary, named after the man who broke the sound barrier. Corpus was home to a huge air base and we regularly saw all manner of state-of-the-art aircraft buzzing our neighborhood. The war in Vietnam was raging and the planes were a constant reminder. Each night on the TV news they would give us the score, how many of our servicemen had been killed and injured and how many of "the enemy's". It was a grim feature of every day from the time I first understood what it meant until my mid-teen years.

Our P.E. instructor was the father of one of my classmates. He was a retired military man and put us through military-style close order drills and calisthenics. That's as close as I ever got to military service. I enjoyed all the "left face" and "double-time march" and "parade rest" training. And the games of kickball were fun too.

I was in Cub Scouts in Corpus too. The first "den" was across the street from the school. The "Den Mother" created fun craft activities for us to do. I made a slide that held my blue and gold scout neckerchief on. It was shaped like the head of a longhorn steer. When her son graduated to the Boy Scouts, we had to find a new "den". A lady a few blocks over offered to become the new "Den Mother". The first few meetings there went fine. Her son was in one of the other fourth grade classes. His name was Marcus Love.

One day, I was sitting waiting for math class to start and I found my desk surrounded by a bunch of boys I did not know and Marcus. They kept asking me if I thought I could beat Marcus in a fight. I told them I did not want to fight anyone, had no reason to fight Marcus, and wanted them to leave me alone. Of course, they began to tease me and call me a coward. I had never been been bullied or harassed before, at least not like this. Where was the teacher? Before I knew it I had agreed to fight a kid didn't know and had never said a word to.

At home, I was surprised how disinterested my parents were in my plight. My dad told me that I had to defend myself and not be a coward. The fact that there was no reason for this fight and that I did not want to fight seemed not to make an impression on either of my parents. I can only chalk this up to the times. I think they thought that a boy should fight as some sort of "right of passage". Maybe they thought is was part of "becoming a man".

And so, the following Thursday, there I was at the "den meeting" sitting around the Love's kitchen table discussing the solar system as part of an astronomy badge activity, across from Marcus. At one point I spoke up to his mother, our "den mother".

"I don't want to fight Marcus. It's not that I'm afraid. (I was.) But we are Cub Scouts. Is it right for Cub Scouts to fight each other over nothing?" I asked, my heart pounding.

There was no response. Soon, the meeting was over and the other scouts dispersed and went home. I waited on the Love's front lawn. My mother sat in our car parked at the curb. Marcus came outside. His mother watched from the porch. And we just started hitting each other. We exchanged blows, mostly missing, but connecting too, mostly in the face. It wasn't like the cartoon, TV, or western movie fights I had seen. No haymakers to the gut, followed by a decisive uppercut to the chin for a knockout. We just kept flailing at each other. It seemed to last a long time and the afternoon was cold. We both got winded pretty quickly. Things slowed down. My face hurt. We were more leaning on each other than fighting.

Finally I said, "I'm done with this. I quit."

"I won!" Marcus shouted. "I beat you up." He raised his hands in victory, but I just turned away.

I walked to my mom in the car. We drove home in silence. I guess she told Dad about what happened. It was never discussed. The next day at school I heard a lot about how I got beat up. I mostly ignored it.

The next Thursday, I told my mother I didn't want to go to Cub Scouts at a place where I got into fights. Surprisingly, I got no pushback. I "transferred" to the "den" that was associated with our church. It was a little further away and none of the scouts there went to my school. Clean slate! Neat, huh? But there is always a catch.

My new den met in the garage of Mr. Billard, a man who went to our church. His son had been a scout but had graduated and was off at college. He was a funny guy who taught us what the football referee's hand signals meant, how to recognize different military aircraft, and how to tell the difference between a poisonous coral snake and the non-venomous scarlet snake. But he had one rule. He did not allow the scouts to talk when he was talking. Repeated violations of this rule were punished by "boot chocks". I didn't know what a boot chock was and was not interested in finding out first-hand, so I kept quiet. Not so, some of my fellow scouts.

After a few warnings, on the second meeting in my new den, I learned what a boot chock was. The offending scout was made to stand at the front of the garage in front of everyone, bend over and grab his own ankles. Mr. Billard then administered a fairly forceful kick to the scout's rear end, knocking the scout onto his face. The scout did not seem seriously hurt, but I was shocked. I certainly would not be talking during the den meetings.

I don't know how aware the parents of the Cub Scouts in Mr. Billard's den were of the boot chock punishment. I mentioned it to my parents and they didn't seem the least bit disturbed by it. Looking back, it's stunning that in 1969 corporal punishment of one's children by strangers was acceptable, as was unsanctioned bare-knuckle fighting between children. I pray that we are beyond that now.

We attended a Presbyterian church in Corpus Christi. Being the late 60s, it was a "mod" church built "in the round". This meant that the minister delivered his sermons while slowly rotating, which was a bit more entertaining than watching non-rotating clergy. The otherwise typical church interior was decorated with colorful banners that were reminiscent of the anti-war protest signs I had seen on the news, but bore slogans like "God is Love" and "Lamb of God". The choir, in which my sisters and I sang, performed more modern-sounding anthems accompanied by organ and xylophone. It was a unique experience, very much of its time.

My older sister went away to summer camp that year. It was strange not having the family all under one roof for several weeks. While she was away, NASA put a man on the moon. Our family watched the blurry, indistinct black and white images and marveled at the accomplishment.

When my sister came home we celebrated by going out to eat and going to the boat show at the Corpus Christi Colosseum. My dad had a newspaper and was comparing the various models at the show and their features to the ones being advertised for sale in the Corpus Christi Caller. I could see we would be getting a boat soon. The following Sunday Dad sat us all down. He had a newspaper under his arm. I knew he was going to tell us about the boat we were getting. I was wrong. He had been promoted again and we were moving to Houston. The newspaper was the Houston Chronicle real estate section. As always, my sisters cried and I cheered. Leaving Marcus Love and boot chocks behind sounded pretty good to me.

6

Houston

EVEN though we had lived in Bellaire a few years before, we were really returning to Houston when we moved there in the spring of 1970. This was the first time I had ever moved back to a place. It felt nice to return to familiar spots. Once again we attended St. Andrew's church. It was cool to reunite with kids I remembered from a few years before. We went to Astros games in the Astrodome. We went back to Felix's Mexican restaurant and Britt's Broiler Burgers. It was great. I started fifth grade and felt right at home.

The school year was only a few weeks old when I got asked to stay after for a few minutes in music class. Miss Neff told me I had a nice voice and wondered if I would be interested in singing in a special choir composed of boys from schools all over Houston. They performed at civic events and even on television. Interested? Heck yes, I was interested. Along with one other boy from my school, I was soon a member of The Singing Boys of Houston. We practiced once a week at an old high school across town and were soon performing original compositions and traditional works at the Museum of Fine Arts and other classy venues. And best of all, we performed during the school day! I got to miss class to go sing! The kids in my class were green with envy! Even the nominal class tough guy, Hart Oshman, would ask me how I got to miss class and what I had to do. He seemed impressed!

We'd do a concert every other week or so and there were articles about us in the newspaper. We sang our Christmas songs on Channel 2, the local CBS affiliate. My family gathered in front of the TV to watch. And there was even a momentary close-up of me! If only there had been VCRs or DVRs back then! OK, it was a blink-and-you'll-miss-me close-up, but there was my face, filling our 19-inch screen as my family watched. I felt like a star.

A month or two before I had been asked to play the title character in the church Christmas play, The Little Drummer Boy. Mrs. Warren, who had been the choir leader when I was a kindergartener, was still there and she decided I could handle the singing and limited amount of acting in the production. The adult lead was going to be Ron Stone, a local newsman. I had seen him on TV plenty of times and now I was going to be doing a play with him! Even though he ultimately had to withdraw due to a work assignment, and Dr. Harper, the minister of the church, filled in, it was a wonderful experience for me. I remember signing autographs for some of the older kids who were in the chorus. I felt so special.

School went well that year. I remember we studied US geography, taking the country region by region and learning the facts and figures about population, chief industries, and agricultural products of each. I was particularly interested in New York City. I still remember learning the names of the five boroughs and having my mind boggled by the enormity of the population. I wondered if I would ever get to visit New York City some day. It seemed like a long shot.

Although we really didn't talk about Dad's career too

much, he did seem to think that this job in Houston might be a long-lasting one. It was, I suppose, a lofty managerial-engineering position compared to the field work he had started out doing just a few years before. The house we lived in was a "custom-built" track house in a new subdivision. I think Dad thought we would be there a long time.

But we had been there less than a year when he came home and made the familiar announcement that he had been promoted and that we were moving to New York! I was beyond thrilled. Of course, my sisters cried. Dad went up to New York to do some advance work and scout the housing market. Mom spent a week with him up north while Nona, our paternal grandmother, stayed with us kids. When they returned, they told us we would live, not in New York, but in neighboring Connecticut. Dad would take a train every day into New York City and work in the Chrysler Building. I knew from school that it had been the tallest building in the world before the Empire State Building was completed. It seemed like the adventure of my childhood would just keep getting better and better.

After the school year ended, the movers came and packed up our household and headed to Connecticut. We went to Louisiana to visit our grandparents and other relatives there before heading off on an epic, week-long car trip to New England in August of 1971! As was his way, Dad had planned a route that would maximize the fun and educational experience for the family. We stayed in Chattanooga and saw the sites there such as Lookout Mountain. Then we drove through the Great Smoky Mountains National Park. My sisters and I tracked our progress on gas station maps as we made our way northeast through Virginia, Maryland, Pennsylvania,

New Jersey, New York and finally into our new home state, Connecticut.

7

NEW CANAAN (FIRST TIME)

MOVING to the little Connecticut "bedroom community" of New Canaan was a little different from any of the moves I had known before. For one thing, I had initially thought we were going to live in New York City, which for me meant that we might be living in the Empire State Building. Such was my knowledge of the big city. So there was a bit of disappointment there.

My sneaky parents took the opportunity to outfit me with a wardrobe of "fancy" clothes because the kids in New England surely didn't play in dungarees and t-shirts. So I ended up with a wardrobe of slacks and button-down shirts from Sears only to find that the kids who lived on our block played in dungarees and t-shirts. There's nothing like dressing differently to make fitting in just that little bit harder.

Also, my parents had informed my sisters and me that New England's climate was cooler than Texas. Air conditioning was not needed and our new home did not have it. When we moved in that August it was in 90 degree temperatures with very Houston-like humidity. Oh well.

New Canaan is one of the wealthier towns, not only in Connecticut, but in the country. We drove around its "Lost

District" area and gawked at huge mansions and gated estates. They had just built a new high school in town complete with a planetarium, TV studio, and twin rotating platforms on the auditorium stage that allowed nearly instant scene-changes in the elaborate productions staged there. The top-notch education was why Mom and Dad had extended themselves financially to live in this town. We lived in the cheapest neighborhood in the richest town in the state. Why so cheap? Our lot backed up against the town landfill. It didn't smell and looked like undeveloped scrubland except for the smokestack that billowed steam when the state-of-the-art incinerator ran. It turned out that it was a great place to play and I quickly tore up those slacks and dress shirts and was happy to see that Mom replaced them with Sears "Toughskins" jeans and t-shirts.

I got to ride a bus to school, which was a novelty. The bus stop was down from our house in front of several apple trees. So it was a bit of Americana to pick an apple or two before boarding the yellow school bus for the twenty minute ride to school.

South Elementary was not so unlike the schools in Texas. There was an odd, early-1970s program being taught called MACOS (Man, a Course of Study). Rather than teaching us about the Netsilik Eskimos (Inuit) by giving us facts to memorize, which was my strong suit, we were shown movies of them hunting for and gutting seals and caribou and given paper clips and told to fashion tools out of them like the native peoples had to fashion tools from bone and sinew. The predictable result was dozens of "fishhooks", "nose-pickers", and "belly button lint removers".

At the end of that sixth grade year, we were taken across

the street to Saxe Junior High School for "orientation". My suspicions were aroused when they kept assuring us how safe it was and how seventh graders were absolutely not beaten up or otherwise victimized by the older eighth graders. Such was my degree of trust in those pre-Watergate days, that I ignored that inner voice that wondered why they were (figuratively) giving us snake-bite kits if there were no snakes.

And snakes there were. Figurative ones, anyway. My two years of junior high were not terribly happy ones. The classes were fine, but for a naive, church-going, former Cub Scout, the handful of long-haired, smoking-in-the-boy's-room, foul-mouthed, threatening classmates were plenty intimidating. Looking back, I wasn't really directly harassed any more than anyone else, but those pubescent years are awkward enough without adjusting to the changing styles of the 70s and establishment of the adolescent pecking-order. And the only advice I got from my parents about dealing with this brave, new world was to ignore anything that was unpleasant. I'm not sure of the wisdom of the "ostrich" approach, but it got me through junior high.

I was happy to make it to high school where there seemed to be a little more room for, and a little less pressure on, the freshman who were just figuring out where they fit in. The fact that there was a "smoking cafeteria" of equal size to the "non-smoking cafeteria" immediately segregated the school into "bad kids" and "good kids", as far as I could see. So all I had to worry about was the worst of the "good kids", which I could handle. Beyond the academic, I turned my attention to girls. Having two older sisters who had friends, I knew quite a few female upperclassmen. These young women were, by and large, unattainable to a freshman like me. But there was a table at which sat a young lady from our church youth group and a number of her friends. I took to sitting with them.

These days the concept of the "friend zone" is well understood, but in those days the uninformed believed that there was a sort of "northwest passage" that, if discovered, would allow one to travel from the "friend zone" into the land of "date-ability". Sadly, that "northwest passage" remained undiscovered, at least by me. It was a year filled with frustration. I wanted to re-invent myself, but how? Everyone in the school knew me as the freshman nerd they had known since sixth grade and through junior high. Sophomore year didn't seem to hold much promise for a breakthrough.

So it was with a heavy heart that I sat in our kitchen when Dad came home one August afternoon in 1975 and announced that he had been promoted again and we were moving to London. I couldn't have been any more excited if he had said we were moving to Mars. This was it! My chance to re-boot my life. A continent away I could become anyone I wanted. And I would avoid the "friend zone" the way an experienced soldier knows to avoid land mines.

My older sister had gone off to college the year before. My other sister wangled a deal to stay in New Canaan for her senior year of high school, so it was only my parents and me that would soon leave for "jolly old England"!

8

LONDON

WHEN you move to a different country everything is different except you. Well, that's a bit of an overstatement. England in 1975 was pretty "American-ized" and getting more so by the minute thanks to TV and movies and even music making its way "across the pond". But it was still foreign enough to be intriguing to me. That first morning I nearly got run over trying to cross Sloane Street. I looked the wrong way before stepping off the curb. But I quickly figured out the basics of city life. I became my parents' designated shopper and interpreter. Yes, interpreter. The residual southern accents of my mom and dad made understanding the thicker Cockney, Scottish, Irish, and other accents hard for them. My younger ears adjusted quickly and I even found I could convincingly fake a few dialects before too long.

And so Mom, Dad, and I settled into our flat in central London and found stores where we could buy approximations of all our favorite American foods and drinks. I hauled Fresca and frozen dinners back to the flat in Mom's little "roller-trolley". I enrolled in the American School in St. John's Wood. The London Underground and famed double-decker buses were quite an upgrade from the yellow school bus in New Canaan.

Our first night out, we found a Mexican restaurant and

discovered that the family at the next table were Americans! In fact, they were Texans! In fact, the father was in the oil business! Eventually, I'd find out that none of this was so amazing as there were literally thousands of Americans living in London and many of them were in the oil business and so naturally, many of them were from Texas. In fact, the American School had a Texas Club.

I didn't join the Texas Club, but I did find a great group of friends very quickly. The American expatriate community was fairly transient and most of my classmates had grown up moving as much as I had, although some of them had travelled more internationally. And not all of them were oil brats. Some had parents in the diplomatic corps and some were the children of artists, foreign correspondents, and actors! And I quickly discovered that the private American School didn't have any "bad kids", at least none that would bother me. It was easy to make friends and even easy to migrate between the various "cliques". It was a relatively small school so you could be a jock-brain-drama guy all at once!

The school had classes that regularly brought the students out into the city for museum and theater visits. We were told to buy a good umbrella and not let a little rain keep us from exploring all the city had to offer. I took those words to heart.

The first friend I made in London, who remains a friend to this day, forty years later, was Mike Colombo. Mike and I were two American teenage boys looking for the things teenage boys look for. A good laugh, a good time and girls. We had already found a few favorite pubs and were deeply into grade-B kung fu movies, which we consumed by the double-feature at London's "finer" cinemas.

One day I saw a flyer on a school bulletin board asking

students to pause in their self-pleasure and debauchery and assist local senior citizens, or as the English so delicately call them, old-age pensioners. I signed Mike and me up. I remember he seemed nonplused when I told him of our afternoon's obligation to visit a little old lady who lived a few blocks from the school. But, kind-hearted guy that he is, Mike shrugged and said, "What the hell?" and off we went.

And as random as my signing us up to do a little good deed might have been, the signs abounded that fortune was going to favor us for following through. The first tell-tale sign was on the slip I retrieved from the school office with our "old-age pensioner's" name and address. Her name was, with God as my witness, Mrs. Beer.

A short walk found us on a quiet lane, knocking on the door of a tidy little row-house. I think it was what they called a "bed-sit", a little flat with a tiny kitchen area, table with four tiny chairs, and a parlor area with a coin-operated "gas-fire" heater.

Mrs. Beer was a little, old English lady straight out of central casting. She had a lovely smile and a quaint, old-world manner. We introduced ourselves and she welcomed us into her home. Mike and I were so accustomed to laughing and joking loudly about everything in the way that teens do. No subject was off limits for our crude, juvenile senses of humor. The world was one big Monty Python sketch to us. But we hushed our voices and found sincere respectful tones when we spoke to this charming, old soul.

We asked her if there was anything we could do for her. Chores, shopping, etc. She had a shopping list and directed us down the lane to a little super-market, or what passed for one in London in those days. She gave us a little money to cover the items and off we went. We returned in short order with the items and her change, carefully counting out the pounds and pence. She was delighted with the time and effort we had saved her and she wanted very much to repay us.

"Would you boys like something to drink?" she asked.

I looked over to Mike and nodded. I had told him that, in addition to the little chores we might be asked to do, we would probably end up drinking tea and listening to endless old stories. This was before we met Mrs. Beer.

"Yes, ma'am. We'd be happy to have something to drink," I said, expecting her to turn to the kettle and tea bags.

Instead, she stood and took a step toward the door. She looked at the two of us as we sat at her tiny kitchen table as if to ask why we weren't following.

"Well, off we go then!" she exhorted.

"Where are we going, ma'am?" asked Mike.

"Why, to the pub, of course! You boys do drink beer, don't you?"

"Oh, yes ma'am!" we exclaimed in unison.

On the way to the Wellington, we met Mrs. Beer's brother Pat. He asked her who her bodyguards were. She responded that we were her new boyfriends. And the four of us entered the pub and settled into a snug corner table.

It is difficult to explain to anyone who hasn't experienced a pleasant afternoon in a quiet English pub, how special it is. There is a warm familiarity about the place as if you've been coming there forever. The people greet you as an old friend and make conversation as easily as you would with family. And of course, a few pints of fine bitter ale don't hurt to make everyone feel even cozier and chummier as the afternoon wears on.

Pat was as delightful as his sister and made funny and lively conversation. Mike and I felt so at home, we quickly forgot the decades in age that separated us from Mrs. Beer and Pat. Pat and Mike played darts and then I played the winner. Mrs. Beer took the change from one round of ales and played the "fruit machine" (slot machine) winning enough for another round! They had stories of how the neighborhood of St. John's Wood had changed since "the war" and how many Americans had come to live there to be near the school. They told us how the Apple Studios on Abbey Road had brought rock stars to the area, but that they were mostly well-behaved.

By the time the sun had gone down, we were all feeling pretty jolly. Pat had to leave and Mike and I walked Mrs. Beer back to her flat. She tried to give us each some money for doing her shopping, but we declined, telling her to put it toward the first round the next time we went out. We set up a return engagement for the following week and bid her good evening.

As we weaved our way back toward the school to get our books, Mike and I laughed and marveled at how the afternoon had gone. We had ended up at a pub having a few laughs as we might have done had I not volunteered us, but we had made two new friends and done a good deed. And more than that, we had connected with people from a different time and place who brought us into their world and peeked into ours. And we wouldn't be able to just stroll past the elderly ladies and gents on the street anymore without a thought that they might actually be wonderfully fun people who could relate to two teens who were mostly just out for a good time.

London was a different world in many ways. The eighteen year old drinking age was not tightly enforced. And so I found myself having the time of my life in one of the greatest cities in the world. I tried out for the school production of *The Odd Couple* and got a part. Amazingly, we were allowed to smoke real (Cuban!) cigars and drink real beer during school hours on school property as we rehearsed the card-playing scenes! And if this wasn't enough, there was a pretty girl working in the stage crew who I noticed seemed to be sneaking looks at me when I was sneaking looks at her.

So, after waiting for what seemed like a long time, the opportunity to have a girlfriend was suddenly in front of me. I was sitting on a bus next to a pretty girl who laughed at my jokes, asked my opinions on things, and looked into my eyes as I replied. It was rarified air I was breathing. I snuck my arm around her shoulder and she snuggled into me. I leaned against her and she put her head on my shoulder. We held hands and it felt so amazing!

My mind didn't even flash back to the few disastrous dates I had when my clumsy advances were roundly rebuffed. I knew what it felt like to have my hand removed from around a girl's shoulder. I bore the scars of incidents when the words "Let's just be friends," and "I don't like you *in that way*," were aimed and fired at me. Those failures eroded confidence like acids eats at metal. It was easy to feel that dating was just one of those things I would never do, like dunking a basketball on a ten-foot hoop.

But there I was, on the very precipice of a relationship. And I did not hesitate. I jumped in with both feet. And here was where, looking back, I made errors that would transform my first boyfriend-girlfriend experience from the learning/growing/maturing/discovering experience I would wish for everyone to have, into an exploration of psychological dysfunction and drama. No one had prepared me for any of what was to come. The TV shows, the movies, Mom and Dad, no one had told me how to become part of a "we", while still being "me". Now, maybe youth and hormones being what they are, all the preparation and advice in the world might not have made much difference, but I was going into this alone, untrained and as innocent as a new-born puppy.

Given the perspective of so many years later, I think that my new girlfriend was equally as unprepared as I was. And she's not here to give her side of this story. She brought her upbringing and experiences of a few prior quasi-relationships with her as I brought mine. Neither of us was well-equipped emotionally for what was about to happen.

We very quickly set up the parameters of our new relationship. First, it was LOVE. I loved her and she loved me. Period. And this was reinforced by frequent, repeated affirmations, interrogations and responses to this effect. Second, we were BEAUTIFUL. No one was more beautiful than she to me and I to her. This was likewise to be repeated like a mantra. Thirdly, there was NO ONE ELSE for either of us. This was an exclusive, binding arrangement that precluded either and/or both of us from ever finding anyone else romantically interesting or physically attractive. Fourthly, this was a PERMANENT circumstance. This was FOREVER. At fifteen, we had both voluntarily made a blood oath to live, each for the other, 100%, until death and beyond. This contract and its details were arrived at and agreed to mutually, willingly, pretty much overnight.

There was a period where none of these parameters created a problem, but that period was, in retrospect, brief. Being "in love" must have made me relax and become confident in a way that others could see. A number of girls who had heretofore been unaware of my existence, sought out my company for casual conversation. But this turned out to be problematic. And so the fights began. Within days of my first kiss, we were having *Kramer vs. Kramer*-worthy screaming matches in the halls, in the lunchroom, everywhere! We soon developed a pattern of incident, followed by fight, followed by reconciliation and a moment of closeness, followed by the next incident. This lasted for two years.

How crazy did it get? One day, my girlfriend wasn't feeling well and had to leave school. I walked her to the bus stop and then went back to class. Later, during our nightly phone call, she accused me of cheating on her. One of her friends had seen me walking arm-in-arm with a girl outside the school! "Where?" I demanded. Out by the ball yard. "When?" I shouted. Just after lunch. I thought for a moment.

"That was YOU", I shrieked. "Your spy saw me walking YOU to the bus stop!" She hung up.

And I must add that I was just as possessive, paranoid and insecure. The outfits my girlfriend wore to school "for me" attracted other male attention. And that drove me insane with jealousy, which I did not hesitate to express in no uncertain terms. I was a nut!

At a school dance, we were having a good night. No arguments. No blowups. We danced and laughed. She excused herself to go to the ladies' room. As I stood there apart from everyone else, a very attractive young lady approached me. My stomach tightened. What if I was seen talking to this girl? Disaster loomed. The lovely blonde asked if I was Steven Yates. I said I was. She told me that she had lived down the street from my family in Corpus Christi, Texas when I was ten! She had a gorgeous smile and flashing blue eyes and her attention was very flattering and sweet. She told me that she had seen me with my girlfriend and did not want to cause trouble so she had waited until I was alone to pop over and say hello. And like that she was gone. Poof. Now I was in a panic. Word was sure to get back to my girlfriend. There was only one thing to do. I had to nip this in the bud. Full disclosure.

My girlfriend returned. I began like I was testifying at Nuremberg.

"I have something to tell you. I want you to hear the truth from me. I was minding my own business, talking to no one when a girl who knew me when I was ten came up and said hello. I was polite and she left. End of story. OK?"

I waited breathlessly for my personal Nagasaki. It did not come. She asked me to point out the girl. I pointed and said, "She's over there."

"Where?" she asked. "Which one?"

"The cute blonde," I blurted. Oh, God, if I could have only sucked those words back into my mouth. But it was too late. I only remember a high-pitched howl and a whirlwind of gesticulating hands. And my girlfriend charged out.

A wise man would have considered walking over to the blonde, turning the page and starting a new life. The thought crossed my mind for the briefest of instants. But I was far from wise. I was committed and in this up to my neck. Teenage love is like riding a tiger, once the ride starts, all you can do is hold on tight and hope for the best.

And so the break-up / make-up cycle continued. Again, since I am the one telling this story, I want to try to be fair. I was consumed by my own irrational fear that I could only ever find "love" with this one person. This was my one and only chance. Looking back, I think we both had issues of self-worth and insecurity. And we had some good times. We saw great plays, great concerts, attended two proms at the famed Dorchester Hotel, and visited Paris in the spring. But it was a whirlwind, a maelstrom.

Apart from the ridiculous drama at school, my "adult" relationship was taking a toll on my relationship with my parents. They observed their son becoming obsessed with "that little girl" overnight. They found it difficult to get me to come home at the end of evenings. They saw little things change. I started parting my hair on the other side. I started questioning the way our family had always done things. It must have been very disturbing to them. And they had no way to fight it. When they suggested I date other girls, I took this as a grave insult to my budding adulthood.

Even impartial observers could see how crazy our relationship was. I recall very clearly our sympathetic American History teacher suggesting to me in private that we should find "a separate peace". After one of our Armageddon-like conflicts at her house, as I stalked away, I had the fully-formed thought, perhaps for the first time, "I gotta get out of this but I am trapped." In spite of that, the vision of her with another guy was just not something I could bear.

Then Dad came home from work one day in the spring of 1977 and made the announcement. He had been promoted and we were moving back to the States. For the first time it was me, not my sisters, who cried. My girlfriend told me I had to stay behind. I'd have to find someone to take me in. I began that painful fight with my parents. A week later, her parents told her that they were also moving back to the States. We hatched a plan. We'd both graduate early, move to Berkeley, go to college, and live happily ever after.

9

New Canaan
(Second Time)

IN no time I was back in New Canaan and my girlfriend was off living with her grandmother out west. Our fathers' jobs that had brought them to London so that we could meet, had taken them back to their respective coasts and torn us apart. But we vowed to "stay together" in spite of the 3000 miles between us. I worked an after-school job and self-isolated, lest I lose focus on our plan or be tempted to stray.

Things in my house had settled into a kind of Cold War stalemate. My parents and I had stopped talking to a large extent. I was prepared to graduate in December and head out west with my few hundred dollars in savings and almost no plan beyond being with my girlfriend somewhere, somehow. I expected my parents to disown me. And I feared that if things didn't work out and we broke up, I would be stranded and alone out west with only a burned bridge behind me.

The weeks went by. We exchanged long letters, had almost daily phone calls and hung onto our promises of eternal love and togetherness and faithfulness. I made plans to graduate early and the fighting with my parents escalated. They did not want me to throw my life away on a girl they did not approve of. I dug in. They dug in. My dad and I argued for the first and only time we ever would. In the rarest of moments of frustration, he expressed incredulousness that I should throw my life away over a girl. He said he had once wondered if I was even interested in girls. I stared at him in shock and anger and hurt. My dad thought I was GAY? I think he would have taken those words back the instant he said them if he could have. I stormed away, furious.

In what turned out to be our second-to-last phone call, my girlfriend mentioned that she was trying out for a part in a school play. I took it as being part of her drama class and really gave it no thought. But in the next call she told me she had gotten a part. I asked what the play was. She said it was *The Fantastiks*. I asked about her part. She said it was the romantic lead. I took a deep breath. Thoughts flooded my mind and I tried to hold them at bay. They weren't jealous thoughts. They were the kind of thoughts you have when you realize you may have been played for a sucker. I asked about the guy she was playing opposite. She said he was a great guy. I took another deep breath and plowed ahead. I asked if there was kissing. She said there was. I asked if she had kissed him much "in rehearsals". She said she had. In my heart I knew I was about to burn, or rather blow up a bridge, the one between the two of us. Had they had sex? She paused for a long moment. I could feel burning and tightness in the pit of my stomach. I felt like I was in free fall and this would not be a happy landing. She said they had.

"How could you?" I asked incredulously into the phone. I poured out my heart and my pain in a flood of words and tears. I told her it was over and I hung up.

Sitting there in my room, surrounded by the mementos of my childhood, I felt as much anguish as a seventeen year old can feel. The worst thing that could happen had happened, I thought. What a fool I had been! How long had I been lied to? I pictured them together, laughing at me. I painted crueler and crueler pictures in my mind until I couldn't think of any more painful tableaus. I raged at the wasted time and the wasted opportunities. I realized how I had lied to myself and let this all get so far out of hand. It was suddenly so clear to me that the two of us had been playing at being adults. As angry as I was at her, I was at least that angry at myself. I had so easily cast off so much of who I was to be with her. Who was I that I baled so completely on my self-image, my self-worth, the values I had been brought up with, and my family?

My family! How damaged was my relationship with my parents, I wondered in horror? In one thought I pictured them happily gloating when they found out that my "adult relationship" was over and in the next thought I knew that, because they TRULY loved me, they would be sad for me. I would have to tell them. I felt like the prodigal son. I had been willing to squander a lifetime's worth of love, care, heartache and upbringing, and for what? I had thought I was so smart and had all but called them stupid. And now I had to crawl back to them. Maybe they'd make me graduate early now just to get rid of such an ungrateful son. Maybe they would say I wasn't their son anymore. Maybe I had forfeited that in my stupidity.

I walked downstairs like I was going to the gas chamber. They were each in their easy chairs watching TV as they did each night, side by side. They had a true love that had stood the test of time. They weren't children pretending to be adults. They knew about love in the way that I had only thought I did fifteen minutes ago.

I sat on the floor at their feet. I told them I had been a fool. I told them I had been wrong. Wrong about everything. I told them they had been right and that I should have listened to them. I told them I was sorry. I cried like a child, uncontrollably. My mom knelt beside me and hugged me. My dad stood over us, a hand on my shoulder. Between sobs, I apologized for every time I had upset them. I asked them to try to forgive me for being so wrong, so stupid, so angry, and so cruel to them. Finally, I looked up at them. I was ready to accept whatever they had to say to me. At the very least they would have to say "I told you so".

But they didn't.

Mom was crying. She said she hated to see me hurt this way. She said that I should wash my face and try to calm down.

It was getting late and I should try to get some sleep. A new day would bring with it a new beginning for me. Dad didn't say anything. He wasn't happy. He didn't gloat. He was just there for me. He didn't turn away. He was there like he had always been. And they never really mentioned it again. They let me learn whatever lessons I could on my own. They hadn't been a part of my "adult relationship". Now that it was over, they had their son back. That was enough for them.

I washed my face and went to bed. Sleep didn't come easily. As I stared at my ceiling, I was surprised that I didn't see visions of her with another guy. I just saw nothing. A blank slate. A void that I could begin to fill with whatever I wanted the rest of my life to be. And I quickly felt a sense of quietude. I had found what that American History teacher had told me I should try to find, "a separate peace".

They say you never know if what you are going through at the time is good or bad. Sometimes it takes the lens of time to reveal if you were at a high or a low point. And you can't control what lessons life will teach you. I hoped to learn a lot about women from my first relationship with a girl. Instead I learned how much my parents loved me. I learned how close I could come to throwing myself away to get something I thought I wanted. And I learned that control of your life is, in part, an illusion. Like a ship at sea, you can't control the tide, the weather, or the unforeseen. But like a wise captain, you can learn from experience and maybe improve your odds of surviving the next voyage.

I changed my plans to graduate in December and decided to take my parents' advice and enjoy my senior year. It was funny to see the looks on a few classmates faces when they realized they hadn't seen me in two years and I was suddenly back in school. I scheduled a bunch of "fun" classes for the spring term and started living.

The church youth group, the Methodist Youth Fellowship, also known as the MYF, was my jumping off point. I know that must sound pretty tame, if not boring, but there was as much, if not more "youthful mischief" of all kinds in those kids as there was in the coolest clique in the school. I had a date in time for the MYF Halloween party.

I quickly became friends with several guys in MYF and joined the church choir. I know what you're thinking. How lame, right? Well, it turns out that the church choir director also directed the high school choir. And the high school choir was traveling to Europe that spring and they needed male singers like me! Those MYF guys and I all turned 18 within a few months of each other and they got me into all the cool parties where we enjoyed more than a few "adult beverages". My social life opened up beyond my wildest dreams. That spring the choir trip to Switzerland and Paris was a blast.

At some point, my parents approached me to ask what college I wanted to go to. I had really good grades, SAT and ACT scores. They had enough money that they could send me pretty much anywhere. But I was not keen to venture too far. I had learned the hard way that my parents were people who would never abandon me, so I chose to stay close to home and applied only to the University of Connecticut. A few weeks later I got my acceptance letter and that was that.

By graduation in June of 1978 I had a great group of friends. We were all going our separate ways, but we all vowed to stay in touch. Some of us did (and still do). And once again I'd be moving, only this time Mom and Dad would stay put. Nobody cheered or cried. This was just the next part of life.

10

UConn - Terra Incognita

WHEN venturing into unknown lands, a man faces unknown challenges. He can imagine and prepare for some eventualities. Others will take him totally by surprise and his fate will rely in some proportion on his wits, his character, the people he meets along the way, and luck. So it was for me when I went off to college. In some ways I was as well prepared for this adventure as I could be. I had attended two of the finest "college preparatory" high schools in the world and achieved excellent grades in almost all of my courses. I had even received six credits that were applied directly to my college transcript in calculus through a cooperative program that my high school participated in. I had no financial pressure as my parents were paying for my tuition and other expenses. And I was attending a college, the University of Connecticut, that was arguably a bit less challenging than many of the schools into which I could have been admitted on the strength of my grades and standardized test scores.

My first semester at UConn, I made the Dean's List. I was the "curve-wrecker" in General Chemistry achieving grades so high that no curve could be applied to the grades of my lower-achieving peers. I had excellent study habits, completed assignments promptly, and even provided help to other students.

That's the end of the happy part of the academic story.

Over the next five semesters my grades declined to the point that I was dismissed from the university for "academic insufficiency". That's the nice way to say I flunked out. I take full responsibility for this remarkable failure. It was all my fault. I skipped many, many classes. I made a few late, lame attempts to pass and got to the point where I ceased caring, except for the terrible burden of how I would explain my meltdown to my loving, trusting parents, who granted me every possible benefit of every conceivable doubt.

Well, if I wasn't studying or going to class, what was I doing? The truth is I wasn't doing much. Most of those lost two and a half years were wasted in a haze of drink and drugs. And don't picture non-stop, wild carousing with others. There was plenty of that to be sure. But there was far more of me sitting alone in a room staring at a 12-inch black-and-white TV for endless hours. Why? What happened?

For me it was a combination of things. I had such a great high school preparation for college that my first semester was just too easy. And when things got harder in the subsequent semesters, I did not seek help or adjust my behavior to succeed. Rather, I turned my attention and energies to my new friends and new, non-academic activities. Some friends were able to maintain a balance between school work and fun. Some weren't. If some of my friends were studying, then there were almost always some others who weren't. And if I couldn't find anyone else, I would just have a "one-man party". Even at the time I knew what I was doing was wrong and I felt guilty. And that just made me "party harder" to try to numb myself to the guilt.

I never embraced my fellow engineering classmates. I became close friends with the guys I lived with in the dorms. I had never had a group of friends like that before. We lived practically on top of each other 24-hours a day. We all were dealing with our classes, yes, but also trying to meet girls, and find out who we were when we were out in the world, away from all parental and other supervision. So when my engineering classmates were forming study groups, I was taking road trips, partying, and trying to have the best time imaginable.

I came to believe that "attendance doesn't count". For many courses, there was no "class participation" component to the calculated grade. I took that as a license not go to class. I tried to half-heartedly "study" my text books, "get the notes" from students who did go to class, and just hope I could get by. And once you stop going to class, it becomes very difficult to start going again. There is shame in facing the professor and the other students.

The final nail in my academic coffin was a combination of not being part of a peer study group and not going to class. I was unable to go to my professors to ask for help. Why should they give a minute of their time to someone who didn't bother to give them a minute of his?

That's how I got to "rock bottom".

And so I found myself facing my parents after I had flunked out. I cried and, again like the prodigal son, asked to be allowed to live under their roof and promised to bag groceries or pump gas until I could afford to move out and disappear. But they didn't curse me. They didn't condemn me.

They didn't want me to disappear. They only reached out to hug me and offer me love and hope and help.

My dad said that I had "swum more than halfway across the river" towards my degree. It made more sense to keep moving forward than to quit and go back. Mom and Dad told me to find an apartment off campus, away from everyone, where I could focus on schoolwork. They told me to take as long as I needed but not to quit. I told them I would try, which I had not done for quite some time. And I meant it. My dad told me one other thing. He told me to get my degree. Once I had that, no one could ever take it away from me. And it would be proof that I could finish what I started.

So, I got an apartment twenty minutes from the campus. I had almost no visitors there over the next two years. At age 21, I became a "non-degree student". That meant I could take whatever classes were not filled by students enrolled in degree-seeking programs. I took summer term classes. I met with an advisor who laid out a path to re-admittance to the School of Engineering. I would have to repeat a couple of classes and take a few more. I did an independent study. I worked hard and alone. After a year, I became, or so I was told, the first student ever to be dismissed and readmitted to the UConn School of Engineering.

Over my last two semesters, I joined a peer study group and graduated in the spring of 1983, a year later than I would have if I hadn't made so many bad decisions. Of course my next challenge would be getting a job. As daunting as the prospect of trying to find a job out of college was in 1983, some students went to extraordinary lengths. In the back of the *Rolling Stone* magazine, next to the ads for services that would make you "an ordained minister" or sell you a term paper on the subject of your choice, there were ads for a service that would send your resume and a "customized" cover letter to the top 100 or 500 companies in the country for a price. I had seen the ads and wondered if they actually did what they advertised. I was speaking about this to a friend who worked in the same college lab I did. He opened a deep desk drawer. It was filled with "flush letters" from the top 100 companies in the country. The assortment of corporate letterheads was dazzling. "Flush letters" were form letters that thanked the job-seeker for his interest in the company but declined to offer a job or even an interview to the poor slob. Almost all of them closed on an oddly optimistic note. It went like this.

"While we are unable to consider you for employment with us at the present time, we are certain, after reviewing your credentials, that you will soon find success in your job search."

I suppose they were trying to offer encouragement, but seeing this reproduced one hundred times on a stack of "flush letters" kind of lessened the amount of comfort one could take from it.

I had learned a lot at UConn, only some of it about chemical engineering. The life lessons were basic. You have to work to get results. Work hard and play hard, but do it in that order. And I learned that God had given me parents that would never give up on me, even if I had given up on myself. They saw something in me that I did not. And from that day to this, I have never cared about anything as much as making them proud of me.

That's the big picture of my college experience. It's the truth and I hope someone reading it can benefit from my mistakes. It would be wrong to try to glamorize those mistakes, right? But, to be honest, as I was spiraling downward academically and piling up a mountain of guilt, regrets and mistakes, I did manage to have a lot of fun.

*****

So let's rewind to September of 1978, when my parents delivered me to Litchfield Dormitory in the North Campus Quadrangle, aka The Jungle, at UConn. I still remember how they tried to hide their surprise at how primitive the accommodations were. They were likely not much different from the accommodations that they had at LSU twenty-some years before. A little ten by ten concrete cell with one window, a steam radiator, two closets, two desks, two steel frame beds, and one dresser, all decidedly Government-issue. This is not surprising when one realizes that the Quad was called The Jungle because it was built to house WWII and Korean War vets who flocked to UConn under the GI Bill. Reluctantly, Mom and Dad bade me farewell and left me to begin this big adventure with an unknown, randomly selected roommate and whatever else fate had in store.

Even though the statute of limitations has long since run out, I cannot in good conscience give a full and accurate picture of what college life was like for me. But there are discrete episodes that may convey something of what it was like.

In 1978, in Connecticut, the legal drinking age was eighteen. This meant that every incoming freshman was able to purchase and consume alcohol openly. And most of us did. The university had few restrictions on when and where alcohol could be possessed or consumed. Several liquor stores near the campus had delivery service. This meant that with a phone call, one could request any amount of any type of alcoholic beverage and it would be delivered to your dorm room in short order. One could pay by check and one could make out the check for up to $20 over the purchase amount thus making the liquor store an ATM before actual ATMs were available in the UConn area. Did this arrangement result in excessive drinking, bad financial decisions, and moral decline on campus? Yes. Yes, it did.

The university itself not only sanctioned, but directly provided alcohol, sometimes free of charge, to the general public and the students. There was an on-campus bar, Huskies, in the student union building. There were bars directly adjacent to the campus. Dorms collected dues that went almost exclusively to the purchase of beer for weekly keg parties and hard liquor for cocktail parties held once a semester.

And then there was "spring weekend". I heard about the upcoming "spring weekend" and imagined all sorts of wholesome activities. Perhaps there was a parade, concerts, sporting events, dances, and the like. There may have been such activities but they were over-shadowed, or rather, blurred out, by the five or six half-kegs that just appeared in each and every dorm on campus at the beginning of the weekend. The predictable mayhem ensued. Property damage, minor injuries, fistfights, unauthorized bonfires, vehicles driving on, and tearing up, the grass in the quad. Students would come from other colleges just to get drunk on free beer at UConn. By Sunday the beer was gone and the whole campus smelled, well, pretty much like you'd imagine it would smell.

At the end of my freshman year, after I had left campus, there was, what became known as, "The End of the World Party". It was reportedly a typical UConn beer-fest except that this one resulted in over $20,000 worth of damage to the property of the university. The response to this outrage was as swift as it was ill-conceived. All of the residents of the South Campus quad, where the party was held, were "relocated" throughout the rest of the campus. The university decided, in its wisdom, to take all of the "bad seeds" of South Campus and sow them, a few in each dormitory, all across the campus. The predictable result was an increase in property damage in every dormitory on campus the following year.

Being the 70s, there was an illegal accompaniment to the alcohol for many students, namely marijuana. Again, in order to protect the identities of so many of us who have gone on to lead productive, drug-free lives, I shall limit my comments. Suffice it to say that for those who wished to indulge in herbal attitude adjustment, the raw materials were generally available. And combined with the aforementioned alcohol, this made all or some of the time spent at UConn an experience to remember, if only one could.

My group of friends and I spent much of our "free time" entertaining ourselves playing cards, watching our 12" black and white TV and having "room parties" in our dorm. Every Monday night, my roommate and I would collect a few bucks from most of the guys on the floor and order a quarter-keg of low-grade beer that was positioned outside our door. We did not play cards for money. Instead we devised a game where the "loser" would consume some form of intoxicant. These games were frequent and quite often went on into the wee hours of the morning.

A lot of fun was had in those wee hours. I recall one evening when there was a Roman candle fight in the "study" across the hall. Bottle rockets and firecrackers were discharged with no real damage. The Resident Assistant (RA) and Head

Resident of the dorm eventually made their way to the smoke-filled room, but by then the perpetrators had fled. Another night, it seems as though individuals had disposed of a number of empty liquor bottles by throwing them against the wall in the "study". My friends and I took it upon ourselves to clean up the mess and imagine our surprise when the RA and Head Resident accused us of having created the mess we were cleaning up! Fortunately, reason prevailed and the event was soon forgotten. There were other more spectacular events however.

A dangerous, time-honored and ill-advised practice of those days was penny-locking a dorm room's door. A stack of pennies was forced between the door and the outside doorjamb thus pinning the bolt of the doorknob in place, locking the door from the outside. The hapless victim might be unaware that this had occurred until he tried to exit and would be stuck in his room until help could be summoned. Removing the receiver from a victim's telephone compounded the difficulty in summoning help. (Warning: This is a stupid and potentially deadly thing to do as trapping someone in a room could be tragic in the event of a fire! Do not do this!)

The following story is true and my friends and I were witnesses, but not directly involved. One particular night an unfortunate freshman was penny-locked in his third-floor room, two floors directly above mine, his telephone's receiver having been removed. The next morning, once he realized his predicament and rather than shout out the window until he could summon help, this frosh (Let's call him Don.) decided to attempt an escape. He tied together a necktie, a belt and a length of baling wire. These he attached to the handle on his upraised window. He climbed out the window hoping to lower himself down to the little portico over the dorm entrance, one floor below. As soon as he put his weight on the makeshift "rope", the window to which it was attached slammed shut. The sudden movement caused Don to lose his grip and he dropped to the portico and then bounced down to the ground. Don had injured himself significantly. I was in my room watching Saturday morning cartoons when I heard the thud from the portico just outside my window. I turned to pull back the blinds, but the humorous antics of Bugs Bunny distracted me and I never bothered to look out.

Eventually, a severely injured Don dragged himself into the dorm to our Head Resident's door and knocked weakly. The Head Resident answered the door and was horrified to see the bloodied Don lying on the floor. Police and ambulance were summoned and Don was taken away to the hospital. He later recovered and needless to say entered campus folklore as "Divin' Don". Epilog: Divin' Don returned to UConn and graduated, although he never escaped his unwanted nickname.

Another night my friends and I were playing cards as we so often did. Outside in the hallway another group of would-be scholars was playing "hall-hockey", which is just what it sounds like. Two or three fellows would stand at either end of the hallway and take turns shooting a regulation, hard rubber hockey puck with regulation hockey sticks full-force down the hallway at each other. Oh sure, the puck might take out an overhead light fixture, destroy the porcelain drinking fountain, or hit some innocent bystander who happened to foolishly walk out of his dorm room into the hallway. But this was just part of dorm life! After a while the hockey game broke up and the players began chanting "H-U-S!, H-U-S!" We had no idea what this meant. We cautiously went outside to see that the hockey players had donned dark clothing and camo face paint, which seemed unusual. They told us to keep an eye on the WHUS tower. WHUS was the campus radio station that no one really listened to. Its odd mix of classical, jazz and other unpopular forms of music appealed only to the DJs who played it. The 212-foot tall WHUS broadcasting tower was across campus and its aviation warning beacon, a blinking red light, could be seen for miles even given the rolling hills of rural Connecticut.

Not really knowing what to make of all this, we returned to our card game and its attendant consumption of intoxicants. The hockey players had been all but forgotten as the hours went by. It was about 2am when we heard the chant again. "H-U-S!, H-U-S!" The hockey players were coming up the stairs. We opened our door as they passed by, still chanting. We tried to ask them what was going on. In response, one of them held out a large, red plastic cylinder with a strobe light inside. Guessing what it was, I ran back to the window and looked out searching for the WHUS broadcasting tower. I couldn't see it! Eventually I made it out in the distance but it was difficult, because there was no blinking red light on top! These idiots had climbed a 212-foot tower and stolen the aviation beacon! An hour or so later, I knocked on their door. When I entered the room, I was amazed to see it bathed in brilliant red light. One of them, an electrical engineer, had hooked the stolen light up to a power supply. I suggested that they might want to douse the light as, once the campus police took notice, it would be a dead giveaway. They just laughed. (Warning: Do not remove aviation warning beacons from elevated structures! This is a stupid and potentially dangerous thing to do! These beacons alert planes so they don't crash into the structures.)

There are endless stories like this from those days.

Eventually, perhaps inevitably, reason prevailed. First, the university put an end to on-campus liquor delivery. They also closed the university-operated bar. They banned individuals from bringing kegs into dormitories. Eventually, they banned the possession of alcohol in "common areas", meaning that students who were of age could only drink in their rooms or the rooms of friends, but not in hallways, lounges or dining halls. Finally, the state raised the drinking age to 21. UConn still has its share of alcohol-related problems, as do all universities, but not like in 1978.

Also, prosperity came to UConn. Shortly after I graduated, UConn hired Jim Calhoun to coach the men's basketball team and Gino Auriemma to coach the women's basketball team. Those two teams rose to become NCAA champions multiple times over the years that followed. With such success, came a great deal of money. The UConn that exists today is unrecognizable to me and my old classmates. And that's a good thing for the most part.

*****

When I was at UConn, their sports teams were not terribly successful, with one exception: soccer. UConn won the NCAA-sanctioned College Cup men's soccer championship in 1981. They played many of their home games on Saturday mornings when the football team played their games. The generally-woeful football team played in big Memorial Stadium. The soccer team played on Gardener Dow Field, an open area with low bleachers surrounding the "pitch". The bleachers held a thousand fans and were always packed. More students stood and many watched from outside the fence that surrounded the field. On Saturdays, fans would even sit in the far upper corner of Memorial Stadium while football games were going on because of the view they could get of the adjacent soccer field.

Now, what I'm about to describe may not strike the reader as being a terribly sportsman-like because it is not. UConn did not have passive fans. They were the Gardener Dow's "home field advantage". From the introduction of the opposing team, the UConn fans would start in. In those days, most of the top teams imported most of their talent from overseas. In contrast, UConn not only utilized players from the US, not only utilized players from Connecticut, but many of the Huskies were from Storrs, the town where UConn was located. So, when the field announcer would introduce a foreign player on the opposing team, the crowd would react.

"At forward for XYZ College, Joe Smith, from Lesotho," the announcer would say.

"WHERE'S THAT?" the crowd would respond as one. And that was just the beginning.

Even if the opposing player was an American, the crowd was tough.

"At fullback for XYZ College, Bill Wilson."

"WHO'S HE?" the crowd would scream. Others would chant "Fresh meat!"

Of course, the UConn players were greeted with deafening cheers. Once the game began, things would get worse. There was something called a "whisper cheer". These were scripted cheers that would begin spontaneously, as if by magic. The effect was oddly unnerving. After a bad call, thousands of UConn fans would repeatedly whisper a word meaning 'bovine excrement'. No one would shout. And it was hard to tell what was being said at first. But then it would become unmistakable. Some of the other "whisper cheers" were just obscene references to one or more of the opposing players. A thousand fans would whisper a much more obscene version of, "Joe Smith is dating Bill Wilson," over and over.

Behind the opposing goalie, the fans had more menacing cheers. They would all but threaten the poor guy, keeping up a steady stream of chants, jeers, obscene suggestions and, oddly, the occasional compliment. Opposing goalies would try ignore the non-stop chatter, hoping to make it to the second half when they would switch ends of the field and presumably have to deal with a fresh group of tormentors. But the UConn fans were more savvy than that. They would relocate to the other goal at halftime so that when the opposing goalie came back out they would greet him.

"Hey, Goalie! Remember us? We missed you! Welcome back! You look tired. Were you kissing the other players at halftime?"

The one uplifting thing I can say is that several of the opposing goalies would, after the game, actually turn and applaud the audacity of the UConn faithful. I guess they could appreciate the passion of the fans, if not their choice of epithets.

*****

After my first eye-opening year at UConn, I returned to New Canaan and besides doing some "industrial labor" temp work, I got a minor part in the local summer theater production of *Cabaret*. It was a fun way to fill some evenings and meet a few girls, but it really wasn't what I was hoping for. My dad had wanted me to have the experience he had working for Texaco out in the oil fields. It would be good work experience that none of my classmates would have. This actually turned out to be the case and it made up for my lackluster grades to some extent. I think citing this experience helped me as I hop-scotched from job-to-job in the years that followed.

11

DOG LAKE

IN between my sophomore and junior years, the summer of 1980, everything worked out so that I could "work offshore" for Texaco. That summer I flew down to New Orleans and stayed with my grandparents as I had so many summers before, but this time there was a difference. Every other week, I'd be working "off-shore".

Digression - When I hear the word "off-shore" I think of one of those giant oil rigs out in the middle of the Gulf, miles from land, with the towering derrick and scores of big, strong men operating the drilling rig 24/7. That's not where I worked. - End of digression

That first week, I had to feel my way to figure out how it would work. Through some personal connection, I hooked up with another young man who was working off-shore and he picked me up from the Houma, Louisiana bus station after I had taken the two hour ride there from Slidell. I had a suitcase filled with work clothes including my steel-toed boots. Josh had a late-model Olds Cutlass and I threw my stuff in the trunk and we were on our way. I was nervous about how it would all go. From Houma it was another hour drive on the back roads to Cocodrie Landing, the point of departure, Josh pulled into a dirt parking lot across from the dock. The boat wouldn't leave for another half hour, so we went inside the little bar where we found all the other guys who would board the boat in thirty minutes "speed drinking". Naturally, we joined them. Since alcohol was prohibited on company property, this was the last opportunity to have a drink for a week before the boat left for our "marsh camps". This little ritual was repeated by every crew, once a week. Ah, tradition.

We staggered out to the crew boat and it slowly chugged down the bayou. Some guys played cards, some read, and others of us got a headstart on our hangovers. Two hours later we arrived at the Dog Lake marsh camp that would be our home for the next seven days. Our crew was made up of a welder, Ed, and three field roustabouts, Hawk, Ray and me. Our "pusher" or supervisor was, I kid you not, a burly man who went by the name of Sue. The camp was a collection of buildings up on twelve foot high pilings situated in a dense marsh. A bayou ran past the camp and connected to a network of other bayous, Caillou Bay, and ultimately to the Gulf of Mexico.

We stowed our gear and walked to the chow hall. There was a generous buffet of southern specialties and a cook standing by to make whatever you might ask for, as long as it was a steak. The company deducted a dollar a day from our pay for room and board. This meant that three times a day you could eat as much food as you could pack away. It was a pretty good deal.

After a giant meal, we walked back to the "crew bunkhouse" where there was one TV. A recreation hall housed some card tables and another TV. All the buildings were, thankfully, air conditioned. And when we were not working, those four buildings made up our world. I never went into the "supervisors' bunkhouse" and only rarely went into the rec hall. So my off-duty off-shore world was the crew bunkhouse with its shower and the mess hall with its bounty. Once I had surveyed the accommodations, I found an empty bunk and passed out.

The light was snapped on at 6am and a loud voice announced that work would begin in half an hour. We all pulled on our work clothes and shuffled to the chow hall. After some bacon and eggs, we carried the camp's garbage to a small "lugger" boat, filled our cooler with ice, and headed out into the darkness of the bayou. A short distance away, we docked on Rat Island, where we deposited the camp's daily garbage in a pile. One man doused the bags with gasoline and then poured the remaining gas down some of the rat holes that perforated the ground. He tossed a lit match over his shoulder as he got on the boat and we pulled away. Looking back, I saw the pile of refuse burst into flames and rats, some on fire, scurrying about, some jumping into the bayou. This was how every workday began.

Leroy was the captain of the "lugger" called Timbalier. He was not a Texaco employee. He was a contractor. Therefore he was not bound by all the rules the rest of us were. His only duty was to drive the boat from job to job. Our crew performed routine maintenance on wells, pipelines, and small production platforms, most of which were out in the open water of Caillou Bay. The Dog Lake field was mostly dormant. Its wells contained gas and oil, but the operations required to pump and transport these to market were not economically viable in 1980. When the price of oil and gas went up, these wells would be tapped. Until then, it was up to us to keep them maintained in a "ready" state. Mostly, we repaired leaks in pipes by applying small clamps, or by cutting out and replacing lengths of two-inch diameter steel pipe. The twelve hour shift was broken up by the boat rides from job to job and back to the camp for lunch.

The work was physical, but only occasionally grueling. The ninety degree heat and ninety percent humidity took a bit of getting used to. And the "greenheads", huge sand-flies with big green eyes that delivered a bite as painful as a bee sting, were always present when the boat wasn't moving. Apart from that, it was pretty pleasant. The marsh and bayou country was beautiful. Birds of many kinds nested, swam and, flew everywhere. Dolphins sometimes accompanied us as we moved from job to job.

Of course, the crew had plenty of time to get acquainted. Ed and Hawk were African-American. Hawk was a college student like I was. He was hoping to make a career with Texaco. He was fun-loving and we talked about music and girls. Ed was quieter and more serious. He would often stay in camp working on welding projects. Ed was interested in my stories of New York City and life "up north". Ray was not terribly friendly. He knew I would only be around for the summer and probably didn't think it was worth his time to befriend a "college boy". He was hoping to become a crew "pusher" like Sue. Sue was a big, tough-looking guy. He didn't talk much and when he did he got right to the point. He'd tell Leroy where to drive the boat. When we got there, he'd tell us what to do. He'd check the work when it was finished, usually without a word. All of us brought our hardhats, gloves, and our orange flotation work-vests with us whenever we got on the boat. Sue brought his hardhat, gloves and a grocery bag filled with girly magazines. Once he had told us what to do, he would sit on the boat and watch Leroy fish, all the while flipping through his stack of mags.

There was one other member of our crew. Babs was 64 years old and he bunked in the supervisors' bunkhouse. I guess maybe Babs' seniority got him his place there. He had been working as a roustabout for Texaco for 35 years. He was a little guy, maybe five foot three. He had a heavy Cajun accent and it took me a while to tune my ear so I could understand him. He lived "down the bayou" in a type of little house that was called a "camp". As we went from one job to the next along various bayous, we would suddenly come upon these "camps". Most of them looked like abandoned shacks. Some of them were used only rarely by fishermen, but others were occupied by full-time residents. Most didn't have electricity or running water. A few did. The people who lived "down the bayou" all knew each other. They all called each other "Cuz". When we would pass a "camp", Babs would give a little wave to whoever looked out. And they all had the same little wave that was a quick back and forth rotation of the hand like putting in a lightbulb.

I found Babs fascinating. Over the course of the seven week-long "hitches" I worked at Dog Lake, we talked more and more. In fact all of us got a little chummier. But Babs told me he didn't like going "up the bayou". He had never been any further north than Houma. He had never been to New Orleans! He said he had no use for cities or the people in them. And Babs would make a little pot of insanely strong, piping hot coffee every afternoon around four. He'd pour everyone a little Dixie cup of it, without asking if we wanted any. And we'd all drink it scalding hot and black, like it came out of the pot. It was just something we did.

Working out on the water in the heat of the summer, we were exposed to some pretty foul weather. It's not uncommon for violent electrical storms to pop up out of nowhere. They'd rage for a few minutes and then dissipate or move away. I remember watching multiple waterspouts form out over the Gulf and dance back and forth on the horizon, sometimes merging into one large twister. I wondered what would happen if one of those hit us in our little boat. But that never happened.

There was one time when I was working with Babs on a large platform over open water. The boat and the other guys actually left us there to work while they worked on a neighboring smaller platform. Babs and I finished our job and awaited pickup. As we did, the sky turned dark. In a matter of minutes low, dark, angry clouds rolled in and rain poured in buckets as hard as I've ever seen. Babs and I huddled under a corrugated metal shelter, open on one side. Lightning flashed all around us with thunder booming at the same instant shaking the whole platform.

"I'm glad I'm with you, Babs!" I shouted over the din of the rain on the metal roof.

"Why's that?" he asked flatly.

"You've been doing this a long time. You've seen so many of these storms I know you know how to stay safe!" I laughed.

Babs gave the slightest smile. He pointed at the silver metal tower right next to us.

"You know what that is, Schoolboy?"

I shook my head.

"It's an oil-gas separator. Lightning hits that and there won't be enough left of us to bury," Babs told me with a straight face. So much for experience.

The weeks went by and I got used to the routine of working one week on, one week off. At the end of a workweek, we'd get into the crew boat and make the trip back "up the bayou" to Cocodrie, hit that little bar like we'd been away from civilization for a year, and then I'd wait for the bus for the painfully long trip back to Slidell and a week-long stay with whichever set of grandparents I hadn't stayed with the "hitch" before.

A direct drive from Cocodrie to Slidell would have taken two hours. But the Greyhound would stop at every bump in the road from there to Houma and then at every crossroads between Houma and New Orleans. Sometimes I'd be lucky to catch the last bus out of New Orleans and my elderly grandparents would stay up until midnight to pick me up at the bus stop in Slidell. One time, I missed the last bus and spent the night drinking coffee and reading *Catch 22* in the New Orleans bus depot. You meet the most "interesting" folks at 3am in a place like that.

Finally, my last hitch was up. As I got off the Timbalier for the last time, I said goodbye to Leroy and thanked him for getting us around safely. Sue took me aside and actually spoke to me, maybe for the first time.

"Well, Schoolboy, I got to say you were a pretty hard worker. You did a good job. Now go on back to school and if you do good, you won't have to come back here no more." Sue cracked a small smile, picked up his bagful of girly mags and walked off to the supervisor's bunkhouse.

As I was about to get on the crew boat a few minutes later, I heard Sue whistle like he did when he wanted the crew's attention. I turned around and he was walking back toward me.

"The superintendent just told me who your daddy is," he whispered kind of angrily. "Why didn't you tell me?"

I thought for a second. "Would it have made any difference?" I asked.

He paused and thought. Turning away, he muttered, "I guess not. You better get on that boat. They're about to haul ass."

Dad got good reports about me. I was happy that I became one of the guys for a while and that I pulled my own weight. I was looking forward to going back to school, but also wondering what the next summer would hold.

12

Paradis

IN the summer of 1981, Dad got me a summer job at a gas processing plant "up the bayou" from Dog Lake. Pawpaw had bought and fixed-up an old Chevy Nova and made it available for my use for the summer, so I wouldn't be riding the Greyhound! I flew down to Slidell and spent a weekend seeing the grandparents. Monday morning I started out at 5am and drove to Paradis, Louisiana where the facility was located.

I got a room at a little, run-down motel near the plant. I didn't do much exploring and didn't sample any of the local nightlife as I was trying to bank as much of my paycheck as possible. I had a styrofoam cooler that served as my refrigerator. I lived on fast food and beer. To be honest, I was a little apprehensive about going out alone in New Orleans, which does have its seedier side. But it turned out that I wouldn't have to leave my room to have a brush with the the Big Easy's "adult entertainment" industry.

One night the phone in my room rang. That was odd because no one knew where I was staying.

"Hello?" I answered.

"Hi. Is Joe there?" a sultry-sounding female voice asked.

"No. You must have the wrong number," I said, ready to hang up.

"Well, you sound nice, what's your name?" she asked.

An alarm went off in my head. In a instant my brain raced through the possibilities. This phone worked through the motel switchboard. This woman was probably in the motel office. And she wasn't a lady looking for someone named Joe. She was probably a hooker looking for a "john". And the desk clerk probably pointed her to rooms where single men were staying, probably for a piece of the action. I was in a panic!

"N-no thank you," I stammered and hung up the phone. If I had any thoughts of going out on the town, they were erased and looked forward to getting to back to work.

Back at the gas plant, I think the word was out about who my dad was. Everyone was very nice to me. And they really didn't give me very much to do. I shared an office with two young engineers, Terry and Mark. Mark was from New Jersey although he had been in Louisiana long enough to call it home. Terry was a Louisiana native. Over the course of the eight weeks I worked at the plant, Mark and I went out a couple of times for a beer at the local spot. He and his girlfriend had a pool party at his place and I was invited. I met a couple of her girl friends, which was nice.

Terry was active on a couple of plant projects. He was pressure-testing a pipeline he had previously installed. The testing was not going well. Every time he would fix a leak, another one would be found. But Terry was persistent and had support of the older, more experienced engineers. I sometimes wondered if they weren't pranking him by creating some of the leaks, but those were just suspicions. When he wasn't working, Terry and I would talk. He was about my age, where Mark was a few years older. I asked Terry what he liked to do for fun. He said he hunted and fished. He asked what I liked to do.

"I'm into music," I said.

"Oh? Who do you like to listen to?" Terry asked.

"Oh, the Beatles, the Stones, the Who, Pink Floyd, Steely Dan, all the classics," I said. "What about you?"

Terry thought about it and said with a smile, "I like Burl Ives!"

I laughed out loud. Then I caught myself. He was serious. There was an awkward silence.

Then I said, "He's a good actor too."

Terry smiled and nodded. We didn't exchange any cassette tapes that summer.

It was a fairly uneventful eight weeks. I mostly learned how the gas processing facility worked. I didn't really make a big mark there. The most remarkable thing that happened was at a routine safety meeting that I attended. An older gentleman was given the Texaco Safe Driving Award. He had operated his own private automobiles and driven Texaco company vehicles for FIFTY YEARS without an accident or citation. FIFTY YEARS! For starters, this guy was seventy-five years old! Not only had he been working for the same company since it started, but he had never had an accident or gotten a ticket. I marveled at his longevity, his consistency, and his staying power. I wondered what my career would hold for me. Where would I be in fifty years?

Part Two

My Brilliant "Career" or Lessons From the "Gotchas"

With my graduation from UConn in May of 1983, came unemployment. Out of a graduating class of 42 chemical engineers that year, two had job offers in hand at graduation. One was from the US Army and the other was from Exxon, who it was rumored, offered jobs to every chemical engineer graduating at the top of his or her class from the top 100 engineering schools in the country. The retention rate after one year for those engineers was supposedly extremely low.

My parents welcomed me home and encouraged me to rest and relax at home for the summer. After a few weeks, I began to get restless and decided to start looking for a job. This being the pre-internet age, my search began not on Google, but at the New Canaan Public Library. I found a Thomas' Register and looked up "chemical engineering" and found very few entries in Connecticut. Not good. I typed up letters to each of these companies and sent them off, never hearing back. I had hoped to at least get an interview before being rejected, but that was not to be.

Plan B in my job search was to consult an "executive recruiter". True, I didn't have the hubris to believe I would get an executive job in chemical engineering, but I had to start somewhere. I put on my best suit, composed my admittedly weak resume, and made an appointment with a firm in nearby Stamford. The gentleman with whom I met was professional and courteous. He listened attentively to my history. He seemed impressed by my work experience during those two summers with Texaco and in the lab at UConn. He told me those were things that set me apart from other recent graduates. Then his tone got serious.

"Steven, let me explain how our business works. We don't find jobs for people. We find people for jobs. Our clients aren't job-seekers like yourself. Our clients are Fortune 500 companies who generally want experienced people. We rarely place individuals in entry-level positions such as you are seeking. You will most likely find your first job through the want ads in the newspaper or through a personal connection. I advise you to pursue those. Once you have some real work experience, come back and maybe we can help you."

And he showed me to the door.

I couldn't just sit around doing nothing, so I called the Manpower temp agency that I had worked for during holiday breaks since high school. They had found me temporary work in warehouses, industrial facilities, and even a law office in the past. If they could find something for me now, it would get me out of the house, give me a little spending money, and possibly end up being my career.

Manpower found me a gig stocking shelves at Bloomingdales. It wasn't a bad gig. Most of the employees and customers were women. None of the lifting was particularly heavy. And I was shuffled from fine china, to housewares, to linens often enough that I didn't go stir crazy. Six months passed slowly.

Then one evening, Dad came into my room and told me he had set up an interview for me with a high-tech company in New Jersey. I got the directions, dusted off my best suit and resume, and headed south.

*****

My father had a *career*. He worked for thirty-nine years for Texaco. He started out as a field roustabout working summers between semesters at LSU. Thirty-nine years later he was Senior Vice-President, basically running the multi-national corporation. That is a career.

I had a series of jobs. I used to wonder how it was that some people had careers and others had jobs. In close to thirty years I did witness a few folks seemingly rocket past me and my peers to big salaries and big responsibilities. Some of them made the switch from technical engineering to sales. Some of them had friends or relatives in high places. But most of us just went to work each day, grinding out the paperwork, completing projects, and hoping for the best.

*****

The first job I remember wanting to have was service station attendant. In 1964, the man who gassed up the family car wore a clean, pressed uniform, complete with a hat. He greeted you with a smile and asked politely what he could do for you. He would not only fill your tank with gasoline, but clean all the windows, inside and out, check the air pressure in all four tires, and check the level of oil and radiator coolant and offer to "top them off" for you. And that was when a gallon of gas cost twenty-five cents. You'd drive away with a full tank, a clean car, a Johnny Unitas beer mug, and a fistful of S&H green stamps, all for less than five bucks. My goodness, I am old!

After that, my career desires went from cowboy to pilot to fireman to whatever it was my dad did before I understood what it was he did. I've since come to believe that when it comes to choosing an occupation, it can be a choice between doing what your are good at or doing what you love. Doing what you are good at may be more likely to result in what most people would see as success. Money. Advancement. Professional recognition. But they say that if you do what you love, you never work a day in your life. If you can afford to, I think this is the better way.

One day, when I was a sophomore in high school, my dad dropped a "Money" magazine on my desk opened to a page describing which college majors made the most money. First and second were doctors and lawyers. Third were chemical engineers. I read the article and it said that students studying to be chemical engineers had to be good in math and science. I had always had an interest in science and I got excellent grades in all my courses. So I decided right then to become a chemical engineer and didn't seriously reconsider that decision for thirty years.

The question of whether I regret that decision is a difficult one to answer, as is the question of what I would have rather done. Some people are blessed with a burning desire to pursue a single passion. I was cursed with being well-rounded. That was something that parents wanted for their kids in the days when I was growing up. So, I worked hard and succeeded in school. But I also sang in choirs, acted in plays, enjoyed cooking, and even took up knitting for a while. I loved watching TV, mostly comedy and movies, listening to music, reading comic books, and watching and playing sports.

I recall my parents and my older sister had several emotional discussions about her future when she turned eighteen. She liked to sing and had a nice voice, but my parents wanted her to have the financial security of a "real career". The decision seemed to have snuck up on them all. I wanted to avoid that.

Among my earliest memories is seeing my dad leaving for work at 6:30am. He would be gone nearly twelve hours and return home tired, but with a smile on his face and kiss my mom and play with my sisters and me. Over the years, I never heard him complain, not even once, about work. His work was stressful and involved travel and time away from the family. He had massive responsibilities, murderous commutes, and a constantly evolving career that required him to take additional college courses and work many nights and weekends. He worked his way from entry-level summer employment between semesters in college to top executive leadership in a multi-national oil company over the course of 39 years.

When I was crying to him on the phone about having flunked out of college, I told him I was ashamed that I would never have a career like he had. He gently told me that there was more to his career than what he brought to it. He had come along at the right time, in the right place and had come into contact with the right people. Yes, he had worked hard and conducted himself well. But that wasn't the whole story. He encouraged me to make my career on my own terms.

13

COMTECH (DECEMBER 1983 - APRIL 1985)

SIX months after I had graduated, through the efforts of my dad, I had my first real interview for a real engineering job with Comtech.

At their offices, I met with an attractive English lady who was doing the hiring and a Chinese gentleman who was a technical expert. I'm not sure if I gave a great interview or if the fix was in from my dad having set it up with Comtech's president, but I got the job! The annual salary was twice what I had ever hoped to earn. The company would put me up in a hotel, meals included, and help me find a permanent place to live.

On my first day, I settled into the office that I shared with Don. Don was a great guy who showed me the ropes and introduced me around. Comtech was a "high-tech" company for its day. And as such it employed a large number of younger people. Of the hundred and twenty-five employees, most were younger than thirty. This was so long ago that there were still a lot of secretaries to do typing, make coffee, and plan travel arrangements. In just a few years, engineers would do their own typing on PCs, make their own coffee, and book their own travel online. And so there were a lot of single young ladies at Comtech. Needless to say, there was an active after-hours scene that I became part of, including joining the company softball team. As a tall lefty, I became the first baseman.

I got assigned to a project that would create a simulation of an ethylene production plant. The complex simulation was optimized based on available feedstocks to make the most profit at all times, based on the real-time conditions. After a test period, the simulation would be used to run the plant. I had learned the programming language Fortran IV in college. These guys were using Fortran 77, which was very similar. In college we had used old, paper IBM punchcards, each of which contained one line of code. It was time-consuming and tedious to assemble a huge deck of those cards and feed them through a card reader, only to find out that there was an error somewhere in the deck. Then you would troubleshoot, or debug, the program looking for and correcting the error. This was repeated until the program ran without error. Then you found out if it produced the expected answer. If not, it was time for more debugging.

Comtech had a big, windowless room where thirty or so engineers worked away at their programs. At the center of the room was the mainframe. All around the perimeter of the room were monochrome monitors and keyboards linked to the mainframe. Instead of coding onto cards, we programmed on the monitors and our programs were saved into the mainframe's memory! Gee whiz! A group of other young engineers had been hired a month or two before I was. They were sent off to a programming school in New York City. They apparently had a blast living in a nice hotel for two weeks and eating out on an expense account and learning all the basics of using a system like the one Comtech used. I was never sent to this training. I was expected to pick it up "on the fly", which I did, kind of.

To be honest, I was not a great programmer. I created one large program that simulated a big heat exchanger. I based it on, that is to say plagiarized from, a pre-existing program that I was given as a model. When I finished my portion of the project, other programmers re-worked my program to make it smaller so it would run faster. That turned out to be the hardest part of the project. The simulation of the ethylene plant had to run several times a minute to give a mathematical optimizer information so various operating scenarios could be tested to determine the optimal economic scenario. If it sounds confusing, it was. Eventually, the project manger and Don got the thing to run. Don spent most of a year in Germany doing customer acceptance testing and training the customer's engineers to run it.

Before I could be assigned to another engineering project, I was presented with the opportunity to transfer to the sales department to be the Proposal Engineer. Instead of working in a windowless room filled with male engineers clacking away at keyboards, I would have a nice, private office and work in a department with six attractive females. I'd do the technical writing for the sales proposals that the group prepared for a small corps of salesmen who were almost always on the road. This was more like it!

I enjoyed the next few months writing and reviewing the slick packages that we put together. The salesmen would call in or have meetings with us to ask for special things to be put into the proposals for certain clients and we would respond. It all felt very productive. I never did ask how many sales were actually made. I just focused on the work I had to do. I thought I must have been pretty good at it too because one day our European salesman asked to have a meeting with just me. He was a Spaniard with a slight accent who had a bit of an arrogant manner, which I chalked up to ego. It seemed to me that salesmen had to have a strong ego as they were in a competitive business. They competed with salesmen from other companies for business and with salesmen within Comtech for bragging rights. He came into my office, closed my door, sat across from me, leaning in and began to talk.

"Steven, the work you do is excellent. I have big plans for you. I am going to ask the VP of Sales to assign you to work only for me. Europe has more opportunity than any other part of the world. The next quarter is going to be huge for me. For us. And I want you to be a part of this. Eventually, I want to take you on a tour of all my clients. Rome. Paris. London. Amsterdam. Oslo. Munich. You will help me make many sales. Eventually, Steven, I want you to be…"

I assumed his next words would be "my successor as European Sales Manager!"

Instead they were, "my *assistant*!"

Assistant? Needless to say, nothing ever came of this meeting. I suspect he never met with the VP of Sales. Unbeknownst to me, Comtech sales were in the dumper. We had been operating in the red for a year. Something would have to be done.

Digression - I mentioned that there was an active social scene at Comtech. This included all of the single, young engineers (mostly male) and all of the single, young secretarial and clerical staff (mostly female). There were a few married folks who would join in too. I had heard a rumor that one married gentleman might be having more than "drinks and dinner" with one of the single young ladies. I don't know whether this was true. I never saw any evidence of it. It was just something I heard.

At Halloween, there was a costume party that the whole group attended at the house of one of the employees. I wore a borrowed karate outfit, mingled, danced, and had a few drinks. I noticed that among all my costumed co-workers, there was one person dressed as a scarecrow. He wore overalls, work gloves and a full-face rubber mask. Good costume. I also noticed that when anyone would approach him and talk to him, he would only mime his response. He never spoke to anyone. Odd, I thought. And I had another drink. I left the party later and would never have thought about it again except for what happened about a month later at the company Christmas party.

My girlfriend and I sat at a large table and witnessed this exchange. Tony, a programmer who had been at the Halloween party was talking about what a good time he had there.

Tony said, "Steve, you had on the karate guy outfit, right? Ellen, you wore the cute little space alien costume. And Ben, you had on that weird scarecrow get-up. Wasn't it hot wearing that mask all night?"

Ben squirmed in his seat. Ben's wife spoke up, "Oh Tony, you must have had too much to drink that night. Ben wasn't even there! He was out of town on business."

Tony rebutted, "Oh, no. Ben was there. Weren't you? You had on overalls and a straw hat. Remember? And those gloves and mask. And you were so funny the way you wouldn't say anything. People didn't even know it was you, but it was, right? I kept trying to get you to talk, but you never did."

All the blood had drained from Ben's face. His wife spoke up again, this time in a tightly controlled tone of voice, "Tony, Ben couldn't possibly have been at that party. He wanted to go, but he had to go out of town *on business*. I drove him to the airport that morning myself. Isn't that right, Ben?"

Ben nodded. The temperature in the room dropped to near absolute zero. Tony stopped talking and we all finished our meals in silence. Yikes! -End of digression.

How blissfully ignorant I was, fifteen months later, when I was called into the Vice-President's office. I thought he might be giving me some new assignment or that he just wanted to meet me because he "liked the cut of my jib". No, he fired me. Actually, he said, my position and twenty others were being eliminated. Same thing. If I had stayed in the windowless room programming, I thought, this wouldn't have happened. Shocked doesn't begin to describe how I felt. I had no idea what I was going to do next.

Gotcha #1: A company must make a profit in order to stay in business.

As I was walking out of the building for the final time, a co-worker I barely knew asked me if I was going to contact Simutronics, our direct competitor, located an hour south, to get a job there. He had heard they were hiring. I almost ignored him. And two weeks later, before I had even spent my severance pay, I had interviewed with them and accepted their job offer at a higher salary. I was on my way to my first day of work at my second real job.

14

Simutronics (May 1985 - September 1988)

LITTLE did I know (or care) that I was moving from one sinking ship to another. I would still have a paycheck coming in. Simutronics was owned by its founder, a jolly, paternal fellow who had been very successful selling an analog operator training simulator to the petrochemical industry for over a decade. Looking back years later, I could tell you that I had joined an analog company just as digital had become the way to go. On what seemed like my second day of work there, the jolly, paternal owner of the company sold out to a lean, mean 1980s energy conglomerate who promptly dispatched two hard-ass, ex-military executives to extract profits from the place.

After losing my first job to a "corporate right-sizing", I feared the same thing was about to happen at my second. The differences in the two companies struck me at once. Comtech had offices in a modern office complex adjacent to the parent company's sprawling campus. Simutronics was housed in what had been a candy factory. Its vast, empty warehouses were sometimes leased as temporary storage for ten million tennis balls or ten thousand lawn mowers. Comtech had a slick, new, image of the go-go 80s. Simutronics was a tired company that was selling to the same customers it had for years, only they weren't buying as much any more. Comtech had a huge corporate parent to fall back on. Simutronics had been owned by a beloved grandpa who started the company with a few engineers in the late 60s. They now had nothing to fall back on except their butts.

Having come from Comtech's sales support group, I was plugged right into Simutronic's marketing group. I became one of five people who did technical writing and sales support. There was a sales staff of a half dozen who had territories as far flung as Asia and Europe. There were a couple dozen engineers who wrote computer simulation programs that ran on the systems that other engineers designed. A group of drafters and techs assembled the systems and documentation. And a small field support group installed and serviced the systems. The product was a computer-based training simulator, similar to what they train pilots on, only for chemical or power plant operators.

The atmosphere at Simutronics was one of relaxed confidence. Back in the 60s and 70s they had sold dozens, if not hundreds, of big, analog simulators all over the world. Companies had trained generations of operators using the things and their after-market needs for updates and additional programs kept Simutronics afloat, barely.

What Simutronics did not see coming in the mid 1980s was the digital revolution that was making their old simulators obsolete. Also, they did not foresee the explosive growth in computing power that, within a decade, would see inexpensive desktop PCs eclipse the custom-built "super-mini-computer" systems they were invested in. The people at Simutronics also didn't see the hard-nosed no-nonsense financial boom of the 80s coming. Barely breaking even was about to become not nearly good enough.

> ***Gotcha #2: A company must keep up with, if not ahead of, the times.***
> ***Gotcha #2a: Kindly, understanding managers can disappear in an instant to be replaced by the other kind.***

I had only been at Simutronics a few weeks when an off-site sales meeting was scheduled. The new owners wanted a look at what they had bought. I was the first to arrive at the nondescript meeting room in a local hotel. A neatly-dressed gent in his mid-40s arrived after me. I had not met him before. I had met, I thought, all of the Simutronics staff, but I wasn't sure. He could have been one of the overseas-based salesmen. He asked me who I was and what I did. I told him. He asked me if I would help him by identifying each of the Simutronics people as they arrived. He had a cool demeanor and I sensed that his request was really an order with which I was happy to comply. He sat next to me. As the room filled, I quietly told the mystery man who each new arrival was and what they did. The room filled. There was general chit-chat until a second smartly-dressed fellow with a blow-dried hair style took a spot in front of us all.

"Who knows when the Battle of Hastings was?" he began.

I raised my hand. "1066," I replied instinctively. My passion for trivia had betrayed me.

"Nobody cares!" Mr. Blow-dry shot back at me.

I slumped in my chair. I resolved to be quietly attentive the rest of the day to avoid further shots.

"From this moment forward, we are not going to dispense information. That is not our job. From this moment forward we are all salesmen. When someone asks us a question, we will ask them a question in return. We will acquire information and use that information to make sales quickly, all day, every day. And we will make…"

He drew a big dollar sign on the flip chart beside him. Mr. Blow-dry went around the room asking what everyone did. Not their names. Only their jobs. Whatever the person said they did, Mr. Blow-dry would correct them, telling them they were now a salesman. When he got to the salesmen, he would ask them their names and tell them he would be speaking to them in private after the meeting.

Mr. Blow-dry then launched into a rambling revival-style sermon that was richly punctuated with homey sayings, cliches and *non sequiturs*. Eventually it became clear he was teaching a method of selling. He never mentioned simulators. He told stories from his past career in which he was invariably the hero. He related tales of great success and huge paydays. He had the smooth line of BS that seemed to me like the prelude to a fraudulent land deal or Ponzi scheme.

Eventually, some the more senior salesmen, who must have felt their jobs were very secure began to push back. They questioned whether Mr. Blow-dry knew anything about the product Simutronics made. Mr. Blow-dry told them he did not and that furthermore he did not want or need to. Then he would ask them the dollar value of the sales they made in the last year. They would tell him and he would say that he could make that amount in a week. If he was trying to ruffle feathers, he was succeeding.

He launched back into his description of how sales should be done. He talked about cold calling, creating prospects, and how to get around secretaries whose job it was to keep salespeople from bothering their bosses. The system he described involved never giving a straight answer, but always answering a question with a question. It used all kinds of pop psychology tricks. Never ask for information, ask for your prospect to "share" what they know. It's nice to share. Mother taught us to share. Open every call by mentioning "problems that may exist" at your prospect's company "that are costing them money every day". Who wouldn't want to talk about their problems? Who wouldn't want to save money?

Mr. Blow-dry was good. He was smooth. And the hours flew by as he evangelized about "the system". The few questions he was asked were quickly turned back on the questioner in a way that communicated that more aggressive questioning might not be in one's best interest. Better to sit back and listen to the snake oil being sold.

Finally, at the end of the day, Mr. Blow-dry had presented the whole system. It almost sounded like he was making it up as he went, but suddenly we all had a book in our hands that described the system in detail. This was to become our Bible, he told us. We were to do everything it said and nothing it did not say. This inspired a crescendo of grumbling from the salesmen and prompted the chap who had been sitting silently next to me all day to stand and walk to the front of the room.

He introduced himself by name and said that he was now The Boss at Simutronics. He shook Mr. Blow-dry's hand and Mr. Blow-dry exited the room. The Boss told everyone in the room that we were failing and that the herd was about to be thinned. Nothing that had come before meant anything. Simutronics was hemorrhaging money and the bleeding was going to stop now. Bill Grant, a senior salesman stood up and said that he had been entertained by Mr. Blow-dry and his show, but that wasting his day like this was not going to bring in any money. He had made more sales than anyone that year and in the five previous years. He knew how to sell simulators and he was insulted being treated like an entry-level underling. The Boss asked Grant to step outside the room with him and returned alone a moment later.

"Mr. Grant no longer works for Simutronics. Does anyone else have anything to say?"

After an audible gasp, no one made a peep.

"From now on, everyone is a salesman. There are no marketers. There are no proposal engineers. There are no sales support personnel. The group I see in front of me is completely expendable. I can save money by firing you all right now. But I will not fire anyone who can pull his own weight and bring in this…" He pointed to the dollar sign on the flip chart.

The Boss explained that tomorrow, when we got to work, each of us would have a 3x5 card on our desk with the name of an industry on it. We were to make ten cold calls every day to top executives in that industry and generate leads which we would pass on to him on other 3x5 cards. Failure to do so would result in loss of employment. I resolved at that moment to do three things. First, I would make ten cold sales calls tomorrow morning. Second, I would drink heavily that night. Third, I would begin looking for a new job immediately.

The next morning, I found a 3x5 card on my desk that

said "Pulp and Paper". Next to it was a stack of ten blank 3x5 cards and a form showing how they were to be filled out with information collected from each call. I wasted no time. My "Bible" had a script that I adapted to fit the pulp and paper industry. I grabbed a copy of the industrial directory for pulp and paper and began making calls.

> Me: Hello, my name is Steven Yates. May I speak to Plant Manager Mr. Smith?
> Secretary: What is this in regard to?
> Me: I need speak with Mr. Smith about problems that may exist there at the mill.
> Secretary: One moment please.
> Mr. Smith: Hello?
> Me: Mr. Smith, thank you for taking my call. I'll get right to the point. I believe there may be problems at your mill that are costing Acme Paper Company money every day.
> Mr. Smith: What kind of problems?
> Me: I'm glad you asked. Would you share with me how you folks do training of your facility operators?
> Mr. Smith: Mostly on-the-job training. Why do you ask? Is this a problem?
> Me: I am pleased that you are as concerned about this situation as I am. Can you share with me your level of satisfaction with safety performance at your mill?
> Mr. Smith: Well, safety is a concern. We have had a number of lost time accidents in the past year.
> Me: Thank you for sharing that with me. Can you share your sense of how pleased you are with profits at the mill?

Mr. Smith: Well, the industry has been hit by a broad slowdown in demand, as you know. Profits could be significantly better. The accidents don't help with that, as you can imagine.

Me: I understand and I share your feelings. Mr. Smith, if I could provide you with a cost-effective means of reducing lost-time accidents and improving your mill's profits, would you be at all interested?

Mr. Smith: Of course. What are you talking about?

Me: I am glad you asked. My company offers training solutions that reduce the accidents you expressed concern about. Further, these same solutions may increase productivity and decrease costs thus improving profits. Would you be interested in getting more information about a specific solution to your problems?

Mr. Smith: Yes, please.

Me: May I share the details of our conversation with a colleague of mine that is in your area and arrange for him to come see you?

Mr. Smith: Yes. I will be in all week.

Me: He'll call you not later than tomorrow. Thank you. Goodbye.

It worked! The plant manager of a huge paper mill had spoken to me out of the blue, giving me details of his operation, and all but invited one of our salesmen to see him! I laughed out loud.

"Fun, isn't it?"

I looked up and The Boss had been standing silently behind me.

"Yes. I can't believe this guy told me about his mill and invited us in!"

The Boss didn't crack a smile. "Nine more," he said.

And I went back to the phone.

My co-workers were not as quick to embrace the cold calling. A few salesmen bristled and refused. One more was fired. The head of the marketing department offered an alternative strategy to the cold calling. He wanted to launch a program of mailings and meetings with our old customers to increase their aftermarket purchasing. He and his department made an elaborate Friday afternoon pitch to the Boss. Monday morning their area was vacant. No cubicles. No desks. Just empty floor space. All four of them had been fired.

By the end of two weeks I had submitted over a hundred 3x5 cards to Sales. The next highest total was less than ten. This was not good. I didn't like doing the calls, but it filled the time and kept me from worrying about getting fired. I was married. We were planning to have kids. I needed this job, at least until I could find another one. After all, I was an engineer. I wanted to get back to engineering.

Maybe The Boss had read my mind. Maybe Mr. Blow-dry had. One afternoon, I looked up from my cold-calling and sitting in my cubicle was Mr. Blow-dry.

"Got a second, Hot-shot?" he asked.

I followed him to a conference room. He shut the door behind us.

"Steve, right?" I nodded. "Steve, how much do you make a year?"

"$32,000" I said.

"Do you know how much the salesmen here make?"

"No."

"Too much," he laughed. "Some of them make sixty, some eighty. Do you know how much you could make as a salesman here?"

"No."

"Ten times that. Easy. Guaranteed. Do you like to travel?"

"Sure."

"How does traveling the world making high six figures sound to you?"

"Sounds pretty good. Is this an offer for me to change jobs?"

"Do you want it to be?"

"I'd have to talk to my wife."

"Talk to her, Steve."

And he walked out of the room. Back at my desk I tried to make sense of what was happening. I knew the salesmen travelled constantly. Most of them were divorced. I didn't want that. I knew that most of their salary was commission on sales. And I knew there was competition. Cut-throat competition. I wasn't wild about that. That night I poured over the want-ads. I saw a couple of engineering positions and sent out a couple of resumes.

A week or so later, I looked up from my cold calling and there was The Boss.

"So, you're a Connecticut Yankee, huh?"

"I lived in Connecticut most of my life. I went to UConn. Yes, I guess I am."

"So, what do you think about taking over sales for me?"

"Taking over sales?"

"Well, I see you taking Far East from Williams. And maybe Middle East from Rogers. Then we'll see. Are ready to make that kind of money?

"What kind of money?"

He barely cracked a smile. "A lot more than you're making now."

I was shaking inside, but tried maintaining a calm facade. I had already told my wife about this "offer" and we agreed that I wasn't going to become a traveling salesman for a company that was losing money and that I should play along for as long as I could and if I got fired, well, I was looking for a job when I found this one. I'd be no worse off.

"I'm not sure I want to travel as much as this job will require. My wife and I are planning on starting a family," I said.

"All that money will make that a lot easier," The Boss fired back.

"But I wouldn't want it to go to divorce lawyers and alimony."

"It's like that?"

"It might be."

"Well, what do you want to do for Simutronics?"

"I'm glad you asked. You know I am an engineer by training. I was an engineer for Comtech. I only got into sales support, I mean sales, for some variety after I had done my first programming project. When they laid me off, I saw Simutronics was looking for technical sales support *at that time*. And so here I am. I spent five years getting a chemical engineering degree. It seems like an asset I should use."

The Boss sighed and walked out of my cubicle. A few days later I transferred to the engineering group and started work on a project of my own. A few weeks went by. I got the hang of the Simutronics process and was making decent progress. Then came an engineering department meeting with The Boss.

It was an odd meeting. The Boss told us that sales were poor and that layoffs were likely in the future if things didn't get better. Some of the engineers asked what we could do to help. The Boss said that we could work faster. This would reduce costs. They asked if we would get raises if we could do that. The Boss cracked a little smile.

He said, "If I can do the same amount of work next week with nine engineers that I need ten for this week, I would reduce staff by one engineer. Logic, right?"

A chill settled on the room. A recently hired young engineer spoke up. He clearly did not grasp what was going on. He asked if the tuition reimbursement program for engineers who were doing post-graduate studies would be expanded. The Boss did not smile. He asked how Simutronics benefitted from having overly-educated engineers. The room got even chillier. Tuition reimbursement was a standard benefit in technical industries, the young engineer ventured.

"You don't seem to understand," The Boss glared. "I could replace everyone in this room with a recent college grad and save half of what I'm paying you all now. And you want me to finance your higher education? What, so you can take the skills I paid for to my competition?"

Simutronics staff continued to slowly shrink. Beyond the handful of firings, anyone who could find another job did. And everyone else was looking. Tough job markets benefit crummy employers. The threat of more firings remained mostly a threat and after a while it became like life during wartime. A grim gallows humor pervaded the place. Everyone expected that every meeting would be the one where the ax would fall. A benefit of the people quitting or being fired was lowered salary costs, giving the company a bit of breathing room.

As grim as the day-to-day was at Simutronics, they did continue to find a very small amount of money for such things as the annual Christmas parties. To save money, they were for staff only. No spouses or dates. One year, there was a Christmas party at a VFW hall in a bad part of town. We assembled there for drinks (cash bar) and snacks (potato chips) and to wish one another the best of the season (and quietly exchange job leads). On a table was a single gift-wrapped box. This was the door prize.

Speculation was that it was a VCR. This was a time when VCRs were just starting to come down in price, but it was still a pretty nice prize. At the end of the evening, The Boss drew a door prize ticket and one of my lucky co-workers won what was in the box. It wasn't a VCR. It was a case of cans of store-brand cola. If you look up the word "underwhelming" in the dictionary, it will refer you back to this story.

The next year, the HR lady was given a small budget for a Christmas lunch. It was held at a nice, but modest little restaurant not far from our offices. Part of the small budget was designated for "entertainment". Now, if it had been my job to organize this shin-dig, I might have hired a DJ, or maybe even a Santa to give out candy canes. But this conservative-looking, mother of two, HR lady was thinking a bit more "outside the box". Keep in mind that we all lived in fear of The Boss and his constant threats of layoffs and firings. He didn't appear to have any sense of humor about anything.

The luncheon was quiet and uneventful. We all ate our chicken divan and drank our one drink. Friends gave each other cards. It was actually quite nice, especially for Simutronics. Then the president called for the entertainment. The HR lady gave a signal and a boom box began to play some sort of loud, non-holiday, electronic dance music. Then, I kid you not, a transvestite stripper entered the room and began to disrobe. He twirled and brushed up against a number of people, transferring an acrid, weapons-grade perfume onto them as he did. Then he zeroed-in on The Boss. The stripper was down to a g-string by the time he started grinding against the unmoving, unsmiling former Navy sub captain. It seemed to last an eternity. The dancer wrapped a feather boa around The Boss's neck and then, as the song mercifully ended, collapsed dramatically at his feet.

There was profound, shocked, absolute silence. The Boss glared at the HR lady. If looks could kill, she would have been a small pile of ash. She hurriedly shoo'ed the stripper out of the room, into a car, and back to wherever he had come from. The party was over. Well, it was memorable at least.

The Boss took an outsider's look at every process at Simutronics. He was looking to cut down to the bare bones. There wasn't much fat left to cut, but he kept looking. There was a Production Coordinator at Simutronics, Bob Henderson. He was a great guy. Scout leader. Baseball coach. Well-liked and popular. His office was a beehive of activity, the nerve center. He had a wall with every active project depicted on it. There were little colored magnets that showed the various stages of completion of the various projects. The magnets showed who was working on what and when the next phase of production would begin. It was like an air traffic controller's radar screen for our business. Bob acted as liaison between engineering and sales, between hardware and software, between production and shipping. Bob had a finger in every pie and seemed to be the glue that kept the business from falling apart. He could handle the demanding salesmen calling in from Timbuktu to ask when their customers would be getting their updates. He would soothe the guys assembling the systems when the engineers would make last-minute changes to the designs. He made sure the tech support guys had the tools they needed to service systems at remote customer sites. Bob was clearly indispensable.

That's why it was such a shock when Bob got the ax one Friday afternoon. The company was in shock. The Boss had gone too far, cut too deep. He must be an idiot not to see that Bob Henderson was the one guy we just couldn't do without. When the new work week started, the production guys had to talk directly to the engineers. The salesmen had to call over to the tech support guys to get their answers. The shipping people had to walk next door to see how the production guys were doing in order to schedule shipments. Basically, the middleman had been cut out and everything ran exactly as before except now there were no little colored magnets being moved on that board any more. I don't know how much Bob Henderson had been making, but Simutronics saved that much and never missed a beat. I never forgot that. Just because someone is busy and seems to be doing something important, if they do not add actual value, maybe they are just dead weight.

Every other week or so, I would look up from my computer to see The Boss or Mr. Blow-dry sitting in my cubicle asking if I was ready to be a rich man yet. The other engineers would come by after they had left and ask if I was in trouble. I told them I didn't think so.

And then one day, one of those resumes I sent out got me an interview, then a job offer, then a new job. I gave my two-weeks' notice at Simutronics. I never saw The Boss or Mr. Blow-dry after that. The engineering department gave me a big going-away lunch. We all got pretty loaded. The normally straight-laced senior engineers made paper airplanes of their placemats and had contests to see whose would fly furthest. The tech service guys and I stayed at the bar deep into the afternoon. Everyone wished me well and quite a few of the guys slipped me their resumes and asked for letters of recommendation. I said yes to every one of them. Their friendship had helped me get through tough times at Simutronics.

Several months later, at my new job, doing actual engineering work, I was joined by a half dozen of my former Simutronics colleagues. I hadn't helped them get their jobs. I hadn't been asked to. But one of them told me that when the first one gave notice that he was quitting Simutronics to go to work at the same place where Steven had gone, The Boss had remarked that Simutronics had been "raided". I wish I could take credit for that.

So, what had I learned so far? Not much. Try to work for a company that sells something that someone else wants to buy and try to work for bosses that have an ounce of human compassion. I wonder if they teach that at the Harvard School of Business?

15

CONTINENTAL E&C (SEPTEMBER 1988 - DECEMBER 1990)

IT'S impossible to say how many want ads I responded to. I would tweak my resume and write a custom cover letter for each opportunity. Eventually, one of these "messages in a bottle" got a response from an engineering and construction (E&C) firm half an hour north and I was on my way to work at my third real job. I applied what I had learned at my first two real jobs and found out that 1) this company was doing marginally better than the first two and seemed to have enough clients and sales and 2) my boss was a friendly but world-weary fellow who seemed to enjoy nurturing young engineers who were just starting out. Whew! Then I learned that there were other "gotchas".

Gotcha #3: Some jobs involve living away from home.
Gotcha #3a Nothing to do can be worse than being too busy.

The "gotcha" at this place turned out to be that most of the engineers did their work not from the pleasant, conveniently-located headquarters office, but from "client sites".

This generally meant trailers on construction sites in bad neighborhoods, dark offices deep in the bowels of shut-down factories, or some isolated corner of a pleasant office building ten hours from where your family was. As a young, married man who was just about to start his family, this didn't seem like a job that would fit into my life plan.

Digression - A word about my experience with HR people. I've concluded that they have a lot in common with salespeople. They typically appear friendly and professional. They make the company they work for sound like a good place to work. And after one has committed and taken a job, they all but disappear. Sometimes they actually disappear.

The HR man who handled my hiring with Comtech, had left that company by the time I started work there two weeks later. The same thing with the HR woman at Simutronics. I was thirty minutes into a meeting with the Continental E&C HR man, when I realized he was the former Comtech HR man who had hired me there five years earlier!

Over the years I've noticed that many companies utilize professional-looking, well-dressed, older men and women to sell their services. It gives a customer confidence to close a deal with a handshake with an experienced, silver-haired veteran of the trade. That's why it's a shock when the work crew arrives looking, well, like a work crew. Young, unshaven, long hair, tattoos, cigarette dangling from their lips.

I don't wish to insult anyone, but I think the average HR person has a "career path" not unlike my own. - End of digression.

But I had just started, and so I was committed to doing the best job I could, at least until I got a better offer. I had only been in the office a few days when I got an assignment to work on a project in Ronkonkoma, Long Island. I would be living there Monday through Thursday nights, coming home Friday after work and returning Monday morning. Not an ideal work arrangement, but since my wife was commuting to a job in Manhattan, we'd really only be losing a few waking hours together per week.

I packed a bag and drove to the facility on Long Island the following Monday. It was a nearly completed trash-to-energy plant, a facility designed to burn trash and produce electricity. A company had built the whole facility and then gone belly-up the last day. Their insurance company was paying my company, Continental E&C, to complete the job. I entered one of the trailers and found two men inside. They worked for Continental, but didn't seem thrilled to see me. I tried not to take it personally. Eventually, I came to understand what was bugging them. Nothing. There was nothing going on. They were being paid to occupy the trailer and do, basically, nothing. And here I was, another guy to help them do nothing. And I wasn't the last of the team. We were staffing up.

A brand new trailer was brought in and five of us set about furnishing it with desks, chairs, office supplies, coffee maker, etc. And then we did…nothing. We sat at our desks from 8am to 4:40 pm, taking a half-hour for lunch. It would have been fun if there had been a TV or if we could have openly read books or magazines. But there was a strange unspoken rule that everyone had to pretend we were busy doing useful work. No one came to check on us. No one pressed us to demonstrate any progress. We just had to be there. I kept a stack of blueprints on my desk. I would open one of them and then put a notebook on top of that and make little personal notes about what I would do on the weekend in my notebook. If anyone came over to my desk, I would put the notebook away and pretend I was looking at the blue print. And everyone else was doing the same thing!

Eventually, I was asked to write a "progress report" each week and turn it in with my time sheet. I wrote a few lines about "reviewing construction diagrams" and turned it in. There was never any feedback. So I kept writing "reviewing construction diagrams" and kept being paid. In fact, they assigned a senior engineer to our trailer two days a week. He praised our work to his bosses and spent his two days a week on the phone to his wife discussing their daughter and son-in-law. He even took us all out for expense-account dinners once a week!

Speaking of expense accounts. I began to bring a large cooler full of food from home to the hotel each week. I would live on that and pocket my *per diem* money. I used it to build a sizable CD collection. It was a nice way to reward myself for the hours of tedium. But over the months it became too much for me. I eventually asked to be reassigned. Obligingly, the company brought me back to headquarters, installed me in an office, and assigned me to a series of projects, about half of which entailed me doing…nothing.

Over time, I came to see that Continental E&C (and presumably all its competitors) overbid on all of its jobs and had to assign excess staff to fill out the hours that they charged to the customers. If there was a sudden need for labor, the staff was already in place. Again, no one talked about this. Everyone acted as if they were busy doing work. But a lot of us were "reviewing construction documents". Now, I must add that some of my assignments involved real, productive engineering work. I learned a lot from a number of excellent engineers. But there was, let's say, plenty of slack time built into the schedules. And I learned that there was a fine art to "acting busy" when I brought in a small radio that I played at a very low volume. A senior engineer who was nominally my "project manager" on a job where I was "reviewing construction documents" for several weeks came into my office and closed the door.

"Steve, I think that you should consider removing the radio from your office," he said.

"OK, Dave. I'll get rid of it. Thanks for saying something. Was it bothering someone?" I asked.

"No. No. It's just that…I think it may…interfere with your…creativity," he finally said.

"Yeah, sure, Dave. No problem. It's gone," I said.

And he left. My creativity? Doing what? I came to believe that this was his way of saying that entertaining one's self somehow crossed a line when it came to pretending to work. There was one other incident whose cause I traced back to the tedium of "work that wasn't work".

I shared an office with a gentleman who enjoyed wearing a lot of cologne and conducted a side business on the phone. You must understand that apart from lunchtime, the office was as quiet as a morgue. People doing actual work were quietly at it. And those of us who were "reviewing construction documents" were doing so silently, certainly without radios. And so over time, my officemate's loud conversations about obviously non-Continental E&C business became annoying. Not to mention his cologne. I asked around and many people in the office were aware of what was going on. They questioned how I put up with it.

I finally asked him in the nicest way I could to please

lower his voice. He did, for perhaps a minute. The next day, I repeated my request. Again, he complied, but only for a brief while. On the third day, after he hung up from his tenth loud, side-business call of the day, I again repeated my request. This time he exploded. He leapt to his feet.

With his back to our opened office door he began to rant and rave using explicit profanity in a very loud voice. If he had been a physically intimidating man, I might have been worried, but he was not. I could see that a crowd was beginning to gather outside our office. He either didn't see or didn't care. He swore at me repeatedly. I calmly asked him what he was talking about on the phone. He screamed that he was a stock day trader and was making a fortune. He could buy and sell me! The louder and angrier he got, the larger the crowd behind him grew. I saw our boss standing behind him.

I asked, "Does the company know you are using their phones to do private business?"

He screamed, "Of course they don't (expletive) know! They are (expletive) idiots!"

"Who?" I asked in my most innocent-sounding voice.

He proceeded to scream the names of several of the managers, most of whom were standing a few feet behind him. Finally, our boss tapped him on the shoulder and took him away. I never saw him again. And I had a private office!

My wife and I welcomed our daughter into the world in May of that year. Nice as parts of it are, we didn't want to raise our kids in New Jersey. We both felt Connecticut was our home. And so I began subscribing to two Connecticut papers and started scanning their want ads and sending out resumes and cover letters to companies there. Finally fortune smiled.

And so, fifteen months after I started with Continental

E&C, I was on my way to my fourth real job. It was at a chemical plant in Connecticut. It didn't seem like the greatest place to work. Its singular virtue was its location.

16

AJAX (JANUARY 1991 - JULY 1994)

THE company I joined, Ajax, had just been saved from failure by an Israeli businessman who bought in as a fifty percent joint venture partner. This meant that rather than being part of the well-known American company I thought I was joining, I was actually joining the bastard step-child of that company to which every windfall did not apply and every misfortune did. Shortly after I joined, there was a two-week furlough. This meant two weeks off with pay in mid-July. Not bad. But since I had not accrued any vacation time, two weeks were deducted from me, so I had *negative* vacation time accrued. For the next two years, I had no vacation at all as I worked to make up for the time off that had been forced on me that first year. There were pay freezes too.

This joint venture was headed by an Israeli gentleman who believed in hands-on management by fear and intimidation. He tried to keep everyone in an state of panic all the time, so that he could ask for things that the average American business would never consider. Did he really have to pay the workers for eleven holidays a year? Could he invite retirees back to do their former jobs in exchange for a free lunch and call it a "family picnic"? Did he have to sign the "Safety is Our #1 Priority" pledge? Wasn't profit the #1 priority?

There were meetings every morning where the supervisors coming off the night shift would have their every decision second-guessed, scrutinized, and criticized by the president of the company who had the benefit of knowing how each decision had worked out. The pressure to produce immediate results with no resources was titanic. I cracked almost immediately. I'd been bitten by "gotcha's" #1 and #2 again! Out came the want ads. But I'm getting ahead of myself.

Gotcha #4: Unions and being trapped.

You have not had a complete, well-rounded career unless it includes some time working in a "union shop". First, I must include this disclaimer in hopes of saving myself from the wrath of those who have enjoyed the positive benefits of union membership. My experience with unions is limited to two work experiences lasting a only handful of years. I am sure that there are many union shops where the workers are enthusiastic, productive, innovative assets to the companies for whom they work. I am also sure that society, our country and our economy benefit in many ways by the presence of unions and all that they do. And maybe the kind of tyrannical management that I wasn't being protected from is why there are unions in the first place! How was that?

My job title at Ajax was Project/Process Engineer. This meant that I would design and execute projects to aid in the production process and work in an ongoing manner to improve efficiency and productivity. My first day at the fifty-year-old facility I was introduced to the concept of break-lunch-break. All of the union production and maintenance staff would take a fifteen minute break in the morning at 10am and in the afternoon at 2pm and a half-hour break for lunch at noon. When I say all of the staff, I should add that some of the production staff would "cover" for the others so that the production units would keep running during these breaks and then take their own breaks on a staggered basis. When I say fifteen minute break, you have to add to that "wash-up time" and the time it takes to get from the work station to the washing up area and then to the break room. So fifteen minutes is closer to 30 minutes. And likewise the lunch break dilates from 30 minutes to somewhere north of 45 minutes.

This is just the tip of the iceberg of the Byzantine official written and unofficial, unwritten rules that governed almost every aspect of work at Ajax. Almost every worker carried a small paperback book in his or her back pocket. This was the union's contract, the rule book for conduct on the job. Over the course of fifty years in business, virtually every aspect of the working experience had been codified to define what was allowed and what was not. One can imagine that over many years, armies of workers had endless hours to study every word in the contract and figure every angle to determine the most financially advantageous way to conduct business. I hasten to add that the management likewise tried to "play" the contract to their every advantage.

For instance, I supervised a small group workers for a couple of years in a "round the clock" operation. They worked eight-hour shifts for ten days straight and then got three days off. Sometimes a worker would call in sick and one of the others would have to cover for him. My guys had perfected the calculus of maximizing the financial benefit to them (and thus the cost to the company) for such coverage. The cheapest way to cover an absence was to hold over a worker from the shift before for four hours and to call and ask a worker from the shift after to come in four hours early. This was rarely done as the on-duty workers could refuse to work the extra hours and the in-coming workers could refuse to come in early. And so the next contract-prescribed step was to call in one of the workers who was on one of his three days off.

The contract specified a premium had to be paid to workers coming in on a scheduled day off. It was "time and a half" for the first day, "double time" for the second day, and "double time and a half" for the third day. Remarkably, my workers almost never accepted an "emergency call-in" on their first or second day off. Instead, they would almost always accept the call on their third day off. In addition to the "double time and half" (i.e. 2.5 times normal) pay, they would receive an extra hour's pay for the accepting the "emergency call-in". So instead of making eight hour's pay, the worker would make 21 hour's pay! Each worker had a maximum number of absences that were allowed per year for various reasons and each worker generally took all of these. So, the company came to expect that it would pay the maximum specified by the contract for the labor it took to run the facility.

As a supervisor, one might be tempted to not fill a vacancy caused by an absence. However, such a decision almost always triggered a union grievance. The grievance procedure, also well established with its own set of arcane rules and procedures, was another bit of theater. One day a week, in a comfy meeting room, the company's managers and HR people would sit across a big table from the union stewards and president and negotiate the settlement of grievances. Of course the stewards and president were plant workers who were paid their usual hourly wage as they participated in these meetings and were consequently not that interested in expediting them.

The union's argument for many of its grievances was based on safety. In the example of not filling a vacancy, they might argue that doing a particular job with one fewer man was not safe and that the company was recklessly cutting corners and endangering the other workers to save a few dollars. Sometimes it must have been difficult for them to say such things with a straight face when the job was to sit at a panel board and record in a log book a half-dozen readings over eight hours. But they would sternly ask what would happen if a solitary worker had a heart attack. The company would have to propose solutions to every such suggested scenario until it became so ridiculous they would simply pay up.

I was at Ajax during a period of waning union power. The facility, once the town's largest employer, was shrinking. The workforce had dwindled to half what it had been at its peak in the 1950s. Generations of local families had worked at, and retired from, the facility. And many had done quite well financially. But as automation and down-sizing took its toll, the union was digging in for its last stand. And the workers, many of them, felt no allegiance to the company. Their interests were looked after by the union. They never seemed to connect the company's ailing balance sheet with their own goal of maximizing personal financial benefit. It was as if they thought the union could and would support them in the style to which they had become accustomed, even after the company closed its doors.

Every two years, the union contract would come up for

renewal. There would be negotiations leading up to the big union vote to either ratify the contract or strike. These negotiations would inevitably go on until the eleventh hour. My first experience with this took me by surprise. One day I was told to come into work on Sunday with a bag packed for an indefinite stay at work. Details were sketchy, but if the union failed to approve the contract, we engineers and supervisors would be locked into the facility and somehow carry on the business of manufacturing. We were not told how long such a situation would last, how much we would be paid, on what basis we could leave to visit our families, or any other consideration such as this. Further, we were not told where we would sleep, what we would eat, if we could drink alcohol in our off hours (alcohol was prohibited on the premises) or how our laundry would be done.

And there was the matter of the safety of our families. Again, I was naive about such things. A union worker, with whom I thought I had a friendly relationship, asked me how things were at 55 Holly Road, my address. He just wanted me to know that he, and presumably the other workers, knew where my family lived. The implied threat made my blood boil. I felt trapped. Our management was silent as to what sort of protection, if any, they were prepared to offer to our families.

Other workers were less confrontational. I remember one of the mechanics, the most capable guy in the facility, came to me and handed me a keyring. He didn't want us to have cut the locks off his toolboxes. He seemed sad to have to have this conversation with me. We shook hands and I told him I would take care of his stuff, if it came to that. Fortunately, while

I was at Ajax, it never did. The union contract was always approved, sometimes by a mere handful of votes.

As a project engineer, work was challenging. We had no budget for projects, but there were projects that needed to be done. So we became "pickers" in the facility "bone yard", scavenging for usable bits and pieces that could be fashioned into solutions to the many problems our ancient production facility had. Since production was ongoing seven days a week, around the clock, projects that required downtime were done on holidays. I worked Christmas, New Year's, President's Day, Easter, Mother's Day and Father's Day one year.

And when the projects dried up, I was told to squeeze maximum production and minimum downtime out of machinery that was much older than I was and in need of major overhaul, if not outright replacement. And to do this, I could not so much as lay a finger on the equipment lest I trigger a grievance. So I had to beg, cajole, and otherwise convince the union workers to help me increase their workload. If my work was successful, it would mean more product for them to package, more attention to be paid to the machinery and more friction from their union brethren, some of whom saw their cooperation with me as fraternizing with the enemy.

And so I began to look for a way out. Ajax was part of a big parent company with other facilities and other locations. The joint venture I worked at was a dark, unprofitable corner of a world-class company. There were opportunities in buildings a hundred yards from where I toiled that promised modern working conditions and chances for advancement. I applied for an open position and crossed my fingers. My boss came to me a week later and asked if I had applied for a job in another department. I told him I had. He told me that was not allowed and handed the paperwork I had submitted back to me. I went to his boss to plead my case. He was sympathetic but told me that the president of the joint venture had forbidden "tampering" with his employees.

I applied for a position in an Ajax pilot plant fifty miles away. I interviewed in secret and was encouraged by a warm reception there. A week later a brown envelope with my application inside appeared on my desk with no note of explanation. I was trapped. That day I received a phone call from the last guy who had been allowed to transfer out of the department before it became a joint venture. There was an Environmental Engineering position open in the most profitable department in our location. They were ready to give it to me. All I had to do was get permission. I went to my boss's boss again. I begged him to beg to the president for me. And he did…to no avail. There was no way out short of quitting or being fired.

*****

For as long as my dad worked at Texaco, we had an understanding that he would help me career-wise as much as he could when needed. But he didn't want me to work for Texaco while he was there. He was so high in the company that he felt it would be impossible for me to make my own way. I'd either be coddled or punished for being "the big boss's son". And he didn't want either for me. And I think he also imagined the poor lower-level manager to whom I might be assigned trying to figure out how to deal with an employee who had the ear of the corporation's Senior Executive Vice-President. He wouldn't want to do that to anyone either. But he had recently retired from Texaco due to poor health. They had held the top spot in the corporation open for him for almost a year, in hopes that he would recover, but that was not to be.

I was becoming desperate at Ajax. And one day I asked Dad, for the first time, what he could do to help extricate me from my professional "twilight zone". He made a few calls. Texaco had a lube oils division that was looking for technical/marketing people. They were located in Houston and he set up a day of interviews there for me. My hopes soared. Even though my wife dreaded the prospect of leaving Connecticut after we had worked so long to get back there, she saw how miserable I was and gave me a kiss for luck. One day I left for work at Ajax, but instead of going home at the end of the day, I drove to the airport.

I flew to Houston and was met by a car that took me to a plush downtown hotel. There was a package at the front desk for me that contained my packed itinerary for the next day. I did not sleep well that night.

The next day was a blur. I was met by handlers who led me through a maze of nice offices. I interviewed with over a dozen people, men and women from each department who wanted to know what I could do to help them. I was a huge motor racing fan in those days and several of the people were involved in marketing Texaco's products through sponsorship of major big-time racing teams! How would I like to be part of that? Yes, please! I took notes of each person I spoke to and each opportunity we discussed. They all sounded wonderful, worlds beyond anything I could ever hope to achieve at Ajax.

Interviews continued over lunch and I saw that I was talking to people who were higher and higher in the organization. I was literally interviewing my way up the many floors of the skyscraper office building. My thoughts flashed back to my days riding my tricycle to visit Dad in his Texaco office in Bellaire so many years before. But there was little time to daydream as I was meeting the next executive and discussing the next opportunity.

Two things stood out to me as I experienced this whirlwind of potential opportunity. First, every person I met, every single one, expressed sincere admiration for my father. Keep in mind, he no longer worked for Texaco. They didn't have to say anything about him, but they all did. They mentioned his integrity, his willingness to work with anyone for the betterment of the company, to make it safer, to make it more environmentally sound, to give its employees the best careers they could have. One man told me how Dad had insisted on a second-chance policy for those who tested-positive for substance abuse and accepted treatment. Another told me how Dad had banned smoking at every Texaco facility after seeing the statistics on smoking-related illness and death among employees. Several of them whispered that the executives who had come before and would come after my dad rarely showed the human touch and common sense that marked Dad's every decision. Hearing those words made me so proud.

Second, every job opportunity I heard about was exciting, promising, and seemed like something I could handle and excel at. I know it might have been the fatigue getting to me, but every person I talked to seemed eager to have me come to work with them and had a list of tasks ready for me to start on. It had been so long since I was excited about my job, since it was anything but drudgery. To have fear and hopelessness replaced by excitement and dreams of future possibilities was intoxicating.

At the end of the day I met separately with the VP of

Technical Development and the VP of Marketing. They had each been tracking my day's activities and getting reports from each of the people I had spoken to who reported to them. Both of them were very serious about the challenges the company faced, but both of them said I could help. As the car took me back to the airport, I felt like I had an excellent chance of being hired. The next day I got a call from the HR Director asking for a copy of my college transcript. My heart sank when I thought of the woeful tale it told. I made a copy and overnighted it to him with a prayer on my lips.

Two weeks passed without a word. Finally, I called Dad to see if he had heard anything. He said he'd look into it. He called me that night.

"Steve, I talked to the two VPs and to the HR Director of the lube oils division. Everybody down there was very impressed by you. They said you showed a technical understanding of their processes and that your experience working offshore and at the gas processing plant was excellent. They said you were well-suited for the technical side."

I took a deep breath. So far, so good.

"The marketing people were even more impressed. They have never seen an engineer who presents himself so well. Your interpersonal and communication skills knocked them out. They would love to have you come on board too."

Even as I could hear the pride in my dad's voice, I could tell that was the end of the good news.

"But…" I said.

Dad finished my sentence. "But, the HR department received your college transcript. And Texaco Corporate HR has guidelines for the hiring of engineers that include college grades. And yours don't measure up."

There was a long, painful silence. Part of me had known this moment was coming since I cut my first class all those years ago at UConn. My stomach churned and I felt dead inside.

Dad continued, "I spoke to the Director of Texaco Corporate HR. He's a good man I've known for a long time. He's a friend. He told me that if you were not my son, you would have gotten a letter declining to hire you because your college transcript is not up to the corporate standard. But he told me that if I wanted him to make an exception for you, he would do it. They would hire you. I told him I would call him back. What do you want me to tell him? I've never asked for any favors from anyone in business, but I'll tell him whatever you want me to."

I knew then that this was one of my life's defining moments. Who was I? Who did I want to be? What was I willing to do to get what I wanted? I thought about my dad and what this process must have done to him emotionally. And then I thought about what all those people in Houston had said about my dad and the words they used. Integrity. Honesty. Fair. Moral. And I thought what I have always thought since I was a little boy eating an ice cream on the hood of his company car in the middle of an endless field next to my dad. I want to be like him. And I want him to be proud of me.

"Tell him thank you, but no," I said.

"Alright, Steve," Dad said quietly. And we never talked about it again. We had walked to the edge of the mesa and looked out over the landscape of what could be. And we had walked back home together. Dad had taught by example and I had learned. Amen.

*****

I continued searching for a job outside of Ajax. And not long after my trip to Houston, I found one. I remember giving notice as one of the most satisfying parts of my time there. My boss told me he understood and wished me luck as did his boss. I didn't hear from the president who had personally blocked my path several times. As I completed my exit interview with HR, the manager there asked if I was sure I wanted to leave. I chuckled and signed my "separation" papers. He stood up and closed the door to his office. He sat on his desk and whispered.

"Steve, you no longer work for Ajax, so I can now offer you the Environmental Engineer position in the other department. Here is the salary and benefit info."

I looked at the seductive numbers and shook my head, "I'd love to accept, but I've committed to my new job. Maybe some other time."

He shook my hand and said he understood and respected my decision. Then he added one more thing.

"Steve, please don't tell anyone I offered you this job. I wouldn't want them to think that you have to quit to get ahead here."

"But that's true, isn't it?" I asked.

"Yes, it is," he said sadly.

And I left Ajax for what I thought would be the last time. I was on my way to work at a regional wastewater treatment plant. For the non-technical reader, that is a sewage plant. And for me it was a step up.

17

TRI-TOWN WWTP (AUGUST 1994 - DECEMBER 1994)

AFTER having worked at a large chemical plant, the thought of working for a small wastewater treatment plant (WWTP) was inviting. I imagined a slow-paced work environment where everyone got along with each other. Since the process of water treatment had relatively few variables, I expected an uneventful, quiet workplace where emergencies would be few and far between. How wrong I was!

Gotcha #5: Smaller doesn't necessarily mean friendlier.

I arrived for my interview at the Tri-Town WWTP, having taken a day off from Ajax. The office was a small, dated 1960's-era building with just a handful of rooms. I was shown into the largest of these, which was modestly decorated. At the far end sat the Executive Director. He was on the phone. His secretary sat me at a table near the door and left. I waited. The Executive Director, who I'll call Derek, held the phone to his ear but said little over the next twenty minutes. He never acknowledged that I was present. In fact he barely moved. The office was as quiet as a tomb. Only the ticking of a wall clock broke the silence. I noted the few professional certificates and awards on the walls and the collection of civil engineering texts in a nearby bookcase. I tried to relax and read over my resume as I waited patiently.

Suddenly, Derek, drew in a sharp breath and said, "Very well," and hung up the phone. He rose from his chair and turned to me. "You're Steven."

"Yes," I said, standing.

Derek walked over, shook my hand weakly, and sat down at the table across from me.

"Who is Deming?" he asked me out of the blue after an uncomfortably long pause.

I tried not to look startled. It occurred to me that he was quizzing me. I recalled that Deming was one of the top gurus of the "quality" movement that was the hot business trend of the 1990s.

"I believe you're referring to W. Edwards Deming, the quality expert. He wrote a number of books about improving workplace performance."

Derek maintained a poker face. He did not respond to my answer at all. There was another long pause.

"What do you know about Penske?"

Realizing it was the next question on this odd quiz, I thought quickly. Derek had not pronounced the "e" at the end of the name, but I guessed who he meant.

"Roger Penske is the owner of Penske Racing. He runs several auto racing teams. He also recently bought Ryder Trucking."

Again, Derek gave me no visible indication of what he

thought of my response. Instead, he stood and walked to the bookcase, took a handful of items from it, and laid them in front of me. There was a civil engineering handbook, a calculator, a college-style blue book and a five page engineering quiz.

"I like to give a little engineering test as part of the interview process," he said. He then stood up and went back to his desk.

I flipped through the quiz and saw that the questions were not too difficult. It was on par with a freshman-year general engineering test. So I opened the blue book and began to fill it up with my answers. One of the problems required a lot of calculation and unit conversions and was rather time-consuming. I was at the end of this problem when I heard Derek walk back over and sit down across from me. I had been working on the quiz for about a half-hour. I started to hand him the blue book, but he waved his hand.

We spent less than five minutes talking in general terms about a couple of the questions. Derek offered me the job of Project Engineer at less than I was currently making at Ajax and I accepted the job. He gave the smallest of forced, fake smiles and went back to his desk without a second look in my direction. I left, excited to be free of my boss at Ajax.

I enjoyed a brief honeymoon period at Tri-Town WWTP, learning the layout and meeting the people. The hourly workers were unionized here too, but they seemed more interested in keeping the facility running well than about maximizing their pay and minimizing their effort. My four fellow salaried co-workers were another story. The Lab Supervisor was a nice enough lady who was in charge of the biological workings of the facility. The Maintenance Supervisor was a pretty easy-going guy with a ponytail who appreciated my interest in the mechanical systems. The Operations Supervisor was kind of an odd duck. He was, in turns, friendly, then standoffish. His words were friendly, but his attitude was cold. I figured I would just do my job and gradually make friends with them all in time.

My second day on the job, I saw the other three salaried workers file into Derek's office and close the door. For the next two hours I heard muffled, occasionally loud voices though the door. I thought I heard my name a few times, but I couldn't be sure. Then the voices fell silent and the door opened and they filed out without a glance in my direction. Days later, the Operations Supervisor was walking me around acquainting me with his routine.

He suddenly blurted out, "That meeting the other day was all about you. The other supervisors and I have not had raises in several years. Rather than finally give us our money, Derek hired you. So we have formed a union. You are not invited to join. You may find that we aren't very friendly or welcoming to you. It's nothing personal."

Wow. I told him that I had taken a pay cut to get out of a bad situation and had no idea my hiring had any impact on others. And the conversation was over. Over the next six months I found my salaried coworkers warmed little to me. Ironically, the union hourly guys were pretty friendly. I did a few little projects and filled the rest of my time studying the facility's plans and drawings, then going out into the plant to see the actual equipment. I talked to a lot of the contractors that worked on-site and learned a lot about how public-sector work was bid, awarded, and performed. There was a possible plant expansion being considered and I began making notes of possible improvements that could potentially be made.

I developed a routine of touring the facility first thing each morning to take stock of any operational issues, familiarize myself with the equipment, and to kill some time. I would start at the "headworks". This is where the raw sewage flows into the facility. It was located in a cavernous room with tiled walls. A large, slow-moving machine called a "bar-rack" pulled miscellaneous debris from the flow. I won't go into detail about the more unpleasant aspects of a municipal sewage treatment facility. Suffice it to say that parts of it are not nearly as bad as you would think and other parts are far worse. The headworks weren't particularly bad.

I would greet the operator whose job it was to remove collected debris from the bar-rack and ask how things were going. Usually it was a pretty perfunctory chat, but one day I noticed a big smile on his face and I asked him why he was so happy. He pointed to the nearby tile wall. Plastered to it was a one dollar bill. He had fished it out of the inflow and slapped it onto the wall to dry (?). Presumably he was going to spend it somewhere. So, when someone tells you that money is dirty, remember this story and don't argue.

Of course one of the outstanding characteristics of a sewage treatment facility is odor. And a fair amount of effort was going into trying to control the odors that escaped the Tri-Town site and impacted our neighbors. Odor science is a discipline that seeks to identify and quantify odors. Tri-Town employed a couple of firms to assist with this effort.

A group of us were trained to compare the intensity of certain odors to different dilutions of an alcohol solution. Believe it or not, we were each given a little leather pouch that contained a number of vials of alcohol diluted to different strengths. We were told to calibrate our noses so that we could provide objective data on odor intensity.

Another time we were assembled and given an odor quiz. The contractor had actually collected special plastic bags of odorous air from different locations around the facility. Each of us had a blast of each bag shot at our noses and we had to guess where it came from. Surprisingly, some of the more experienced employees were able to do this with a very high degree of accuracy.

But in order to direct our odor control efforts to the source of the odors which elicited the most complaints from the public, we utilized what is called an "odor panel". One day after regular working hours, I stayed at the facility overnight to collect a couple of dozen bagfuls of odorous air from various processes and various areas of the facility. At dawn I brought the bags to the contractors suburban offices in a lovely office park an hour away from Tri-Town. There technicians would hook each bag up to a complicated device that could control the dilution of the sample with air. In this way the "threshold of odor detection" could be determined. The noses that would try to detect the odors belonged to a half-dozen paid volunteers.

The volunteers were retired elderly ladies who lived nearby. For five dollars an hour they would sniff samples and report their impressions on little forms. Odor panels are used by perfume manufacturers to test reactions to new fragrances or by food companies to measure how tempting the aroma of a new flavoring was. The panel members were never told what they were sniffing. Today it was a selection of odors from Tri-Town's sewage treatment processes. Maybe it was the lack of sleep, but I took a shameful joy in watching these nice, old ladies earnestly sniff a sample and then remark on it. The remarks included,

"Ooo, this one is sweet, like a cake baking!"

"Is this fudge? It smells like dark chocolate fudge."

"Oh, I don't like this one. It smells like burnt coffee."

I'm not sure what we learned from this, but I got to take the rest of the day off.

In early December, Derek called me into his office for my six-month review. In his usual deadpan, emotionless delivery he told me I was a poor engineer and was ineffective. He didn't like the way I did the few things he asked me to do and basically told me he was disappointed in every aspect of my job performance. I was stunned. It seemed clear to me that I was about to be fired. This was the first mention he had ever made to me about how I was doing and it was devastating. I had been through many performance reviews at each of the other places I had worked and was almost always highly-rated across the board.

He concluded my verbal evisceration, "So, I am putting in your file that you are an unsatisfactory employee and I am recommending that you be retained at your current salary."

It took me a moment to realize that I was not being fired. Then it hit me. This was his way of freezing my salary, probably for a very long time, just as he had the other salaried employees. Maybe it was some sort of gesture to them or maybe it was just his way of holding down costs.

Digression - I had attended a few Board of Directors meetings at Tri-Town WWTP. The Board was composed of old men from the three towns that the facility served. When I say they were old, the average age was well over 70. Derek orchestrated the Board meetings down to the cookies that were served. The Board members each got a slick package of memos and graphs showing the excellent performance of the facility. Costs were always held flat or decreased. Productivity was always high and increasing. There was no mention of the salaried staff other than Derek. The facility not only processed the waste of the member towns, it brought in sewage sludge from other towns and from septic tank cleaning companies. It had been over-designed by Derek so that it could take in this other waste as a very lucrative "side-business". In this way, the plant was rapidly paying off its construction loans and excess cash was being invested in a then-booming stock market. It was whispered in the facility that Derek got a percentage of the side-business profits and also received regular, large pay increases, all approved by the Board. And why not? Derek was carefully controlling the information the Board received to make him look like an infallible genius. Aside from the unanimous "yes" votes on all of the proposals Derek brought to the Board, the only words I heard from them were questions about the type and number of cookies that had been provided for the meetings. I kid you not.

So this was Derek's plant. He made the rules. He made the money. He controlled the Board that was supposed to oversee his work. It was a pretty sweet set-up for Derek. - End of digression.

I left my performance review in shock. I closed my office door. One thing was clear. I had to get out of this. I thought back to my exit interview at Ajax where they had offered me that dream Environmental Engineer job in the non-joint venture part of the company. I called them to see if, by some chance, the offer was still open. It was! I could come over to interview that afternoon. It was a Monday. I had a job offer within a few days and tendered my resignation to Derek that Friday. He didn't bat an eye. He offered his weak, fake smile and a weaker handshake telling me he hoped I would find my niche. Me too, Derek.

A week later I read in the local paper that the wastewater facility's latest monthly board meeting had been crashed by the maintenance supervisor who brought a reporter with him and presented the board members with a not-so-slick package of graphs and tables that described a number of problems that Derek had not been so forthcoming about. These included "an unplanned discharge", what laymen call "a spill", from a piece of processing equipment. The discharge had gone unreported. He had correspondence showing that Derek had been aware of the situation, but had taken no action. The Board might now be liable, possibly *personally* liable, for fines and cleanup costs. I understand that Derek's resignation was accepted at the next Board meeting. I wonder what kind of cookies they had?

18

SYNTECH (JANUARY 1995 - MARCH 1999)

I am pleased to report that my return to the chemical plant and my sixth real job had NO GOTCHA! (At least not for a while.) I was working for Syntech, the parent company of Ajax, in a profit-making division, doing real engineering work for a normal boss who oversaw my efforts and provided resources and guidance. It felt like I might, at long last, be starting my *career*.

I had two part-time engineers and two summer interns working for me. (More about them later.) As Environmental Engineer, I was tasked with creating an air emissions inventory and I went right to work. The plant had a bunch of different pieces of production equipment that could be used in various ways and in various combinations to create a large number of products. The air emissions of a given batch of a product could vary depending on which combination of equipment was used. I had to create a complex matrix that covered every possibility. I assigned one of my interns to create a list of all the products and the other to create a corresponding list of the different combinations of equipment that could be used to make each product. I began studying the operating instructions to determine when in the production process the air emissions would occur. We would hire a consultant to estimate what the air emissions were using vapor-liquid equilibrium (VLE) calculations and create a user interface so that each year we could simply input the production numbers and the computer would spit out the air emissions information. Simple, right? Maybe I wasn't such a terrible engineer after all, Derek.

I was about to go on vacation when I was approached by the two summer interns assigned to work for me. I had struggled to find some benign make-work task for them. They were super-smart Ivy League engineering students who were eager to put their newly-acquired skills to work. They asked about the air emissions inventory project. I reluctantly gave them an overview and they began bombarding me with questions and then suggestions that were surprisingly astute! I told them that we were about to bring on a consultant to do the "heavy lifting" VLE calculations and to create the user interface. They begged for a chance to do that work. I couldn't believe that these two kids could begin to understand it all, much less do it, but I told them to work on their own computer drive using copies of everything so that, if they messed up, all that would be lost was their time. I assigned one of my part-timers to keep an eye on them and I took off for a week on the Outer Banks of North Carolina with minimal expectations of these youthful go-getters.

When I returned to work, tanned and rested, I took a morning to clear away the accumulated mail and administrative tasks that had piled up, then called "my staff" together. The Ivy League guys were beaming like cats who had just eaten canaries. They asked me to move the meeting into their work area. We moved.

"OK. Here is the user interface we came up with. Sorry. It's a little crude," began young Mr. Dartmouth.

He showed me a slick graphic screen that had the company logo on it and listed my name as creator of the "Facility Batch-Specific Air Emissions Calculation Tool" or FB-SAECT. He hit a button and the screen changed to show a year's worth of production data.

"Here is last year's production data. We got this off the Accounting drive. Hope that's OK. It took a while to massage the format, but now you just access their file and it dumps into the calculation package. Their code tells where each batch of each product was made. We feed that through the list of products and equipment combos you guys put together. Those were really helpful," continued young Mr. MIT.

"We threw together a bunch of VLE data that we had from school and used the emitting step info you gave us, Steve. Again, that was super-helpful. That gave us all the emissions for all the production, but not which vents emitted what," said Mr. Dartmouth.

"Yeah, if we hadn't found the roof vent map on your desk…Was it OK that we borrowed that?" asked Mr. MIT, fearful.

I nodded, not really believing what I was hearing and seeing.

"Oh, good. We thought you might be pissed. Sorry, angry. Anyway, that actually took a couple of hours to trace out the pipes from the emitting sources to the associated roof vents, but it was a nice day, so we did that," said Mr. Dartmouth. He hit another button.

"And this is the air emission data per pollutant, per vent for last year's production. We correlated it with the reported data. It's a rough match. Most of our numbers are lower, but the reported numbers used a bunch of super-conservative fudge factors, you know? So, what do you think?"concluded Mr. MIT.

The two young whiz-kids looked up at me like puppies hoping for a treat.

"Guys, this is amazing! We'll have to go through this all, but if it does what it looks like it does, then we're not going to need to hire the consultant," I said, thinking about the $35,000 that had been budgeted for that.

"We know it's a little clunky, but we wanted to get it up by the time you got back. How was the vacation?" asked Mr. Dartmouth.

"It was good, really good. Guys, who have you shown this to?" I asked.

"Nobody. Just you," replied Mr. MIT.

"Well, you guys have gone far beyond what I expected. This is really great. I don't know what to say!"

"So, you'll give us a decent assessment? We'll be heading back to school next week," they asked.

They got the best assessments I could write! In the weeks that followed, my part-timers and I went through the FB-SAECT and only needed to make minor tweaks. I presented it to my boss and the Director of Environmental Services and they were blown away. I gave the Ivy League guys the lion's share of the credit, but they told me that I must be a great manager to get that kind of work from "college kids". I got the best performance review of my career!

When the year ended, I used the FB-SAECT to prepare

the air emissions numbers. It worked like a charm! I made a presentation on the FB-SAECT to a national company meeting and became the unofficial corporate "air emissions inventory guy". I was developing a reputation! A good one! It was hard for me to believe.

Back at the plant, I was doing some emissions measurements on the roof to double-check the values that FB-SAECT gave me. They all checked out. All except one. There was a very plain-looking two-inch steel pipe that vented a methanol holding tank that shouldn't ever produce any air emissions. It was pouring out a steady flow of a cool, alcohol-smelling vapor. I put my hand over the vent and it was under more than a little pressure. Something was wrong. I studied the drawings and the FB-SAECT output. I made some flow measurements and tested the vapor composition. It was almost pure methanol vapor. This was a potential fire hazard. I called my boss up to the roof.

He saw what I saw, checked the drawings and called the building supervisor. The building supervisor was polite but said he was sure there was a mistake. Then he put his hand over the vent as I had and felt the pressure and smelled the methanol that had condensed on his hand. He radioed the production supervisor to shut down the building. This was big. Shutting down the building started an imaginary meter running that counted up dollars for every minute of lost production. Before long there were maintenance, production, engineering, and business managers gathered in a conference room pouring over the drawings and going over the facts. I sat quietly fearing that somehow this was going to turn out to be a false alarm or otherwise my fault. The plant manager entered the room. He sat right next to me.

"OK, what's going on? Why are we down?" He was asking me.

I nervously and cautiously recounted the sequence of events that had occurred.

He asked me, "How much methanol are we losing out that vent?"

"By my calculations, it could be eighty-thousand pounds a year, assuming the building is up 24/7," I said quietly.

"Jesus. OK, what's causing this?" he looked at the maintenance supervisor.

"It looks like the pipe to the holding tank is sized too small. It's supposed to self-vent. If it's too small then it just pushes the vapor out of the tank up the vent," he maintenance manager said.

"How long to fix it?" asked the plant manager.

"We've ordered the bigger pipe, we'll work 'round the clock. Should be back online in 72-96 hours." replied the maintenance manager.

"Make it the 72 hours. I guess the good news is that, based on the methanol we won't be spewing out the roof, we'll pay for the lost production and downtime in a couple of weeks." the plant manager said soberly. Then he looked at me and smiled. "Good job finding this, Steve."

And the meeting disbursed. It was the oddest feeling I ever had. From that day on, all the managers looked at me a little differently. They hadn't been cold to me before, but now they saw me as a valuable member of the team, instead of just part of the plant's overhead cost, which is how they generally regarded environmental work. It felt really good to be respected by guys who were experienced, no-nonsense professionals. I got a letter from the plant manager "for the file" commending me on my work and the pollution prevention and economic savings that would benefit the company as a result.

At the end of my second year there, the division held a conference at a resort in Westchester, New York. It was a very fancy place and no expense was spared. Champagne receptions and deluxe accommodations were provided to thank us for the great job we were doing. The theme was, "Save Some Time For Dreaming". This seemed too good to last. And it was.

It turns out that the reason they were able to have such a nice, fancy corporate party was that a competitor had stopped production of a certain chemical that was needed in the manufacture of automotive topcoats (also known as car paint). That meant we became the sole supplier of that chemical worldwide. The salesman who handled that product made the bold move of tripling the price to all of his customers over night. Consequently, he and the company made boatloads of money that year. But like the cartoon where Daffy Duck outdoes Bugs Bunny in a vaudeville act by blowing himself up, it's a trick you can only do once. Other suppliers moved in and the massive profits evaporated. That salesman took his windfall fortune and left for greener pastures.

A year later they held the conference in the Newark Airport Ramada Inn. The theme was, "Snap Out of It!". I kid you not. Profits had dipped and that was unacceptable. Last year's boom meant nothing. And here was where I got a new lesson in business. We were told that the purpose of our chemical manufacturing business was not to make chemicals. It was to make money. The investors who owned the company only cared about the return on their investment. If they couldn't get eight percent back every year from us, they might as well put their money in a certificate of deposit or a mutual fund where they could. It was further required that we increase profits every year, without fail and without limit. We had to grow and grow and spend less and less and make more and more money, or we were a failure. Every employee, in every department, in every location, in every division of the company had to be a "profit center" to justify his or her continued employment every year. Or else. Snap out of it, indeed.

Now, about those part-time workers that I inherited when I rejoined the company. One was a young man, Tim, with a ponytail and leather jacket. He was very smart and easy to work with. He was into heavy metal music and I was a fan of classic rock. We talked a lot about music. We also talked about the internet. I knew nothing about the new "information superhighway" that was supposed to change our lives. We had just gotten email at the company. But Tim, knew all about he internet and was a very quick learner when it came to technology. He really helped me make sure that FB-SAECT worked. And he had worked with the Ivy League boys as they were putting it together. I eventually lobbied for Tim to be hired full-time and he was. Great.

My other part-timer was Alice.

Digression - My grandfather was a retired GM master mechanic. He could fix any problem on any car, period. He had a toolshed full of tools, many of which he had made to fix particular problems on particular models of cars. If a 1968 Ford Galaxie 500 air conditioning unit was particularly difficult to remove, he had made a tool that allowed him to remove it by himself, with one hand. Knowing as much as he knew about cars, and what could go wrong with them, he took extraordinary care of his own cars and was as prepared as possible for trouble when he took a long road trip. The spacious trunk of his 1969 Chevy Impala was full, not with suitcases or hanging clothes. Those were in the back seat. The trunk contained two full-sized spare tires, two one-gallon jugs of water, six quarts of oil and an oil filter, jugs of radiator fluid, washer fluid, cans of brake and transmission fluid, a full set of belts, gaskets, and hoses, and, of course, the tools he would need to perform any emergency repairs.

I heard some of his friends tease him that the weight of all the stuff in the trunk might be too much for his car's engine to handle. Maybe all the precautions he took to guard against being stuck because of a breakdown would increase the chances of a breakdown! Maybe. But Pawpaw believed that you could never be too careful.

In the course of my nearly thirty-year career, I saw a lot of changes in the business world. Smoking went from ubiquitous to rare. Employees were required to be educated about everything from "managed medical care insurance" to workplace violence, diversity and sexual harassment. I'm old enough and have been in enough mostly-male workplaces to have seen girly calendars and posters ranging from cute to explicit. I've seen mimeographed "jokes" ranging from silly to obscene. I've heard dirty jokes whispered in confidence and broadcast on facility-wide walkie-talkies. My attitude has changed from ignorant acceptance to irritated intolerance of this kind of nonsense in the workplace. End of digression.

I have a working wife and daughter. The thought of them being harassed at work makes my blood boil. So it was in this context that I was put in charge of Tim and Alice. When I first returned to the company, the HR guy took me aside and carefully chose his words as told me her history on the job that went back two years. Apparently she had been doing her job well and not creating any issues when a group of employees went out for pizza and beer one Friday after work. Alice, ended up seated between two managers. Both were long-time company employees, one married and one single.

The following Monday morning Alice began her day at HR reporting that both of the men had made improper remarks and advances toward her, including physical contact. Both men were summoned to HR and questioned about the events of the previous Friday night. Neither man had any history of any kind of improper behavior in many years at the company. By the end of the day, both men had been discharged for sexual harassment.

The HR guy told me to be very careful in my dealings with Alice. He told me to document every conversation and communication I had with her, just in case. I quickly discovered that there was widespread animosity toward Alice among many employees who were friends of the discharged managers. Many of these folks told me to "watch my back".

Alice worked on her own for the most part and I had few dealings with her. We talked a few times so that I could acquaint myself with her work and track its progress. In the course of these chats, she told me that she knew she was hated by many people because of the incident. She did not go into detail about the incident or about the expressions of this perceived hatred toward her. I told to tell me or HR if she was made to feel threatened in any way. After our chat, I documented it in a notebook I kept for that purpose.

A month or two later, as Alice's time with the company

was coming to an end, I got a call from HR that I should come down to see them asap. The HR guy told me that Alice had made him aware of a situation that needed to be investigated. My chest tightened. The HR guy told me it did not involve me. I sighed in relief. It involved a manager who worked near where Alice did her work. This manager, I'll call him Chet, was the quietest, most easy-going guy in the company. He was a family man who coached Little League and did volunteer work at the community soup kitchen.

The next day, the HR guy, Chet, Alice and I all met in a conference room. Alice said she was unable to work because of the change in Chet's attitude toward her. Whereas he had previously been cordial and friendly, he was now "all business". We asked for examples of this and Alice could only say that Chet used to greet her with a "hello" and "How's it going?" and now he did not.

"And you cannot do your job because of this?" the HR guy asked.

"It's difficult. No, I can't," Alice said.

We tried not to look as mystified as we all were. I could see Chet was dumbfounded. He knew that two of his former co-workers had lost their jobs because of their alleged interactions with this young lady and now he was fearing the same fate awaited him. What would he tell his wife and daughters?

The HR guy asked Chet if he had changed his behavior toward Alice.

Chet said, "I work two doors down from where Alice works. I see her a couple of times a week in the hall. Sometimes I say "hello" and sometimes I've got my mind on my work and I guess I don't. I've got a lot on my plate and I'm here to work. I'm unaware of any change in my behavior."

The HR guy again asked Alice what the problem was that was causing her to be unable to do her job. She repeated that Chet's slightly less-friendly occasional greetings were the problem. And that was it. We all went back to work. The HR guy called me to his office later that day.

"What did you make of that?" he asked me.

"Hell if I know," I told him. "What do you do now?"

"I'll write it up and put it in the file. Nothing Alice says Chet did or didn't do is in our policy on sexual harassment. Let's all sit tight. She's leaving at the end of next week."

On Friday of the next week, Alice came to my office. She handed me a sealed envelope. Then she told me how hard it was for her to work here. After the incident with the two managers, everyone in the office had steered clear of her. No one spoke to her. Only Chet had remained cordial for a while, but then he had stopped greeting her. She thanked me for being a good supervisor and then she left.

I nervously opened the envelope and read the four-page hand-written letter. It detailed how isolated she felt and how drastically a once-friendly work environment had changed after the incident. It was a strangely sad letter. But there was only praise for me in it. And all I had done was collect her time-card once a week.

I passed the letter on to the HR guy along with a copy of my notes from all my conversations with Alice from my notebook. I never learned the details of the alleged sexual harassment incident that cost two men their jobs from Alice, nor from the HR guy. But I wondered how overt the "improper acts" were in light of the odd "complaint" she had made about Chet. Had those two managers done anything? The company had terminated them with such speed and without any review.

I could only imagine the impact it had on their families and professional lives. Chet must have feared the same.

I don't know how to balance the protection of victims with the rights of the accused. The company took quick, decisive action, trying to protect itself from litigation and bad publicity, and presumably trying to do the right thing. And surely generations of women have endured outrageous harassment before any thought was given to protecting them.

And I thought of Alice. And of my wife and daughter. I once thought that you couldn't be too careful about protecting women in the workplace from sexual harassment. But maybe there was a point when too careful became too much. And my thoughts drifted back to Pawpaw's trunk.

*****

It's difficult to be generous if you are broke. I understand that. I worked for several companies that were so close to bankruptcy for so long that pinching pennies became a way of life. When a company that I worked for moved its offices, cases of notepads that carried the old address became obsolete. Did they get thrown out? Given away? No, they did not. The CEO decreed that the company would not purchase Post-It notes until all of the old notepads had been used. Each employee was given a stack of the notepads with the old address, a pair of scissors, and a roll of tape. We were to "make our own Post-Its" until further notice. I kid you not.

In healthier companies, there are what are known as "perks". In my experience, certain people are particularly adept at finding perks and exploiting them. It's good to get to know such individuals. Bob Griffin was one at Syntech. He had been with the company for a number of years and he was wise to the ways of not only our facility, but the business of our parent company. He asked me if I wanted to join the ERIM team. ERIM was Emergency Response and Incident Management. I asked him what that involved.

Bob took me to a building I had never been in before. In it was a brand-new, beautiful, fully-equipped chemical emergency response vehicle. He told me that the ERIM team had been around a few years and it tapped into a corporate budget to purchase and equip this truck. It had everything in it. Tools, chemical protective gear, generator, banks of lights, communications equipment, you name it. He told me that a few times a year, they would get a call that some warehouse or other had spilled one of our products and, as part of Syntech's commitment to "product stewardship", the ERIM team would drop what they were doing and drive to the site and clean up the mess. They got special premium pay for their trouble, of course. And if they had to stay over, they got hotel and meals paid for. And everyone on the team got to go to training in Colorado for a week annually. The guys on the team were all friends of mine, so I joined immediately.

As a part of working in a chemical plant, I had already received copious amounts of safety training. In fact, I actually conducted safety training on certain topics for the guys who worked for me. Two of the guys on the ERIM team were full-time safety guys. Two of us were full-time environmental. Bob was production and Earl was a maintenance supervisor. A few weeks after I joined, we got a call. A fork lift had nicked a drum of one of our products in a warehouse in New Jersey. We were on our way.

But first, there were a few details to attend to. The three of us who were responding grabbed our "go bags" from the trunks of our cars. We assembled at the ERIM truck and loaded up. The first stop was Dunkin' Donuts for coffees and pastries. An army travels on its stomach, after all. The second stop was for cigars. And then we hit the road. The ride to the Jersey warehouse was three or four hours, plus traffic. But it was far from boring. Earl could talk endlessly on almost any subject. He'd lived a full life although he wasn't that much older than I was. So, to pass the time we had our coffee, cigars, the radio and Earl. It wasn't bad.

At the warehouse we found a single drum of one of our products that had a little hole a few inches from the top and had leaked less than a gallon of clear, sticky goo onto the concrete floor. We put the drum in an "overpack", a large yellow plastic drum that would contain the damaged steel drum. We put the overpacked drum in the truck. Then came the mopping up. As new man, I got to literally mop the floor and clean up the thankfully non-toxic goo. An hour later we were headed back to Connecticut.

"Where do you want to eat?" asked Earl.

"How about the Chart House in Greenwich?" replied Bob.

The Chart House was a top shelf, fancy steak house in Greenwich, one of the ritziest towns in wealthy Fairfield County. I couldn't believe they were talking about eating there. It would cost a fortune and we were not exactly dressed for it. But I kept quiet. Bob explained that since the warehouse fork lift had damaged our drum, the warehouse company would be billed for our response, including our meal. If the drum had leaked because of something our company had done, Syntech would have had to pay the cost of the response and we'd have probably had some fast food for dinner.

We pulled into the waterside parking lot at the Chart House and parked right in front. In our jeans, workshirts, and jackets, we entered. The hostess didn't blink.

"Three for dinner?" she asked.

And like that we were led to a table with a water view. The guys ordered cocktails and I followed suit. As we were sipping our martinis, the manager of the restaurant approached our table.

"Excuse me for interrupting, gentlemen, but is that your truck outside?"

"Yes. Is there a problem?" Bob took the point on this one.

"No. No problem at all. I was wondering if I could trouble you to park it on the side of the restaurant. Would that be possible?"

"Of course," said Bob, tossing me the keys.

As I walked outside, it suddenly seemed obvious why a tony eatery might not want a huge red truck with the words "Chemical Emergency Response" in big letters parked in front of it. It could put off potential diners. I moved the truck and we enjoyed a sumptuous feast.

That was a simple response. Quick. Relatively clean. Not even very inconvenient. There were others.

There was another warehouse on the New Jersey waterfront that we were called to months later. A bag of our product had split and spilled granular plastic molding compound. Simple enough. We mobilized and got there just after midday. Now, I don't know what a mafia stolen merchandise warehouse looks like. And I'm not saying this was one. But inside was an unusual collection of goods. As we walked around looking for our pallet of bags, we passed several pallets of cases of Jack Daniel's whiskey, many of which were opened, a half dozen Ducatti motorcycles, mountains of electronics, Italian suits on racks and more.

We found a pallet of our product with one ripped-open bag that had spilled about half its contents on a loading dock. Earl grabbed a broom, a dustpan and a haz waste drum. We began to clean up the mess. As we worked a group of "warehouse employees" assembled around us. They were kind of a rough bunch, as you might imagine. At first they were just curious, then they started to heckle us, probably out of boredom. Earl put the broom down and motioned for me to follow him back to the truck.

He opened one of the many compartments inside and handed me a white, Tyvek jumpsuit, safety goggles, a respirator and rubber boots. He told me to put them on and he donned the same get-up. Back we walked to the clean-up site.

The crowd of dockworkers were still there, but seeing us dressed as we now were, they fell silent. Finally, as we began cleaning up again, one of them spoke.

"Hey, what's with the space suits? This stuff isn't poisonous is it? Is it safe to be here?"

Through his respirator, Earl's muffled voice called out, "It's perfectly safe…for us."

The crowd dispersed in seconds. We finished cleaning up the innocuous mess in peace and were gone not long after.

Not all of our company's products were benign. One was a white powder that contained acrylamide, which is a neurotoxin. It can be dangerous to inhale, consume, or touch. We were called to a distribution warehouse in rural Pennsylvania where we were told a bag had opened in the back of a trailer. We arrived after midnight. The place was all but deserted.

Digression - A distribution warehouse is where tractor trailers shuffle their loads to make for more efficient transport of goods throughout the country. Our company, like others, I presume, took great care to load trailers according to every safety standard under the sun. At the distribution warehouse, those loads were taken apart and split up and put onto other trailers with other goods for further transport. I'm not saying the regulations are not followed, but who knows? - End of digression.

The trailer in question was backed up to the warehouse dock. It's doors were closed. It was isolated with "CAUTION" tape creating a perimeter around it. I could sense from the other team members that this was way more serious than our usual jobs. We huddled and discussed the hazards of acrylamide. This would require "Level A" personal protective equipment and decontamination after the job was complete. As the youngest, fittest one of the team, I volunteered to go in. The guys assisted me in donning the "space suit". I had an air tank on my back inside the suit. When they zipped and taped me in, it became clear to me that this could be dangerous. But the guys and I were all trained and well-equipped, so I didn't panic…yet.

I walked past the "CAUTION" tape and up to the door of the trailer. I undid the latch and lifted the door. Inside the trailer was a jumble of boxes, some on pallets, steel and cardboard drums, and bags. As I passed my flashlight over the mess, I could see that everything was covered in a fine layer of white powder. I glanced back at the guys. They had all donned respirators and were standing well back behind the "CAUTION" tape. I didn't blame them.

I had a walkie-talkie inside my suit. They were giving

me some instructions and asking questions. They wanted to know if I could see our company's product. I couldn't. But the trailer was big and I would need to find them. According to the manifest, our stuff was the only hazardous material on board. I began to make my way deeper into the trailer. I had to push things out of my way and climb up over other things. It was a slow process. The guys had stopped talking and all I could hear was the regulator on my air tank as I breathed. One of the guys was keeping track of the time and my air supply. Depending how much air I used, I might have fifteen or twenty minutes before I'd run low.

Finally, I made my way to the far end of the trailer, lit only by my flashlight. And there is was. One pallet loaded with forty fifty-pound bags of acrylamide-containing product. It had been shrink-wrapped before loading in the plant. I reported back. They told me to examine every inch of the shrink-wrap and see if it was intact. It was a tight squeeze, but I managed to work my way around all sides of the pallet. I was as careful and thorough as I could be. It was intact.

Well, then, what was the white powder all over everything? As I made my way back to where I had entered, I saw a partial pallet of bags that I had not looked closely at on my way in. The bags didn't bear our company logo, so I had disregarded them. I saw at least one bag had a huge rip in it and powder from it was everywhere. What was it? It could be anything. I reassured myself that I was wearing the highest level of protection that would protect me from many common industrial chemicals. I trained my flashlight on the bag's label. "Pizza Flour", it said. Sure enough. Once I saw the source of the white powder, I could see the heaviest coating was nearest these bags of flour. I headed out to the team.

Out of caution, they had set up a decon area and proceeded to wash off my suit before taking me out of it. They bagged it and made sure the area was clean before removing their respirators and helping me with mine. We could laugh about it now although transporting a neurotoxin with food products is illegal and not a laughing matter. But since our company was not at fault, this call would be charged to the transporter. So it was off to the Marriott to sleep and for a champagne brunch the next morning before heading home. I was glad I didn't have to do that every day.

I went to two sessions of Emergency Response training at a facility in Pueblo, Colorado. The first was for "highway response" and the second was for "railroad response". The training was straightforward and excellent. The facility had several old tank trucks and they used these to teach us how to deal with spills, rollovers and everything in between.

The week-long railroad course climaxed with a night exercise. A thirteen railroad car derailment had been elaborately staged. It was plumbed with water gushing from "damaged tanks" and propane gas to create great plumes of fire. And the worst-kept secret of the week was that they had rigged an explosion to go off at some point during the exercise. Sure enough, as our group approached the derailment to copy down the numbers of the damaged railcars, BOOM! Even knowing it was coming, I still jumped out of my skin.

Most of the attendees at these courses were firemen. They generally didn't care for chemical emergencies. They preferred to fight fires. I felt just the opposite, of course. They were, by and large, good guys. They enjoyed teasing us "college boy engineers" and telling us how our chemical protective suits would be no more than "shrink-wrap" in a fire.

I remember pulling up to the Holiday Inn in Pueblo on the Sunday before the highway course began. The radio mentioned a huge snowstorm expected the following Friday. I thought it was odd that they thought they could predict the weather so far in advance. It was late October.

The week went by. Classes were long and we took a bus back and forth from the hotel to the training area. The days were warm. I had a rental car and went out for dinner each night, sometimes alone, sometimes with a few of the guys. On Friday we got our certificates when the class was over. We had one last dinner and a few drinks. I packed my bags and went to sleep. I woke early for the two-hour ride back to Denver and my midday flight. I opened the curtain and looked out to where my car was just a few feet away. White. Nothing but white. No ground. No sky. No car. Just snow. White-out blizzard. I could barely make out the snow mound covering my car. It was buried.

I walked to the lobby and all the guys from the class were milling about. I heard snippets of conversations.

"highway closed"

"four feet of snow expected"

"only building in town with electricity"

"airport closed"

Then one of my fireman friends grabbed me by the arm and walked me to the front window and said gravely, "You see over there? There's a gas station and they have beer. Everybody's loading up because we're going to be here for a while longer. You should too."

I followed his gaze. I couldn't see any gas station. I vaguely remembered one being on the corner out there in the white. For some reason, stupidity, I guess, I flipped up the collar on my light jacket and walked out into it. I could barely see the hotel once I had taken a few steps. But I trudged on, relying on my fuzzy recollection. Eventually I could make out the outline of the gas station. I was about to charge in that direction when I paused for a reason I can't explain. I strained to see the ground in front of me. But there was none. I was at the edge of a wide, deep drainage ditch, which was more like a crevasse. One more step and I'd have been at the bottom of it. And with the wind howling as it was and near-zero visibility, I'd have been down there for a while.

I carefully inched along the edge of the ditch and found myself at the gas station. I bought a case of beer and made the return trip, this time watching more carefully for deadly obstacles. After I got back to my room and warmed up, I joined some firefighters from Terre Haute in a room and we watched college football and drank 3.2 beer, trying to catch a buzz, for the rest of the day.

Two days later, the airport had cleared its runways and I-25 was reopened. I dug my rental car out. As I exited the parking lot, I took note of the huge ditch that I was glad not to be at the bottom of and slowly drove to Denver and my flight home.

*****

Although most of my later professional engineering career was devoted to environmental affairs, some of it was actual hands-on project work. I worked for two years in a chemical plant. One of the key raw materials we used was formaldehyde. Most people think of those frog specimens in biology class floating lifeless in jars of formaldehyde, but due to its chemical structure, it turns out to be a pretty useful "building block" in a number of every day products like paints and plastics.

It's true that formaldehyde can be dangerous if mishandled. So can water, air and every other substance on earth. One good thing about formaldehyde from a human safety perspective is its "warning properties". Think of the rattlesnake's rattles. If you are walking in the desert and hear that sound, it might be a good idea to slowly reverse your course and move away from it. A rattlesnake has good "warning properties". Formaldehyde's warning property is a particularly pungent smell. That smell is readily detected by the human nose at very low concentrations. Formaldehyde can be irritating to the human upper respiratory system at higher concentrations. Long term exposure at certain concentrations may cause serious health effects. At high enough concentrations it can be immediately dangerous to life and health (IDLH).

A bit of chemistry. Formaldehyde is most often used industrially in a solution with water. At certain concentrations, if it is not kept warm enough, a waxy solid will precipitate out of the formaldehyde solution. Our facility had a million gallon concrete underground storage tank for formaldehyde that was many years old. Over those years lots of the waxy solid had precipitated out of the formaldehyde stored there and deposited itself on the bottom of the tank. The tank was huge, more than a hundred feet across and maybe twenty-five feet deep. After many years the waxy solid (paraform) build-up was close to twenty feet deep. At that point a new aboveground storage tank was put into service. But what to do with the massive amount of paraform in the old tank? Disposing of it as a hazardous waste would be extremely costly.

An ingenious solution was devised that involved "mining" the paraform, digging it out by hand and putting it into big bags. The contents of the bags would eventually be used in place of formaldehyde solution to make certain products. Neat, huh? A complicating factor was that the atmosphere inside the tank had a very high concentration of formaldehyde, above the IDLH-level. So, the whole mining, storage and reuse thing would have to be done by people wearing face-covering, protective respirators and plastic suits. And those folks would have to be decontaminated whenever they left the work area. There were gas monitors used to determine where the area of hazard was and procedures were written and people were trained so that the work could be done safely. And it was. Remarkably, over many months the entire tank was emptied and all the recovered paraform was eventually used up, going into products that were sold. Pretty cool.

Oh, there was one incident. One of the workers doing the paraform mining was a contract employee that I will call Bobo. Bobo was an experienced contractor who had done work in many chemical facilities around the country. He received the training that all the workers got and worked for a few weeks without incident.

Digression - One of the principles of safety is "awareness of the hazard". Most people know to be careful when they climb to a high place so they won't fall off. But if someone climbs to high places every day, he may become less careful because his familiarity with the hazard of height has numbed him to it. - End of digression.

Bobo was exiting the contaminated work area for a lunch break one day. As he had done many times before, he stood in the decon pool (a plastic kiddie wading pool) as another worker in protective gear, including a respirator, hosed him off. Paraform is water soluble and once it was all washed off, the worker would remove his protective suit and move to an uncontaminated area where he could safely remove his respirator. This day, however, Bobo didn't follow the procedure. He pulled off his respirator in the contaminated area and got a very big whiff of concentrated formaldehyde vapor. He collapsed on the ground in convulsions. Fortunately, another part of the procedure called for trained emergency personnel to be on hand and they donned respirators and removed Bobo from the contaminated area and began treating him. He was taken to a hospital and suffered no lasting injuries, thank goodness. Lesson learned for Bobo, right?

About a year later, I transferred to this department. My boss, who had supervised the clean-out of the underground formaldehyde tank, assigned me to supervise the clean-out of the new aboveground formaldehyde tank. We were not going to allow paraform to build up in this tank. So, a procedure was written and workers were trained so that the work could be done safely. I was attending the final training of the crew that would enter the tank, making sure that everyone knew everything they should and that all of the paperwork was in place.

We went outside to the tank. The workers would don protective hooded tyvek suits with boots and gloves and supplied-air respirators. A supplied-air respirator has an umbilical line attached to it and to a special air pump that brings fresh air to the mask of the respirator. It frees the worker from having to carry a heavy, bulky air tank and provides unlimited fresh air.

The first worker to go into the tank was to be a big fellow named Dan. He reminded me of a football player. He was all suited up and ready to enter the manway hatch at the base of the tank. From there he would climb up a twenty foot scaffold that had been erected inside the tank and use a high-pressure water hose to clean the paraform from the tank walls. Inside the tank he would hook his harness up to a rescue line. In case of trouble, the facility's rescue squad would pull him out through the roof hatch of the tank.

Elevated work in a confined space with an IDLH atmosphere was serious business as so many things could potentially go wrong. The work permit had to be signed by a half-dozen supervisors including me. Our signature meant that we had observed that all required precautions had been taken.

I was a few feet away from Dan, who appeared to be balking at entering the tank. His supervisor was standing next to me. I looked at him and he told me that Dan could sometimes be a little claustrophobic. I told him that wasn't good for a guy who was about to spend a day inside a chemical storage tank wearing a rubber gas mask. The supervisor walked over to Dan and they talked. I didn't hear every word, but after a minute I moved closer.

I heard the supervisor say these words, "Relax, Dan. Just stay calm. And when you get inside and get up on the scaffold, if you feel any panic, just crack your mask and take a few deep breaths."

I was stunned. Dan's supervisor had just given him advice, that if followed could easily kill him. If Dan had "cracked his mask", that is, pulled it away from his face, and taken a few deep breaths, he would go into convulsions and possibly fall off the scaffold. By the time we could get him out, it might be a body recovery rather than a rescue. In an instant I pictured Dan's lifeless body, his grieving family looking at me, the police inquiry, the newspaper headlines, and a judge sentencing me for negligence in Dan's death.

"Get out!" I heard myself shout at Dan and his supervisor. They looked up at me, confused.

"This job is suspended. Get out of my plant. Pack your things. Get in your truck and get the hell out of here, all of you. You're fired! Get out! Now!"

The supervisor started to tell me I couldn't do this and that everything would be fine. I cut him off and grabbed the work permit and tore it in half.

"Get out now or I will have you forcibly removed."

"Why?" was all the supervisor could say.

"Why?", I echoed. "Because you just gave Dan here permission to kill himself on my jobsite and that's not going to happen. You're an idiot and I want you out of my sight now!"

The contractors packed up their gear and got into their truck and drove out of the plant. As he removed his respirator and other safety gear, Dan looked up at me. I couldn't tell whether he was mad at me or relieved that he wouldn't have to go into that tank. But he didn't say a word.

Then I realized that I had, without authorization, shut down a time-sensitive job. Every hour that the tank was empty reduced the entire facility's output by up to 50%. I called my boss who had signed the work permit hours ago and was in his office. I told him what had happened. He told me to call the plant manager. The plant manager was also a senior executive vice-president in the corporation and didn't get there by being a nice guy. He was notoriously hot-tempered. He did not like bad news. I dialed his extension and told him what had happened. There was a long silence.

"You did the right thing. Secure the sight and go back to your desk," he said.

Back inside, my boss met me in my cubicle and patted me on the back. Then he told me the story about Bobo and the underground storage tank job. I thought he was just sharing a "war story" when he told me that the supervisor I had just fired and kicked out of the plant **was Bobo**. Why hadn't he told me before? Why was Bobo allowed back in, as a supervisor no less? He just shook his head.

A number of people congratulated me on my action. Some guys from the rescue squad thanked me for saving them from a potentially dangerous and gruesome chore. The facility safety manager, Gary, a man I respected immensely, called me to his office to praise my action and tell me that I might be nominated for a corporate award for safety. I was flattered and proud. Inside I knew that I had done what I did partially out of self-interest, but it was one of those moments in my professional life when I had clearly done the right thing.

Another contractor came in and performed the tank cleaning without incident. I supervised their safety training and many of the shifts they worked to complete the job.

That event faded into memory until one day nearly two years later when I got a call from Gary, the safety manager. He asked me if I recalled the incident with Dan and Bobo. I told him I did. He told me that the president of the company that Bobo worked for had called him and described the two-year retraining program that had been given to Bobo at great expense. He told me that the president had pleaded with him to allow their company back into the plant. Gary wanted to know what I thought.

"Gary, as long as Bobo doesn't come into our plant, I don't mind. The only mis-step I ever observed was his."

There was a long pause. Gary told me the president wanted to bring Bobo back to our plant.

"If you are asking my opinion, I am completely against it. And I am surprised you would consider it," I told him. "We've both got friends here. And Bobo has the kind of foolish ignorance that could get one or more of them hurt or killed. I wouldn't want that on my conscience and I don't think you would want it on yours. "

*****

I was sitting at my desk one day and a soon-to-be-retired manager came by to chat. Out of the blue he said, "I understand you're going down to the wastewater plant to supervise. How do you feel about that?"

This was news to me. I went straight to my boss, who sent me to see the plant manager. I found myself in his big office, sitting across from a man I knew to be tough, but fair. He apologized for the way I had found out about my new assignment. And he told me that it was only to be for a year or two. He said that the management in our plant was made up of "old farts", most over 50 and many over 60, and that there were precious few competent young men like me (I was 36.) being groomed for plant and corporate management. I had a college degree. I had worked in two of the four departments in the facility. I had an environmental background. I was well thought of. He mentioned my discovery of the leaking rooftop methanol vent, my dismissal of the negligent contractor Bobo, and my overall good performance. The only thing I lacked was "front-line supervisory experience". A year or two at the wastewater facility would give me that. And he said that he knew it might not be what I wanted to do, but if I could hang in for one or two years, I could call him and he would create a staff job for me to keep me from walking away, until my turn at plant management came around.

My head was spinning. I walked into his office bummed out about having to work at the "ass end" of the facility and he had spun it so that I was walking out picturing myself as a future corporate VP, like he was. And so I was off to the wastewater treatment plant (WWTP).

Located at the very back of the property, away from all of the operating units, were two large "lagoons" where the liquid waste from the facilities' various processes was rendered harmless for discharge into a river. There were physical and biological processes that produced potable water, which was sent to the river and a "sludge" that resembled oatmeal which was dried and burned in a furnace. Oh, and the whole place smelled like poop.

The WWTP was staffed by a motley assortment of fellows. A couple of them were nice guys who cared about their work and wanted to do a good job. The rest of them were looking to do as little as possible while being paid as much as possible in exchange. They had been almost entirely unsupervised for decades. In a company where everyone else, secretaries included, was required to attend monthly safety meetings, attend productivity seminars, and adhere to the corporate mantra of "continuous improvement", these guys had been allowed to pretty much do what they pleased as long as the WWTP didn't violate its permit.

I introduced myself to my new staff and told them that all I expected was minimum adherence to company policies.

Safety, their safety, was my top priority. Permit compliance was number two. And beyond that I wanted to give them what they needed to do their jobs and would stay out of their way. How could they not love me?

They hated me. I got push-back on everything. They each carried a copy of the union contract in their back pocket at all times. They would accept or decline overtime requests in a way that cost the company the maximum amount possible. Some refused to wear the company-provided uniforms. Others refused to wear protective gear. Still others wondered aloud why they couldn't sleep on the job. After all, if something went wrong, an audible alarm would sound and awaken them, right? One would lie and another one would swear to it. Outgoing workers would "punch in" for the incoming crew, sometimes hours before they would arrive. It was a nightmare. But I hung in. One year came and went and then another.

On my second anniversary at the WWTP, I called the plant manager to tell him I was ready to take that staff job and await my rise to plant and corporate management. He didn't answer his phone. I headed to his office only to be told he had quit the company the day before. Gotcha! I spoke to his successor who of course knew nothing of the plan to move me out of the WWTP and up the corporate ladder. When might I expect to be assigned elsewhere? There were no plans to do so.

Gotcha #6 The rungs on your ladder to a successful future may disappear before you get to them.

And so I went back to the want ads. I must have been getting better at finding new jobs because within a month I had interviewed with the state solid waste authority (SWA).

They loved me! I was just what they needed! They would hire me at once! Hallelujah! Although it turned out that "at once" meant six months. I didn't consider that a "gotcha". But I knew there was likely to be one coming.

19

THE SWA (MARCH 1999 - JUNE 30, 2011)

MY final professional engineering job was to be doing "air compliance work" for the four trash burning facilities in Connecticut and several of the landfills. Yes, I now had worked with both "wastewater", commonly called "poo", and "municipal solid waste", known to most as "garbage". Yes, it was a glamorous "career".

The quasi-public SWA, also known as "The Authority" had been created to assure that the criminal elements that are sometimes attracted to the trash hauling business would be excluded from it. Trash combustion in The Authority's facilities generated electricity, for which a premium rate was paid as it was considered "renewable energy". The Authority also got paid per ton of waste accepted from the various towns in the state that used its services. Although The Authority was supposed to be a non-profit enterprise, or "cash neutral", it was hugely "cash positive". It invested its money in bonds, presumably for future construction of new trash disposal facilities when the existing ones became obsolete. There was a dedicated investment analyst who worked for The Authority who was evidently very good at his job and The Authority was flush with cash.

This is what I was told when I interviewed there. One day I left the Syntech chemical plant in my jeans and workshirt and met with a gentleman a few years older than I was. He was a fellow UConn alum named Carl and we got along well. Before we had talked for long he all but told me I had the job. Then Carl started telling me about The Authority. He explained the many facets of its operation and then told me that The Authority had money, lots of money. And they were well connected politically. Our Chairman worked for the Governor. We also employed three lawyers who happened to be state legislators. When the Authority needed something, it got it. If need be, a statute could be written, pushed through the state legislature and signed by the governor to expressly permit The Authority to do what it wanted to do. So, I should pursue any project that I thought could benefit The Authority as money was no object.

In fact, Carl told me, he was working on a top priority project that would alter the face of downtown Hartford. The owner of a nearby NFL team wanted to move the team to Hartford and build a new stadium with all the latest features including tons of "luxury boxes" which generated gobs of revenue. And The Authority was putting together all the plans for demolishing a sizable chunk of the capital city's downtown area and building a stadium there. But that wasn't all. While they were at it, there would be a new upscale shopping mall, ritzy apartments, and of course tons of parking all located along the neglected riverfront. It was a massive project. For a moment I wondered why the solid waste authority was redesigning a city center and building a football stadium, but the prospect of being involved in such a huge, high-profile project made me giddy!

He told me to come back for one further interview with his boss, Dean.

"Do you have a suit? A really nice suit? From now on, you have to wear a nice suit any time you are doing anything for The Authority, OK?"

"Yes, sir!"

After I was hired Carl would tell me that he almost laughed me out of his office when I had come in wearing jeans. I quickly saw what he meant. I wore my best suit to interview with Dean. He only seemed interested in how I presented myself. I was quiet and professional. That was all he cared about. I was hired.

By the time I started, there had been a reshuffling at The Authority. Carl was not to be my boss. Instead I worked for a woman named Betty. When I asked about the change, it was as if I was asking about some shameful, awful scandal. To this day I have never gotten a straight answer about what happened. It seemed to involve a power play that Dean had won and in the aftermath Carl was shunted to some lesser role and Betty was given control of the environmental group. I got a private office in an historic downtown building that would house The Authority until the new, high-rise, "Class A" office space could be made ready for our move there. Our new digs would overlook the proposed new football stadium. It was whispered that we would be able to watch the games from our office windows! I soon noticed that everyone in the office seemed to be on edge. The hallways were silent. People whispered when they talked. No one laughed. Strange.

I got busy familiarizing myself with the state air regulations that applied to municipal waste combustors and going through a huge stack of accumulated correspondence. The Authority believed in very formal correspondence and I was taught the "proper" way to write memos and letters. Then, one day, Dean called me into his office. He had a project for me. He told me it was a "loser" project, but to handle it as if it was a winner as he would be presenting it to the Board of Directors.

One of the directors had the idea of capturing the massive amounts of carbon dioxide that billowed from The Authority's largest trash burning facility and making dry ice from it. It would reduce "greenhouse gas emissions", years before the regulatory agency would even begin talking about such things and selling the dry ice could be a lucrative "side business" for The Authority. It seemed insane to me, but I began gathering data, making calculations and consulting with commodities people. I presented a draft to Dean and he told me to beef up the financial analysis.

As I refined my report, I realized I needed to do financial calculations that I was not that familiar with. So I walked down the hall and introduced myself to the CFO and asked him for advice. He took five minutes and showed me what I needed to know. He was nice to me. I thanked him, thinking I had made a new friend, and went back to work armed with the new knowledge. I figured that Dean would be impressed by the financial calculations. When I presented the next revision of the report to Dean, he seemed pleased. Then he asked me about the financial calculations. I told him that I had used the methodology the CFO had shown me. Dean raised his hand to silence me.

"Never go into the CFO's office again. Never talk to him unless I specifically direct you to do so. Do you understand?"

"I'm sorry, Dean. I had no idea I was doing anything wrong," I pleaded.

"Did I say you did anything wrong? I did not. I'm taking your report to the Board. I'll let you know if further work is needed. That will be all." Dean said.

By the way, my analysis showed that if we had captured all the carbon dioxide from the trash burner and turned it into containerized CO2 gas or dry ice, we would have become the world's largest producer of both commodities and our potential production would have destroyed those markets driving the prices through the floor. I never heard back from Dean about it.

The Authority took up residence in its new downtown, high-rise offices. We were told that we could not eat or drink in our luxurious cubicles, nor could we display so much as a picture of our children without the approval of the Authority's "decor specialist". The "suits-only" dress code was reiterated. Quietly, the football stadium plan went away. It turned out that the team owner had just been "playing" Hartford to get what he wanted from his Massachusetts landlords. If The Authority had been capable of being embarrassed, its face would have been red, but The Authority simply moved on to its next project, energy.

Fuel cells were the new thing. A fuel cell is a device that produces electricity from an electro-chemical reaction, usually between hydrogen and oxygen. For some reason, The Authority was planning to buy and install these little power plants all over the state. There were whispers of all sorts of other projects involving real estate deals and other work that had nothing to do with disposing of the state's solid waste. It was all very hush-hush.

Christmas was approaching and I put in for a week off. The Authority had a very generous "comp time" policy. In short, if one wanted to work extra hours beyond the normal work day, a portion of these extra hours could be saved and taken as time off, with the approval of one's supervisor. Mine, by that time, was Dean. I had been told that everyone did this and I was encouraged to do so. I came in early, left late, and worked through lunch. As a result, I was earning a full day off every month, for which I got approval from Dean. So I was surprised to get his email asking me to "reconsider my time off request" as I had "taken more time off than any other Authority employee".

I was livid. My father had died two weeks after I started at The Authority and I had to take the time off to attend his funeral without pay. Authority policy. Real compassionate, huh? And, based on the way the "comp time" worked, I had given the Authority far more than one hour of extra work for every hour I had ever taken in compensation. That night I wrote a detailed analysis of my hours worked and "comp time" taken since I began at The Authority. I referenced a draft employee handbook, that was never finalized, nor distributed, that described the "comp time" policy not under "leave", but under "working hours". I concluded my analysis by saying that not only had I taken no leave at all since I started at The Authority, but that I had contributed more uncompensated hours than any other Authority employee. I reiterated my request to take a week off at Christmas.

Dean's reply was terse. "I didn't expect such a comprehensive response. Leave approved."

When I left for my Christmas holiday, I was feeling the stress of working in the odd Authority environment. Dean was sometimes loudly verbally abusive to some employees (although never to me) within earshot off all of us in the cubicle area. The Authority's president was likewise vocally profane in meetings and would storm out if he heard things he didn't like. I was beginning to think about the want ads again. I fretted about the day when Dean's wrath might be directed at me.

In the weeks leading up to Christmas, it came to light in the newspapers and online that The Authority had apparently made some sort of deal that some politicians were calling "an improper loan of state monies" and the Authority was calling "an investment". It all came to a head when the "investment", went bad and a quarter of a billion dollars evaporated.

I braced myself as I returned to work in the New Year. I greeted the receptionist and she asked if I had heard that Dean had quit. I was shocked that she would make a joke like that, especially as it would have been my most fervent dream come true. No, she said, it was true. He would be leaving at the end of the week.

Now Dean was a chess player, so to speak. He was always planning three moves ahead. But that week, a wistful, smiling Dean was casually chatting with us as if we were old friends. He said he had no idea what he would do after he quit. Yeah, right. Maybe he would travel, he said. But he was gone at the end of the week. His replacement was a genuinely nice man, Paul, who would become one of my closest friends over the next ten years.

I don't know, but maybe Dean was getting out before he would have been made to get out. The "SWA debacle", as it became known, resulted in the replacement of The Authority's board of directors and upper management. Amazingly, all of this turmoil passed me by like when you dive under water and avoid a breaking wave. The new board and management were straight-shooting businesspeople who just wanted to deal with solid waste disposal and seemed to appreciate my work.

For a total of twelve years I did my job there. I became known and respected in the "regulated community" and by the regulators. I worked with local, state and federal environmental people. I served on subcommittees that helped draft new air regulations. I even won the Connecticut Department of Environmental Protections's 2004 Green Circle Award for one of the projects I had worked on. And within The Authority, I was friends with everyone. I had no nemesis. My boss Paul was a smart, funny, reasonable guy who valued my counsel and let me do my job the way I wanted. My co-workers were smart, funny, hard-working guys who looked out for each other and formed a great team who could do just about anything we were asked to do.

So, was there a "gotcha" in this job? For a while after I first started, before the "clean sweep" that followed the "SWA debacle", it seemed like the "gotcha" was about how politics and alleged corruption can make an otherwise normal job surreal. But that never really "got" me. No, the "gotcha" was different this time. As I worked at the Authority, I turned forty and then fifty. I watched my kids go from grade school to high school, and then college. When I turned fifty, the reality of how I had spent my life came into focus. I had worked all those jobs for all those years kind of keeping my head down and pushing ahead. I guess I was good at my jobs, but this was my life. Had any of it made any kind of difference? I had kept my family fed, clothed, and housed comfortably. That was something, wasn't it? But had I been happy?

I thought back to the vacations we had taken and the dread I felt when they ended and work loomed ahead of me. Even most weekends would end with me depressed about the inevitability of Monday morning and the return to work. I know everybody feels these things to some extent, but they haunted me. There were times when I found myself having an extra drink or more to numb the feeling of desperation that was becoming familiar to me.

Like so many other people, I went to the doctor and was put on anti-depressant medication. It alleviated the symptoms of depression for a little while, but I quit taking them when I came to the conclusion that my sadness wasn't an illness, it was the result of a decision I had made long ago to make my living doing what I was good at rather than doing something I loved. What would that have been? Writing? Stand-up comedy? Who knows? I hadn't been miserable non-stop for the last twenty-five years, but I hadn't gotten much satisfaction either. I found I re-lived the most upsetting episodes of my life again and again in my mind. My ill-fated high school romance, flunking out of college, my disappointing series of jobs rather than an ever-upward career climb like my dad's. I needed to get out. I needed to quit.

I talked to my wife, who had seen how unhappy I had been off and on over the years. She had gone back to work a few years before. She wasn't making a fortune, but with the smart way she had invested our savings, we could manage. Most of all she said that she just wanted me to be happy. So we decided that I would retire in the summer of 2011.

I told the guys I worked most closely with what I was contemplating. They were as supportive as my wife had been. They had seen how unhappy I was, as much I thought I had been so good at hiding it. They told me they used to worry about the way I would put myself down as an engineer, as a father and husband, and as a man. I thought about how often they would tell me they couldn't see why I was so down on myself. They were happy that I was making a move for myself. They wanted me to be happy. Good bunch of guys. True friends.

When I announced my retirement, my boss Paul was delighted for me and the office staff was only sad because they would miss me. At my retirement luncheon, Paul praised my work and said that I had more heart than anyone he knew. As I looked at all the friendly faces, I quoted the Tin Man from *The Wizard of Oz* and told them that I must have a heart because I could feel it breaking just little bit at the thought of not seeing them every day. June 30, 2011 was a Thursday and my last day of work as an engineer.

20

"Career" Epilog

MY career was a long, strange trip, a long and winding road. It was a little less than thirty years of incidents and accidents that seemed to have mostly just happened to me. When I think of my dad and his 39 years with one company. I couldn't help but wonder if I had been successful. What did that even mean?

I hadn't built any bridges or skyscrapers. I hadn't left any tangible legacy. But I had remained gainfully employed and supported myself and my family. I had been honest and fair. I made many friends and few enemies. And I had survived a lot of "gotchas" that I list below for the benefit of future generations.

> *Gotcha #1: A company must make a profit in order to stay in business.*
> *Gotcha #2: A company must keep up with, if not ahead of, the times.*
> *Gotcha #2a: Kindly, understanding managers can disappear in an instant to be replaced by the other kind.*
> *Gotcha #3: Some jobs involve living away from home.*
> *Gotcha #3a Nothing to do can be worse than being too busy.*

Gotcha #4: Unions and being trapped.
Gotcha #5: Smaller doesn't necessarily mean friendlier.
Gotcha #6 The rungs on your ladder to a successful future may disappear before you get to them.

*****

I sometimes think of the reams for paper I used up on resumes and cover letters sent out as SOS messages over the years. And I think of the vacation days I wasted interviewing with all manner of companies. One must swallow one's pride sometimes. Following is an extreme example of that. Some readers may wish to skip ahead a page or two.

I responded to an add from a venerable, well-respected engineering firm that had a nice office headquarters nestled in the woods of New Jersey. I knew several people who had worked for them and it seemed that they were free of many of the "gotchas" I had identified. I presented myself to the receptionist a few minutes before the scheduled 8am interview. She offered me coffee. I declined and took a seat in the waiting area. One hour passed. Then another.

I asked the receptionist if there was a problem. She was surprised I was still waiting. She thought I had gone into the offices and was being interviewed. She apologized and again offered me coffee. I declined again and took a seat in the waiting area as she called someone to see what was taking so long. Another two hours passed.

I approached the receptionist and she had me stand by her as she called someone to inform them that Mr. Yates had been waiting patiently all morning. She handed me the phone and a voice apologized and told me that there was an emergency that was being dealt with by all of the people with whom I was scheduled to speak. Just my luck. Could I come back tomorrow? I told the voice I could not, but I was willing to wait if I would have a chance to interview. How long would this take? I was asked to be patient. The receptionist offered me lunch. I declined and took a seat in the waiting area. I did not want to risk being unprepared should the opportunity to speak to someone suddenly appear.

I waited all day. I had seen most of the staff arrive that morning. And I saw most of them leave as the winter sky got darker. The receptionist started packing up to leave when she looked over and saw me sitting where I had been for over eight hours. She called back and begged someone to come talk to me. She listened for a long while and then hung up the phone. She told me that if I would wait, the Senior Engineering Director had promised to speak to me. He apologized and was embarrassed and said he would understand if I left. I waited.

Sometime after 6pm, a weary, wizened-looking old man in a rumpled suit appeared and called my name. I followed him back into the office. I had been waiting for ten hours. My hopes soared as he began talking to me as if he was planning to hire me. He had seen my resume and was impressed. He knew some of the people I had given as references. He showed me where the engineers' offices were. He told me a little about the emergency they had been dealing with at a Mexican customer's site. I asked questions and even tried to suggest possible solutions, as if I was already working for him. We had just arrived at his cluttered office, the walls papered with certifications and licenses that this man held, when he said he had to go to the bathroom. He asked me if I would go with him so that we could continue our talk. Wait. What?

I was old enough to remember the old *Candid Camera* TV show. Was this a put-on? Was I being *Punk'd* ? No. He was serious. I asked myself how badly I wanted this job. Having waited ten hours and feeling that this might actually be a good job and that my persistence on this day might earn me some extra consideration, I followed him into the men's room and we continued our interview through the toilet stall door! (I wish I was making this up.)

Several minutes later, he emerged, washed his hands, shook my hand, and told me he would be in touch. I exited the empty building alone, tired and not knowing what to think. A few weeks later I got a "flush letter" from them. How appropriate!

*****

For about half of my career, I was actively looking to escape the job I had for one reason or another. I had to keep telling myself that there were good jobs and good bosses out there. And I actually found a couple of good jobs and good bosses. But the journey was an odd, disconcerting one. I often wondered how things would have been different if I had graduated at the top of my class at UConn, if I had persevered as a programmer at Comtech, or if I had become a globe-trotting salesman for Simutronics. I think about a lyric from a Jim Croce song. "After all it's what we've done that makes us what we are." I'm a happy man these days. And the long, strange trip, the long and winding road of my "career" got me here. So, I guess it's true, you never know if what you're going through at the time is good or bad.

When it comes to a career, you can either do what you are good at, or do what you love. For close to thirty years I did what I was good at. I advise my kids to do what they love. We'll see how that works.

Part Three

Essays

Ghosts of Slidell

It didn't occur to me until I was grown that most people would consider spending July and August in South Louisiana a form of cruel and unusual punishment. I grew up looking forward to summer and the trip we would take there every year. I have been richly blessed in my life. One my major blessings was to know my four grandparents from my earliest memories until well into my thirties. Not many people get this gift.

We called my dad's father Pops. His mother we called Nona, a corruption of Leona. When Dad was ten, they had a daughter, Linda. Mom's mother was Meemaw and her stepfather was Pawpaw. Mom's father had died when she was a child. Her mother remarried ten years later and they had a daughter, Carol Ann.

Meemaw

Of my four grandparents, the one I had the longest relationship with was my mother's mother, Velma, who was always Meemaw to my sisters and me. It was only late in her life and even after she passed away that I really considered who she was and what events shaped her life. It was only then that I considered the strained relationship my mother had with her and how that affected who my mom was. And the truth is that, of all my family, I am most like my mother. Who Meemaw was determined a lot of who I am.

At the end of our family's annual, long car trip to Slidell from Texas, we would finally turn up the long oyster-shell driveway of Meemaw and Pawpaw's house. They were always there, side by side, to greet us. Pawpaw had an ever-present smile and was child-like in many ways, playing little games with us, sharing his little "sayings", and whistling to us. Meemaw always greeted us warmly. She was a tiny lady and so she was about our size.

Like most grandmothers, she loved to feed her grandchildren. Both she and Nona had similar specialties. They both made regional favorites like gumbo, red beans and rice, and fried chicken. And like most grandmothers, she loved to spoil her grandchildren by buying things for us. However, Meemaw tended to give us only practical things like school clothes, rather than the toys we might have preferred. And she could be insistent and scolding at times. This was in sharp contrast to Nona who hardly ever showed us anything but sweet kindliness and generosity. As a child I would note this difference, but never thought too deeply about where it might have come from.

Both sets of grandparents were on relatively fixed incomes and both were careful about money. But Meemaw, although at times quite generous with us, would sometimes make a point of being frugal. She would drive her gas bill payment to the gas company office, rather than mail it to them, presumably to save the cost of the stamp. She would say it was on her way, but it seemed odd to me. And the biggest difference between staying with my dad's parents and staying with Meemaw and Pawpaw was air conditioning.

Slidell, Louisiana in July and August is hot and humid in the way that only Louisiana can be. Temperatures in the nineties and humidity of ninety percent are not uncommon. Now, I was born and raised in south Texas, so I was no stranger to warm, even humid weather, but every house I ever lived in had air conditioning. The older houses such as the ones my grandparents lived in did not have central air. But Nona and Pops had big window unit air conditioners throughout their house. And when we came to stay with them, those units hummed from morning until bedtime. In contrast, Meemaw and Pawpaw had two window units that they almost never ran. They had an attic fan and a big kitchen window fan that they ran from time to time to "move the air".

And I don't think I would have ever seen those window units operate except that Carol Ann had a baby, Jennifer. She was the first new grandchild for Meemaw and Pawpaw since I was born ten years before. Meemaw invited a bunch of her friends and relatives over to her house to see the baby. Carol Ann arrived, that sweltering day, before they all showed up and basically said that unless the air conditioning units were put on, she was taking the baby home. And God bless her, Carol Ann stuck to her guns. Meemaw closed off her living room and put on that one unit. And for the first time ever, it was really comfortable in that room with its vinyl upholstered sofa and chairs. Of course, by the time you packed a dozen people in there, it was still pretty stuffy, but it was a landmark occasion.

It was only years later that I began to think about how Meemaw got to be the way she was and, by extension, how that affected my mom and me. I have a newspaper clipping that describes some of the circumstances surrounding the death of Meemaw's first husband, my grandfather Everiste Levy. He was a young man, just 28, when he died leaving behind a young wife and a five year old daughter, my mom. The headline to the story was "Popular Young Man Is Found Dead At Home". He died of a gunshot wound at 6am on a Wednesday morning when his young wife and daughter were off visiting relatives in Slidell. Based on my reading of the story it was either an odd suicide or a motive-less murder. "Boots", as he was known, is described as the popular and good-natured operator of the local market who had been in good spirits the night before. He rose early, shaved, dressed, and then either shot himself or was shot with his own shotgun in the bedroom at close range in the abdomen, falling between two beds with the shotgun resting at his feet.

The newspaper account read, in part, "Legions of Boots' friends cannot find any motive for the rash act, which has caused many to believe that his death was accidental. He was a young man of sterling qualities and if he had any worry or troubles, it was unknown to his intimate friends. He had a happy family life, a splendid business, and was of an unusually cheerful disposition. He was taking treatment for a minor illness but seldom ever mentioned it to close friends."

As I was growing up, I heard only about a 'gun accident'. My sisters told me they heard whispers of suicide. I can only guess at the circumstances, with little more than the newspaper story to go by. If there was life insurance, perhaps charitable authorities reported the shooting as an accident so that the young widow and child might not be left wholly destitute. Surely, if there had been a hint of foul play, the murder of a popular local merchant would have at least been investigated. The one clue in the article is the "minor illness" that he "seldom ever mentioned", even to close friends. If it wasn't so minor, Boots may have decided to take this "rash act" to save himself pain and suffering and his young family the cost of a long course of expensive treatment. I'm sure we'll never know.

But I do know that Meemaw left my mom with loving relatives in Bogalusa and went to Slidell to find work. Among her endeavors was playing piano at the White Kitchen, a well-known restaurant, bar, and package store that featured live entertainment. My mother always spoke of the kindness of the Bogalusa relatives and took us to visit them. (I never enjoyed those visits as the local paper mill utilized the "kraft process" that blanketed the town in an acrid "burnt bacon" smell.) Five years later, Meemaw married Carroll C. Pravata, who became known to his grandchildren as Pawpaw and they had a daughter, Carol Ann. I think my mother then joined them in Slidell in the house on Teddy Avenue.

I don't know for sure because this was not something that was freely spoken about as I was growing up, but I can imagine that my mom was sort of the odd-man-out in the newly-formed household. And she took refuge in her education becoming the Slidell High School Class of 1951 valedictorian. It's no wonder that when she fell in love with my dad, while in high school, she never looked back. And I can only imagine Meemaw's guilt at having to abandon her first child so that she could make a living in Depression-era Louisiana. When she remarried, it was probably a difficult decision to bring Mom back into the fold as another mouth to feed for her new husband. That may explain why Meemaw always worked, eventually becoming the long-time office manager for a local insurance company.

In any case, the times and the events certainly created a far-from-happy situation in both my mother's and grandmother's lives. And that may account for Meemaw's pragmatism, toughness, and the edge she sometimes displayed. And fate wasn't finished hurling sadness her way. When Carol Ann passed away at age 50, shortly after Pawpaw had died, Meemaw was distraught. She lived alone in the house on Teddy Avenue. Her circle of canasta-playing friends and the Church of Saint Mary-Margaret gave her support, love and attention. And there were some good times even then. Meemaw lived to become the oldest alumna of Slidell High School. The Fifty-year Club met each May and I made the trip to Slidell to escort her to the reception more than once. She was the belle of the ball! A non-stop parade of old folks, many of whom had watched me grow up over the summers we visited Slidell, lavished attention on Meemaw and me. There was even an article in the paper with a picture of her! And there was one more milestone to be celebrated a few years later. When my mom turned 68, she and Meemaw became the first-ever mother and daughter to belong to the Fifty-year Club! Once again, I escorted not one, but the two most-celebrated ladies of the event to the big reception! There were more well-wishes from the senior crowd and another article in the paper with pictures. In some way, perhaps that moment brought a kind of closure to the strained mother-daughter relationship after all the years and twists and turns. They were both widowed, Meemaw for the second time. They shared the loss of Carol Ann, one as beloved half-sister and the other as "baby daughter".

It was only a few more years until the Alzheimer's disease that had affected her mother, began to affect Meemaw. She never forgot who I was, even if my name didn't come to her lips quite as fast as it had. Meemaw eventually gave up her driver's license and home with the reluctant anger and fight you would expect.

Aside from the gala dinners, I would visit Meemaw in the lovely assisted-living facility she lived in. It was small and neat and she had friends who lived up and down the hall from her. They played cards and enjoyed the activities that the facility offered. One of these was afternoon concerts by various local musicians, some of whom were quite talented. I escorted Meemaw to one of these events. She took my arm and we took the long way to the facility "living room" so Meemaw could show me off as her escort, her baby's baby, and "new bodyguard" to the other residents. We settled into a comfy sofa as the music started. It was a pianist. He played several classical numbers to polite applause. Meemaw became less and less polite with hers. During one number she made faces and squirmed in her seat to indicate that she did not approve of the music. I even feared that things might get ugly. But this piano player knew his audience. He cut Mozart short and launched into a spirited version of "When the Saints Go Marchin' In", a huge local favorite in south Louisiana. Meemaw immediately shifted from sour to ecstatic. She raised her arms and bounced in her seat. She clapped and insisted that others join in, which they did with gusto. I clapped and bopped along. I had never witnessed the transformative power of music with the elderly. It is an incredible REAL phenomenon. The years rolled back and Meemaw and her friends became kids again. Vacant stares became joyous smiles. Laughter and singing filled the air. The piano man put all he had into that number. He played chorus after chorus, stretching the brief ditty into a concerto. It was amazing, a miracle. But all good things must come to an end and this song could not last forever. It ended with a great crescendo and the pianist began another piece, but he would not finish this one. After a few bars of the slower, classical piece, Meemaw made a face and said, "Let's go back to the room, Stevie-boy." And we did. Our leaving triggered the same notion in all the others. The pianist just quit, thanking the residents for their attention. He gathered his sheet music and left. Note to that guy: Save your big number for your "closer".

A few years later at a similar performance, the same pianist saw Meemaw seemingly mesmerized watching him play. He invited her to sit next to him. As she sat beside him, he asked her if she could play piano and she said no. He played a bit more, then paused. Meemaw lifted her hands to the keyboard. And then she began to play. Not "Chopsticks", not even the only song I had ever heard her play, "Heart and Soul". No, she began to play a beautiful, swirling, melodic piece. She played *piano*, then *forte*, with wonderful emotion. Finally, she stopped.

The visiting musician said, "I thought you said you couldn't play."

Meemaw smiled a little smile.

"I didn't know I could," she said. Then she stood up and made her way back to her room. Maybe there are miracles inside us all.

When Hurricane Katrina destroyed the assisted living facility she was in, an "Angel Flight" took her to North Carolina to another facility near my mom. Mercifully, Meemaw never knew she had moved or she'd have probably raised hell about that. She passed away peacefully a few years later, at 94.

A long life is like a long road. They both have a lot of twists and turns. There are rough stretches that seem like they never end and beautiful parts that you wish wouldn't. When needs must, what might have been a hobby becomes your last, best hope to put food on the table and to pay the rent. And though the years give and then take away husbands, children, and even parts of your mind, that hobby can still allow you to create beautiful art unexpectedly out of nowhere. Music never dies. It always plays, in some remote corner of our minds, waiting to blossom into a duet with a companion. Or sometimes a single note may drift in a window left open.

There's a connection between mathematics and music. And there is a connection between music and something so deep in us that it defies the passage of time. Mathematics, its said, was not created by man, but was discovered by him. If true, then mathematics has always existed. That makes it an aspect of the divine and that divinity applies to unforgettable music. Maybe that infinite music is the sound of heaven.

Pawpaw

When I was staying with Meemaw and Pawpaw, the days had a reassuring rhythm. Meemaw left for work at the insurance company very early. Pawpaw also woke early and headed out to his workshop to continue work on whatever automotive project he had going. I'd wake up a bit later and eventually make my way out to the workshop to "help" Pawpaw. My "help" mostly consisted of handing him tools and making small-talk. Once we were talking about the TV shows I liked and I remember him expressing surprise that we, in Texas, watched the same shows that they did in Louisiana.

Digression - We take for granted in the 21st century the degree to which we all are "media savvy". Everyone from children to senior citizens of today have an understanding of things like prime time, major networks, mini-series,

DVRs, Netflix, and more. My grandparents had been raised in a time before nation-wide radio broadcasts, much less TV networks with local affiliates across the nation. And they were much more concerned about winning world wars, defeating the Communists, and making sense of the social turmoil that erupted in the late 50s and continues today. - End of digression.

Pawpaw was particularly keen to know if we got *Let's Make a Deal* on our TVs in Texas. I told him we did and he and I shared noontime viewings of that show through the summers for many years. Pawpaw was a retired master mechanic who had worked for General Motors as a regional trouble-shooter and trainer. He was, to the Rochester carburetor, what Eric Clapton is to the Stratocaster. He could fix any make or model of automobile. Period. When he "retired" from GM, he simply continued to fix cars out of his well-equipped home workshop. Local people would bring him their cars and he would repair anything from transmissions to body work. When I was there, I became his helper, although I don't think I was ever much help to him. But I could hold a flashlight and fetch tools that he needed. He always made me feel important when we "worked together". I can see his smile in my mind's eye as I write this.

At lunch time Pawpaw would wash up and open a can of pork and beans. He would dump the contents into a saucepan. Then he would open a tin of Vienna sausages that he would place in another saucepan that had about an inch of water in it. Once both saucepans had heated up he would serve us each a plate of pork and beans and dole out the Vienna sausages between us. Always accompanying this was a slice of white bread spread with a liberal smear of margarine. Pawpaw made us this same lunch hundreds of times and although I have dined in some of the world's most acclaimed restaurants, I have never enjoyed a meal any more than I enjoyed those lunches with him.

Once he had filled each of our plates, he would wheel in their 19-inch black and white TV set and put on *Let's Make a Deal*. We would watch attentively and comment on the wisdom of the choices made by the contestants. Sometimes a contestant would choose a door or box that contained a joke prize or "zonk". Pawpaw would call these joke prizes "the jackass". And he would smile and laugh a loud "hee hee" every time someone got "the jackass". I can still hear it and see his smile.

Often, during *Let's Make a Deal* there would be a commercial for a baseball game that was to be broadcast that night. Pawpaw would ask if I wanted to watch it with him and I would always say yes. After dinner, he would sit back in his big recliner and I would take my place on the sofa in their back room. Meemaw would take her place in her recliner beside his and sew or do crossword puzzles as we watched. Invariably, by the time the game had started, Pawpaw's giddy excitement would have yielded to a deep sleep. Meemaw and I watched many baseball games with Pawpaw asleep in his chair. She would often point to him and sarcastically say how much he enjoyed his sports. And also invariably, the moment the game was over, Pawpaw would awaken refreshed, with a smile on his face and Meemaw would ask him if he had enjoyed the game. And he always said he did.

My first memory of Pawpaw is of our family arriving at the house he and Meemaw had on Teddy Avenue in Slidell. It must have been 1965 or so. He was all dressed in a nice white, short-sleeved shirt with his grey hair neatly combed. After we all hugged and greeted each other, I remember hearing my dad congratulate Pawpaw on his retirement from General Motors. I wasn't sure what retirement was.

Pawpaw and his brothers had come to the US from Sicily in the late 1920s. They opened a barber shop in Slidell where they all worked for many years. Little by little each brother educated himself and found other employment. Pawpaw and his brother Joe became mechanics. Joe was a good mechanic. Pawpaw was a *virtuouso*. I've known some excellent craftsmen over the years, but Pawpaw was the undisputed best. He could fix ANYTHING on ANY CAR built from 1900 through 1970, probably 1980. Body work, transmissions, air conditioning, you name it. But he was renowned for his mastery of carburetors.

When I was in fifth grade we studied the various systems of a modern automobile. I wrote to Pawpaw and told him that I would be of great help to him that summer. Pawpaw had a corrugated tin shack attached to his garage. It was chocked full of every imaginable part, gadget, repair manual, and tool you can imagine, including the "special tools" he had made. He called these his "patents". Over many years of repairing everything on every car, usually alone, Pawpaw had found that he sometimes needed an extra hand. He would fashion a tool to act as that extra hand. Was the last nut on a 1971 Plymouth alternator impossible to get at? Pawpaw had a "patent" that would reach it. Did it take two people to properly tension the fan belt on a 1965 Chevy? Pawpaw had a "patent" that allowed him to do it all by himself.

People would bring their cars to "Uncle Carroll", as Pawpaw was known to others, and he would fix them. He didn't charge much more than the parts cost him. He took his time. And he often fixed problems he found that the owners were unaware of. He was methodical. First, he would steam-clean the engine. He and I would drive the car to the local car wash and he would clean the car inside and out. He would not work on a dirty engine. Then he would dash back inside to start the car up before water could get into the distributor cap make make starting the car impossible until it dried.

Once an engine was clean, he would begin to troubleshoot and repair it. He was like a detective. He would call me out to help him by holding a flashlight, pumping a brake pedal, or telling him if the taillights came on. Sometimes he would call me out to crow about finding the most elusive problem. I remember coming out to the shed and seeing him beaming from ear to ear.

"Listen to this," he told me.

He had his finger over a tube deep inside a carburetor. Then he moved his finger. There was a little sound of air being sucked in. Pawpaw hooted like he had discovered gold! He repeated the process several times, hooting each time. I smiled and hooted too. I didn't know what it meant. Apparently, the air being sucked in was a problem. And now that he had discovered it, he would fix it.

He and I would journey around Slidell looking for parts. If the needed part was not available locally, we would go into New Orleans. I can still smell the oil and gasoline of the dozens of garages, parts houses, junkyards, and stores we would go to. And everywhere we went, they knew Pawpaw. They'd ask him if "his little helper" (me), was ready to start working on cars by himself. He'd laugh and tell them how smart I was and what a good helper I was. It made me feel so special. Sometimes they'd give me automotive stickers.

Often, when we were in New Orleans, we'd go to the General Motors Training Center. Pawpaw was a rock star there! They would stop whatever they were doing and introduce him to the classes. They would ask Pawpaw to share some of his knowledge with the class. And he would. He'd go from the Buick classroom, to the Cadillac classroom, to the Pontiac classroom and on and on. In each room, there would be a lecture and demonstration going on and the instructor would stop and defer to Pawpaw's greater knowledge and experience with a smile.

"We have a celebrity here today. This is Mister Carroll Pravata. He has forgotten more than all of us instructors know. If you're smart, you'll listen and learn from him," they would say.

I saw Pawpaw talk about electrical systems, body work, suspensions, and every other part of a car. And after he had dazzled the students and instructors, he's go back into the offices and meet with the men who ran the center. They would invariably ask him to look at a car that someone had brought in that they couldn't fix. Pawpaw would look at me, wink, and ask if we had time to look at one more car. I'd scratch my chin and nod. And he would always diagnose the problem in no time. Sometimes he'd fix it. Other times he would tell them how and leave it to them. Then he would take me to lunch. I can still see him smiling as we sat together.

Pawpaw died at 89 when I was in my early 30s. At his funeral there was a pretty good-sized crowd. I knew many of the people and recognized many of the mechanics and others from the Training Center from years before. A small man came up to me and introduced himself.

"My name is Mutt Miller," he said. "I remember you when you were only so high." He held his hand out waist-high.

"Mister Carroll was a great man. He fixed my mother's car for no charge more than once. He did that for lots of the older folks in town. He and his brothers started the volunteer fire department in Slidell in the 1930s. I bet you didn't know that, did you?"

I shook my head.

"I didn't think so. He never bragged about things like that. Yep, before that no one in town could get homeowner's insurance. After that, they could. And the town started to grow. This town owes Mister Carroll a lot. And I'll tell you another thing. He was the best damn mechanic there ever was, maybe the best there ever will be."

I nodded.

"Many was the time Mister Carroll would say to me, 'Show me a Rochester carburetor I can't fix, and I'll kiss your ass on Canal Street and I'll give you ten minutes to draw a crowd!'"

I chuckled at the inappropriate joke made just a few feet from my grandmother and the priest. We took our seats and the priest said some prayers and gave a eulogy. After that, one of Pawpaw's nieces stood up to ask that anyone who had a remembrance of Uncle Carroll please stand and share it with those assembled.

A few people stood to say how kind he was, or that he had helped them with one thing or another. One lady talked about how he liked to dance with Meemaw and how happy he was the day Carol Ann got married. Another talked about how much he loved his grandchildren. Then there was a pause and a silence. And then Mutt Miller stood up.

He walked to the front of the room beside the casket and began to speak.

"Mister Carroll was a great man. He fixed my mother's car for no charge more than once. He did that for lots of the older folks in town. He and his brothers started the volunteer fire department in Slidell in the 1930s. Before that no one in town could get insurance. After that, they could. And the town started to grow. This town owes Mister Carroll a lot. He was the best darn mechanic there ever was, maybe the best there ever will be. Many was the time Mister Carroll would say to me, 'Show me a Rochester carburetor I can't fix…'"

And he paused, looked right at me, and continued.

"…well, it ain't broke."

Mutt Miller smiled, the assembled crowd chuckled, and I nearly fainted.

My memories of fixing cars and watching TV with Pawpaw are among my most treasured. Everything you would want a grandfather to be, he was to me. (That's true about all of my family. They all took their roles seriously and excelled.) I can see his dark, friendly eyes as he would listen to me talk about my little life. His smile was ever-present. I could feel the love. If there are cars in heaven, they are well cared for.

Nona

I don't think I have a first memory of my dad's mother, Nona. It's like she was just always there. But I do recall being six or seven and waking up in her house to the smells of a full bacon and eggs breakfast. She was a small woman with a big smile who always had her hair done and her makeup on. She'd give you a big kiss on the cheek and then lick her thumb to wipe the lipstick from it. If love was a person, it was Nona. She loved my father and treated him like royalty. She loved her sometimes irascible husband, Pops, is spite of his occasional crabby moods. And she loved her grandchildren with an energy that belied her years.

I've met a lot of people and had a lot of good friends, but I've never met anyone who I felt was so completely on my side, right or wrong, as Nona. My sisters like to tell about how Nona would invite them into her bed for morning girl-talk when she was staying at our house. She would ask about their schoolmates and boyfriends and want to know all the details about their lives. And as she listened to what they had to say, she would smile, a sparkle in her eye, as if she could not get enough of it. She made you feel like what you were telling her was important and that you were special.

When I would stay with Nona and Pops, Pops would go out to work early in the morning and return for lunch. Then he would go back to work until the mid-afternoon. So I had plenty of time alone with Nona. I'd help her with the chores like folding the clothes and some of the cooking. But we'd also just sit at the kitchen table and talk or play cards. She was just the best company you could want. She loved to tell stories about when my dad was young, always smiling as she recalled the details.

When the Vietnam War was raging I would tell Nona how afraid I was that I'd have to go. I'd tell her how the nightly news reports with their body-count score-keeping frightened me and how I didn't want to die. I remember having one of those conversations when I was eight and the draft was ten years away. And I remember having one when I was ten and the draft was eight years away. It seemed inevitable.

Digression - I think I was thirteen and watching the nightly news with my dad and after the nightly "body count score", I asked him what I would do if my "number came up" in the draft when I turned eighteen in five years.

"You'll go," he said matter-of-factly.

"But, if I go, I know I'll die," I said.

"They'll train you and you'll go," he said.

"So, there's no way to avoid it. I'll just go and get killed," I said, resigned to my fate.

"You're not going to Canada. You're not going to desert. You will do what your country asks of you," he said.

And so I figured I had five more years to live until I would be shipped off to the jungle and be killed there. I lived with that fear in the back of my mind until the day the war ended in 1975. - End of digression.

Nona would listen quietly and ease my worried mind. She told me that Pops and my dad had both been born at just the right times to be too young for one military conflict and too old for the next. She was sure the same would be true for me. (And it was!) Then, she'd suggest we run some errands. Those trips often included a stop at the donut shop for a half-dozen glazed donuts that I would gobble down with a big glass of milk.

Nona and Pops ate their big meal at midday and often had just a sandwich for supper. So there would usually be work to be done in the kitchen and I would help Nona cut up the vegetables, mix cake batter, and prepare whatever was on the menu for that day. Years later, as a bachelor I ate much better than I would have because of the training she gave me.

One day she was preparing her southern fried chicken. I was in the den playing with my young cousin Raymond. He must have been about three. Nona got distracted with a phone call and got back to the kitchen in time to see her frying pan full of oil ignite and flames shoot toward the high kitchen ceiling. I remember seeing the light from the blaze reflected off the wall and I ran into the kitchen to find Nona paralyzed in panic. I grabbed the lid of the pan and slid it on, smothering the flames. Nona turned off the stove and moved the pan off the burner. We opened all the doors and windows and fanned the smoke out.

"Let's clean this up before Pops gets home," she said to me.

I got on a step stool and used a mop to clean the soot from the kitchen ceiling. The smoke dissipated quickly and before long all traces of the near-catastrophe were erased. Nona discarded the burnt oil and began cooking the chicken again, this time without incident. By the time Pops returned home, everything was back to normal. It would have been "the perfect crime" except for Raymond, the weak link in our conspiracy of silence.

Pops asked Nona, "How was your morning?"

Before she could answer, Raymond chimed in, "We had a FIRE, Grandpa!"

Nona's confession poured out of her. I feared Pop's temper might show itself. It did not. He listened to her tale, laughed, and said it was a good thing I was there. I was so proud.

Nona had a sense of humor too. When we would arrive at her home, she would ask how my hand was. My hand? It's fine. Why? She would say she assumed I had broken my hand because I hadn't written to her in a long time. Guilt and humor in one shot.

Nona was the most loving, accepting, encouraging person I ever met. She loved her family collectively and individually. She made you feel like the most special, important person in the world and that you had wonderful things ahead of you that she was excited about. She loved all her grandchildren, but made no secret that she loved the boys more. She had so much love to give us all that it didn't matter to my sisters. I wish everyone could have a Nona in their life. That kind of unconditional love and warmth and safety is the unmoving mooring in a stormy sea of life, a safe harbor in my memory, where I can always find a smile and big kiss on the cheek… followed by her wet thumb rubbing off the lipstick.

Pops

My father was named after his dad. His dad was Elton Orlando Yates. My dad was Elton Gottlieb Yates. Nona called them Elton O and Elton G. I called Elton O "Pops". Pops was a Slidell native. In his younger days he had a full head of red hair, loved to hunt and fish, smoked cigars and enjoyed a drink from time to time. By the time of my earliest memories of him, Pops was mostly bald, still enjoyed fishing, had quit smoking, and enjoyed a "high ball" whenever he went to New Orleans to visit his affable brother, Clarence David, who we called "Uncle CD".

He saw the world changing around him and he wasn't happy about most of the changes. I think he was of just the right age that the changes that happened in the 60s must have seemed aimed at him. He was watching a world where white men of a certain age ran everything and had everything pretty much go their way for what seemed like forever being attacked from every side as disenfranchised groups fought for and won their civil rights and voice in society. Nowadays these stories are told, properly so, as these underdog groups overcoming historical, institutionalized oppression through struggle and hardship. It's not popular to pause even for a moment and think about men like Pops who didn't create the inequality that existed but were born into it. Seeing that world change so much in so few years must have been mind-blowing. How realistic is it to expect men of his generation to swiftly and happily welcome revolution after revolution, even if we can clearly see today these revolutions as long-overdo corrections of so many historical wrongs?

Pops was part of that generation that saw Slidell grow from a bump in the dirt road to a "space-age" city through countless cycles of boom and bust. He told me stories of lynchings and moonshiners back in the 1920s and 30s. And there were stories told about him that would make a pretty good movie.

The one that I enjoy most is the story of Pops and the alligator. Sometime in the 1940s, Pops and another man were out hunting for quail or pheasant in the marsh. Slidell has lots of marshland that most people would call swamp. The two men split up to increase their chances and each hunted alone for several hours. If you've ever spent any time in the south Louisiana swamps as I have, you know that they are vast, humid, infested with snakes and bugs, and the "ground" is often little more than crusted-over dead vegetation over mud or water. It's not quite the quicksand of old movies, but it can work the same way. One misplaced step and the hapless hiker or hunter may find himself nearly submerged in water that resembles the *cafe au lait* served at the Cafe du Monde in New Orleans, but is much less tasty.

Pops apparently took such a misplaced step and found himself almost up to his neck in a thick muddy slurry. And he was not alone. The first thing he saw once he wiped the muck from his eyes was a six-foot alligator heading his way. His Remington 16-gauge shotgun was all that could potentially keep him from becoming gator food. He waited until the gator was practically on top of him and poked the barrel of the gun at the gator. It opened its mouth and Pops shoved the gun inside and pulled the trigger killing it. The shot alerted Pops' hunting partner who came running. By the time he got to where Pops was, Pops had gotten out of the muck and dragged the dead reptile out as well. Today I am the proud owner of the shotgun in question. I have looked for gator tooth marks on its barrel but none are evident.

(I'm not saying that the previous account is factually accurate to the smallest detail, but I do insist that that's if that's not the way it happened, it sure as heck is the way it ought to have happened.)

Pops's career was a patchwork of jobs, kind of like mine. I think he did what he had to do in a time and an area of limited opportunity. His jobs included working as a haberdasher in New Orleans, selling real estate, serving as Slidell's Superintendent of Schools, supervising the town department of public works in Slidell and collecting taxes.

He told me about the challenge of collecting taxes from people during the depths of the Great Depression in rural Louisiana. As you might imagine, many people weren't exactly glad to see him coming. He had little leeway in the matter, acting as an agent of the state. Either he collected what was owed or he dispatched the sheriff to arrest the property owner. He said that he had looked down the wrong end of more than a few shotguns, but was able to talk sense into the folks that simply had no money with which to pay.

"There was a fella over on the North Shore, who lived in one of those little shacks out over the water. I knew him like I knew just about everybody in town. And knew me and why I was there. He invited me inside and I saw his wife and two kids all in the one room that was their home. They were as poor as folks could be. But she and the kids greeted me politely calling me 'Mr. Elton'. The man showed me a cigar box that held a couple of dollars and a little change. It was all the money they had in the world. He told me he fished for what they ate and whispered that the church would leave a small box with bread and other food on the doorstep on Sunday mornings."

"I was about to give him the speech I gave so many folks when he told me he might have something to convince me not to sic the sheriff on him. He lifted a floorboard and reached down for what I assumed would be a gun. It was a rope. He pulled the rope up and attached to the end was a big old jug. He poured some of its contents into a little glass and offered it to me. It was white lightning. Moonshine. And it was strong!"

"I thanked him, but told him I still had my job to do. He said he wasn't trying to bribe me. He wanted to know if I wanted to buy any of his hootch. He'd use the proceeds to pay his taxes. I told him I would buy a little jarful, but that wouldn't cover his tax bill. Then it hit me that I knew enough people around town who might buy a little of his 'tonsil varnish' to allow him to pay up. That night I made the rounds and a few of my friends must have headed down to the North Shore because the next day, when I came calling, that cigar box had enough in it to pay his property tax!"

"It never crossed my mind to report him for moonshining. I wasn't a 'revenuer'. Besides, I had a big, old crockery tub in my garage that I made beer in!"

Pops was known, in his later years, as a tough, old bird with a bit of an edge to him. The neighborhood kids were afraid of him, but he was loved by his family.

My mother tells the story of how she was not immediately accepted by my dad's family. Dad's family was far from wealthy, but I guess Mom's situation, losing her father and having to go off and be raised by relatives, put her even lower on the social pecking order. And one of the hoops she was expected to jump through was the ritual of having watermelon with Dad's family one hot summer evening. When this was "sprung" on her, my mother, to her credit, said simply that she didn't care for watermelon. This left my dad's family, particularly his material grandmother, a stoic mountain of a Swiss woman, dumb-founded.

"Jo Ellen doesn't like watermelon!" was passed from person-to-person around the big table like that scene in *The Wizard of Oz* where the munchkins whisper one to another, "Follow the yellow brick road!" My dad offered to buy her ice cream and the two walked off hand-in-hand to the malt shop.

Apart from Mom, we all loved watermelon. The ritual went like this. The big kitchen table would be cleared by the women-folk. One or more of the men would go outside to the shed where an ancient refrigerator hummed noisily. Inside it they would find two cold watermelons and bring them back inside. By now the women would have prepared the table by spreading layers of old newspaper to fully cover it. Pops would take out a silver butcher knife and begin to slice the ripe watermelons. I can still hear the ripe melons as they cracked and popped at the touch of the knife on the rind that would split them almost completely in two.

He always sliced the watermelon lengthwise in half and then lengthwise again and again until full-length pieces, each an eighth of the melon were distributed to everyone. These melons were "red to the rind", sweet as sugar, dripping with sticky juice, and studded with countless black seeds. Everyone was armed with a butter knife and would begin the process of de-seeding and consuming his slice.

Digression - Be careful what you wish for. As a child I was eager to take big bites of the delicious, cool, sweet fruit. But the multitudes of seeds made for slow, tedious going. I used to wonder why they couldn't make a seedless watermelon. How wonderful it would be! Flash forward fifty years to the present when it is nearly impossible to find a watermelon that is NOT seedless. It is sadly also equally impossible to find a watermelon that is a fraction as sweet and juicy as those I remember from my childhood. Convenience sometimes carries an unacceptably high price-tag. - End of digression.

I would fairly mutilate my slice of of watermelon trying to de-seed it as I cut it into bite-sized pieces. But I enjoyed it nonetheless. And even then, I felt that I was taking part in an ancient and important family ritual. I would declare my piece finished and Pops would scarcely give me a glance and say, "There's plenty of good melon still on that rind, Steven. Keep eating." And I would obey. That twelve-inch silver butcher knife that Pops waved as he spoke was awfully persuasive.

There were other rituals and rights of passage.

One summer, when I was eight, we went on an all-day

fishing trip. My dad woke me up at 5am to join Pops and him in the car, already loaded with the fishing gear. We drove out to Palm Lake, which connected via bayous to Lake Ponchartrain. We met my Uncle Ray and Uncle Charlie there at Charlie's house. Charlie wasn't really my uncle. He was a friend of the family who had married Sis, Nona's best friend. Charlie was Norwegian, a retired sea captain, and one of the nicest people I ever met. The five of us piled onto Charlie's boat with a big cooler full of soda, beer, and sandwiches. The sun was just beginning to rise as we set off down Bayou Liberty.

Charlie guided the boat, meandering down the twisty channel pointing out gators and various marine birds as we went. When we got to the open water of the lake, he gunned the motor and off we went. We stopped under the old railroad trestle that connected Slidell to New Orleans. Everybody put a shrimp on a hook and we dropped our lines in the water. We each stood quietly against the side of the boat until somebody got a bite. Mostly we caught croakers. These were considered good eating. They got their name from the sound they made when they flexed their gills once they had been pulled from the water.

After a while Charlie told us to pick up our lines and we moved to other spots along the shore and under the larger, 'new bridge'. We caught croakers all day pretty steadily. At one spot I caught a sheephead, a larger fish with black and white vertical strips and a somewhat sheep-like face. This impressed Charlie and the other men. They asked me for details of my technique. I hadn't done anything different, but I made up something to explain the secret of sheephead catching.

The only other thing we caught were "hardheads". These little catfish-like creatures were ugly and had three spines that poked out, one to each side and one straight up from their back. The spines delivered a poison, I was told, that was the hardhead's natural defense. When I would hook one of these, my dad would carefully use the pliers to remove it, beat it against the side of the boat and toss it overboard. However, around midday I hooked a hardhead and it flipped off my hook, landing at my feet. I panicked fearing the poisonous fish would somehow attack me in retribution for its murdered comrades. Not thinking, I stomped on the fish! There was a long second in which I realized what I had done and what the possible consequences might be.

Getting my foot punctured by a hardhead spine where we were would mean a long trip back to Palm Lake. I wouldn't get to medical help for hours. Fortunately, the vertical spine had passed through the rubber sole of my tennis shoe and neatly up between my toes. Talk about luck!

It was one of those wonderful, endless summer days that made a childhood memory as fresh in my mind now as it was then. The sun began to get low in the sky. Uncle Charlie gunned the engine and headed back to the bayou and Palm Lake beyond. I remember watching my dad as he scanned the lake with a serene calm. I thought that this must have been as good a day for him as it was for me. He was with his father, his son, his brother-in-law, and a family friend he had known since childhood.

Back at Pops' house they cleaned one hundred and two fish, all croakers expect for my sheephead. There was a huge fish-fry that went late into the night. Everybody took fish home. Later, Pops brought out a huge watermelon, put it down on layers of newspaper on the kitchen table and used his big, silver knife to cut slices for everyone. It was the end to about as perfect a day as an eight-year-old can think of.

Mom and Dad

They're Right Here

I see my mother appear on a fog-shrouded beach. She is in her nightgown and unsteadily making her way forward along the sand with her walker, making difficult progress in halting, shaky steps. Her white hair is wind-blown and her facial expression is pained. In the distance, barely visible in the mist, is my father, looking very much as he did the last time I saw him. He is in his wheelchair, slumped and grey. He cranes his neck upward so that he can see in front of him and he is struggling to inch the chair forward.

I look back at Mom and notice that she has changed. She is wearing a neat pants-suit and now is walking much more surely forward. Her hair is neatly done and has considerably less grey in it than it had a moment before. I turn to look at Dad and see that he too has changed. He is now standing, walking toward Mom. He appears stronger, his hair has only the smallest hints of grey. He is smiling and moves purposefully along the sand.

Looking back at Mom, I see her now looking much younger. Perhaps she is forty. Her hair is dark and stylish. Her skin is smooth and she is smiling sweetly too. Her eyes twinkle as they always did when she looked at my dad. She wears a nice summer dress and is gliding across the sand toward Dad. Turning toward him, I see that he now looks even more youthful. He is slimmer, taller and wears the dark-rimmed glasses of his youth. He has on a plaid short-sleeved shirt and khaki slacks. I think I hear either keys or change jingling in his pockets as he strides closer and closer to Mom.

I barely have to turn to look at Mom, as they are approaching so close to one another now. She looks very young, like the high school picture of her that I always carry in my wallet. Her hair of dark chestnut is long and wavy. She has a big smile and is almost giggling. She wears a white sweater over a blue dress. Dad appears to be no more than eighteen now. His jet black hair is neatly combed back. His glasses are gone. His boyish face is beaming. His hazel eyes dance, locked in a gaze with Mom.

Each of them reaches out a right hand and they pull together with a peck on each other's lips. Holding hands, their faces now inches apart, each is all the other can see. They smile at each other as if they can see the lifetime of happiness that each will provide the other. Time means nothing now. Neither does age, infirmity, sadness or loss. As they walk arm-in-arm together away from me into the mist, I hear God's voice saying to them, "Well done, my good and faithful servants. You will never be apart again. That is the heaven I have prepared for you."

And then God says to me, "Don't be sad. There is no death with me. And they are with me now. Go and live your life the way you know they would want. And tell their family and friends to do likewise."

Love, like energy and matter, is never created or destroyed. There is an infinite supply of it that circulates endlessly all around us. Mom and Dad are alive and well in that flow, as are all of those we love but see no longer. And I will tell you a secret. You can close your eyes and see and feel them any time you like. They're right here.

Boy Scout

My father was a Boy Scout. He didn't attain the rank of Eagle Scout, but he was a fine Boy Scout. I know this because in the summer of 1976 we returned, as always, to Slidell, Louisiana, the hometown of both of my parents, and my dad took me with him to visit his old scoutmaster.

Slidell is a typical small southern city of perhaps 25,000 people and it has seen good times and bad over the years. What was once the center of the town has fallen into disrepair and rather than renovate, townspeople have simply built anew on land a bit further from away from Lake Pontchartrain. That newer construction is the generic concrete, steel and glass variety that seems soulless when compared to the smaller, wood-frame buildings of Old Slidell that are full of personality and evoke another age. Granted, the central air conditioning of the New Slidell is welcome on the July and August days when we were usually in town, but the slow-moving ceiling fans rotating silently overhead or old-fashioned steel oscillating fans humming in the corner do a fair job of moving the air in those dark, enclosed Old Slidell buildings protected from the powerful midday sun by awnings and tall white pine trees.

In one such Old Slidell house lived an ancient fellow, tall and lean, with wire-rimmed glasses and thinning white hair. He appeared at the wood-framed screen door before we had even stepped up onto his porch.

"Is that Elton Yates?" his old voice croaked.

"Yes, sir, Mr. Beecham," my dad replied crisply.

"Well, you fellows come on in and sit with me a while," the old man said, his voice alive with the happiness that only recalling the good times of days gone by can spark.

We entered the dark little home, sparsely furnished as it was. A console radio played that station that every small town seems to have, the one that plays old tunes from the 40s and 50s. I recognized the Andrews Sisters chortling. There was a parakeet on his perch in an rusted cage hanging next to the radio. On the walls were photos, old portraits of formally-dressed ancestors, long dead, I imagined. The sepia-toned photographs seemed like they had hung there since photography was invented. Did everyone always wear brown or grey back then? And didn't anyone ever smile? Maybe there wasn't much to smile about. Or maybe they didn't enjoy putting on their Sunday best and sitting for a portrait.

Mr. Beecham motioned toward a rattan couch with thin, fabric cushions in a faded floral pattern. Dad and I took our seats.

"How are you, Mr. Beecham?" my dad asked.

"Oh, I shouldn't complain," the old man began. "There's people out there who have real problems. I've just got the aches and pains you get when you've lived as long as I have."

His particular southern drawl was light and lyrical. He spoke in a cadence common to the area, but with a dignity that was not quite as common. At least not these days.

"Tell me about yourself, Elton. I read in the States-Item that you have done pretty well for yourself. It said you were running an oil company. Can that be so?"

My dad explained about his recent promotion and the travel his job required. He was naturally modest and made the international travel and meetings with heads of state and business tycoons sound like picking up the dry cleaning down at Gozanos' shop.

Unbidden, Mr. Beacham turned to me, took a deep breath

and I could almost see him peering back through thirty-odd years.

"Your daddy was the best scout I ever saw. He was so eager to learn and to earn each new merit badge, I had a hard time keeping up with him. You know our troop only met twice a month, but your daddy would come here to my house between meetings to ask me to show him how to tie fancy knots or who in town might want him to clean up their back yard as part of a service project. I recall he was keenly interested in identifying various types of woods by the grain patterns, isn't that right, Elton?"

"Yes sir, Mr. Beecham," Dad replied.

"I suggested that he assemble samples of various woods into a display, labeling each type. I figured that would keep him occupied until our next troop meeting. Well, the next afternoon, there was your daddy knocking at my door with the display almost complete asking my advice on how best to afix the labels so as not to obscure the grain of the various samples."

Mr. Beecham's voice trailed off. His eyes twinkled and moistened. He cupped his hand as if he was holding the wood samples, admiring the work that had been done so long ago.

Mr. Beecham and Dad talked for a while about the other boys in the troop, most grown and moved away, some dead and gone. They talked about Old Slidell and a downtown fire that happened more than twenty years before as if it had burned last night. It was a polite, easy conversation. My dad unfailing called Mr. Beecham "sir" and Mr. Beecham spoke to my dad as if he was a boy, but in a respectful way I will never forget. He offered ice water and brought out a tray with three glasses. There were long pauses in the conversation, but the radio filled them until Mr. Beecham would offer another old story or ask another question about my dad or his parents.

After a while, Mr. Beecham said how good it was to see my dad again. He stood and my dad and I stood too. We all walked the few paces to the door. Mr. Beecham held the screen door and Dad and I walked from the cool inside out onto the porch where the heat and humidity hit us again. As the screendoor closed behind us, I spoke for the first time.

"Mr. Beecham, sir, my dad still has that display of the different kinds of wood. It's on his workbench at home. I've looked at it a thousand times."

"I know he does. When a scout puts his time and effort into building something of quality like that, he doesn't just throw it away." The old man smiled at me. "What's your name, young fellow?"

"Steven," I said.

"Well, Steven, I hope you grow up to be as fine a man as your father here. Pattern yourself after him in the things you do and you won't go too far wrong. Goodbye." And Mr. Beecham turned and walked back inside his cool, dark home. Dad and I walked to our car.

It occurred to me that what we had just experienced was time travel. Mr. Beecham held inside his mind a bit of spacetime, Slidell 1950. And with a wave of his weathered hand, he took us there and back. I didn't check my wristwatch, but it would not have surprised me if not a minute, not a second, had elapsed in our visit with Mr. Beecham. Good, honest men still pass on the skills of scouting to the boys who seek to learn them. Scouting hasn't completely disappeared. But sometimes, to get at the purest form of it requires a bit of time travel.

The Last Lesson

Growing up in the 1960s and 1970s I probably saw hundreds, if not thousands, of deaths. Not real deaths, of course, but dramatic depictions of death in TV, movies and cartoons. Usually, they were deserved, like when the bad guy got shot as he was about to shoot the good guy. Mostly the deaths were quick and even clean with little or no blood or gore being shown. This was, after all, a more innocent time. But there were "war movies" and "gangster movies" and westerns and sci-fi "space operas" and sometimes scores of troops or gangs of alien hordes would be wiped out to advance the plot. And a youngster like me didn't give any of it much thought.

There were scenes in some of those old movies and TV shows when the good guy would die. Often this was required in order to be historically accurate, like when Davy Crockett died at the Alamo or President Lincoln was shot at Ford's Theater. Or sometimes it was for some kind of dramatic balance. The hero had to die so that his friend would live or to pay off some earlier misdeed of his youth. A youngster like me was sometimes given pause by these deaths, but after a commercial break a new show would come on or the following week John Wayne would be back from the dead playing a slight variation of the hero who I had previously seen go off to meet his maker.

One evening when I was ten years old, I was watching a movie on TV. It opened with a realistic depiction of a modern funeral. The mourners were all somberly dressed in black, many sadly weeping as the shiny black hearse pulled up to the gravesite and the pallbearers lifted the casket and carried it to the grave. A minister read a brief passage from the Bible, "ashes to ashes, dust to dust," and the casket was lowered into the ground. I had never seen anything like that. I had never been to a funeral or a wake or a burial. I hadn't really ever known anyone who had died. And suddenly I was struck by the most awful thought conceivable. My parents were going to die some day. Never mind that everyone is going to die. Or even that I was someday going to die. But my parents were going to die. They were everything to me. Safety. Security. Continuity. Home. Everything. I began to cry in panic.

I had a wonderful childhood, right out of one of those old 50s or 60s sitcoms and my parents were my Ozzie and Harriet, my Ward and June Cleaver, my Donna Reed and whatever her TV husband's name was. They provided everything for me from food and shelter to information about how the world works. They told me what to worry about, like homework and choir practice, and what not to worry about, like Vietnam and monsters. I didn't know much about the world, but I didn't need to. They were my source, my filter, my protectors. And now I became aware of the unescapable fact that someday they would be gone. They weren't permanent. It was as if the ground wasn't solid for me any more. I felt like I was falling. My stomach flipped and flopped. I had to see them right away.

I ran downstairs to the living room as fast as I could, I found them both sitting reading. They looked up and could see I had been crying. I asked them if it was true that they would someday die. After a pause, Dad said it was true, but that it wouldn't be for a long time and I didn't need to worry about it. Mom, too, assured me that they would be around for a long time to come. She offered me a hug and feeling her arms around me gave me comfort and reassurance.

I bounced back from this realization as kids usually do. Death remained a distant stranger to me although the nightly

Vietnam War body count was hard to ignore. I knew it was real, not like the TV western shoot-em-ups. I had friends whose older brothers were over there. Through the years I knew of kids who lost grandparents and pets. As a teen, two of my close friends lost a parent. I was blessed to have all four grandparents live until I was in my thirties. So, death didn't really touch me for many years. A second cousin who I was close to was killed in Detroit. My mother's half-sister had a stroke and was disabled at 40, then ten years later another stroke killed her.

I remember being at Auntie's funeral. Her mother, my grandmother was distraught, grieving openly, consumed by loss. "A parent is not supposed to outlive their child," she repeated. "My baby is gone," she wailed.

My parents were there at that funeral. They consoled me and my sisters. They comforted my grandmother too. Shortly before, we had lost my two grandfathers, old men who lived full lives well into their eighties. Slowly, as mercifully and gradually as one could hope for, death was creeping into my consciousness. It was becoming real enough, but not too real. It had touched our family, but not clobbered me as I had feared it would when I saw that movie when I was ten.

About a year after Auntie's funeral, I got a call from my mother while I was at work. Dad had been giving a speech at his office. He worked for a big corporation and they had a big, fancy media studio/theater where they could broadcast these executive speeches to their offices worldwide. My dad was a great public speaker. He was forthright and direct. He knew how to use humor to help him make his point. People liked to have him speak at company events. Well, this day, they had introduced him and he had bounded up onto the stage from a seat in the front row of the audience and he had passed out as he reached the podium.

Mom said that the company medical staff had been right there and quickly provided care for him. He quickly regained consciousness and seemed to be fine. He went to the best medical center in New York to be evaluated, just in case. Over the weeks that followed, that medical center and others ruled out cause after cause for the wonky blood pressure fluctuations they had detected. He was sent to more specialized centers for more tests. He developed occasional pain in his legs. Something was wrong.

Months went by and he eventually ended up spending a week at Vanderbilt University medical center. They had an expertise in diseases of the autonomic nervous system. A week or so later, on a beautiful spring afternoon, my phone rang again. It was Mom. They had heard back from Vanderbilt. The doctor there, who was the world's foremost expert on this condition diagnosed Dad with something called Shy-Drager syndrome. That turned out to be correct. She told me that what Dad had wasn't life-threatening, nor was it life-shortening. That turned out to be incorrect. And somehow, as I sat on the bathroom floor looking out the window at the flowers blooming and the trees bursting back to life after a cruel New England winter, I knew that I was being told that my dad was going to die.

It felt like I had been suddenly strapped into an awful roller coaster that was going too fast, too high and too far. I hung up the phone and began to cry. In truth, I actually resumed the crying I had suspended back when I was ten. Dad had been right, he wouldn't die for a long time, but now that time had passed and he was. I curled up on the cold tile of the bathroom floor and cried like a little boy for a very long time.

Ten years before, when I got my first real job out of college, I had moved out of my parents' house. Dad's work had taken them far away from where mine had taken me. But they eventually moved back to a town nearby and with the birth of our daughter we had become regular visitors at their little townhouse. They got to see their granddaughter grow from infant to toddler to little girl and now that we had a son, they got to see their grandson often too. I drove to see them alone the next day. I hugged Mom and then hugged Dad. I didn't want to let him go. I kissed his cheek. I hadn't kissed my dad in years, not since I was a child, but I wouldn't pass up the chance to kiss him again. I knew there was a finite number of hugs and kisses in our future.

Before long, Mom and Dad moved down to Carolina to their dream retirement house on a golf course. Dad was only able to play a few rounds before he was too weak to walk the course, even with a cart. Over the next three years, he got weaker. His fine, then gross, motor control worsened. Mom said he spent hours practicing his once-impeccable handwriting just so he could sign "Dad" on our Christmas and birthday cards. I still have every one of those cards. Eventually, Mom signed for him.

We took every chance to go down and seem him. On the last visit, I brought our son. He was five. I made sure he hugged and kissed my dad just like I did. On our last night there, Dad called my sisters and me into his bedroom. He was hunched over in the wheelchair. His hazel eyes were still piercing and strong as he looked at us. We sat at his feet looking up at him. He kept parting his lips, but no words came out. A tear formed in his eye and ran down his cheek. I wiped it away. We sat quietly, patiently. We would have waited forever. Finally, he hung his head and waved us away. I left early the next morning with a final hug and kiss.

A few days later the phone rang. It was Dad. He hadn't called me in ages. He sounded stronger than he had during our recent visit.

"I wanted to tell you what I couldn't tell you the other night. Sometimes I can't get the words to come out. I wanted to tell you and your sisters to take care of Mom when I'm gone."

"I promise we will," I told him. "Is that it?"

"That's it," he said. He sounded relieved.

"I love you, Dad."

"I love you, Steve."

And that was the last time I heard my dad's voice. He died two days later. And I've missed him every day since. It was strange to me, that after he was gone that I didn't wail and agonize over the loss. I had pre-mourned him for three years, starting the day I had gotten that call as I sat on the bathroom floor. Maybe I had started back when I was ten and saw that movie. Though the slow deterioration of his health was extra sad in its way, Dad had softened the blow of his passing by letting me get used to the idea. And he had taught me the lesson of how to let go, without ever really letting go. Thanks, Dad.

Lost and Found

Feeling lost and being lost are two different things. You can be lost without knowing it. There is no fear, no disorientation. It is the essence of 'ignorance is bliss'. You can feel lost without actually being lost. You can be in a place you know like the back of your hand, but due to circumstances, you can suddenly feel like you don't recognize it. I remember approaching a neighborhood in Slidell, Louisiana, the hometown of both of my parents, a town in which I spent every summer of my youth, but approaching this neighborhood from a direction I had not come from before and suddenly panicking before I eventually deciphered the familiar landmarks and regained my composure.

When I am lost I feel very small, very vulnerable and very, very anxious. When I was a child, I rarely felt that way. My parents took such good care of their three kids. We were rarely out of eyesight or earshot of one of them. And my mother was the living embodiment of security and comfort and love to me. I wouldn't learn about her childhood, the tragic death of her father before she could get to know him, and subsequently being passed to relatives who could afford to take care of her, for years. Notwithstanding this, my mom made my childhood so perfect and so without trauma that I took it for granted that my life would always be like that.

I have a late birthday, December 30th. My parents made the decision to hold me back from kindergarten an extra year so I would not be the smallest kid in class. Instead, I spent a wonderful, extra bonus year at home with my mom. Mostly, I watched kid's shows and cartoons on TV, played with my Tonka trucks and ran errands with her. I loved running errands with her. It made me feel so special to walk into the shops beside her. In the dry cleaners, the clerks would give me a piece of candy and call me a 'little shaver'. In the drugstore I would watch the little slide gizmo that gave her our change, like a little slot machine jackpot every time we shopped there. But the biggest place my mom would take me was the supermarket.

I had just outgrown sitting in that little rear-facing seat in the grocery cart and was now able to walk beside my mom as she collected the items on her list. Of course, there were many things on those lower supermarket shelves designed to capture my youthful attention and they did. Little by little, my confidence grew as the colorful boxes of cereal commanded my attention. But what made me completely forget about my mother, for a little while anyway, was something I have not seen in many years now. It was Easter time. In that supermarket, set up on a large table, near one of the aisle end-caps, was a display of live baby chicks! I recall there was a little glass wall that ran around the perimeter of the tabletop that kept the chicks from falling off of the table. As one approached this display, the cute little peeping sound that the chicks make grew louder. And there were not only yellow chicks, as nature had intended, but some of them had been dyed, through some process that I now suspect may not have been particularly beneficial to the chicks, green, blue, and even pink. The store let you touch and even pick up the little peeping balls of fluff. I was so entranced by them that I didn't notice as my mom pushed her shopping cart further and further down the aisle, away from me.

At some point, I think I wanted to ask my mom if I could have one of the chicks. I looked up and realized that my mom was not with me. The impact of the realization hit me like a freight train. Sudden, blind panic ensued. I forgot all about the chicks and I dashed up and down the aisles desperately, but saw only strangers. I could feel my heart pounding and my throat tightening. This was bad. This was very bad. For the first time in my life, the possibility that I would not have a loving, comfortable home with a family who loved and protected me came into sharp focus in my mind. I would be alone and cold and I knew that bad things were bound to overtake me.

Still dashing up and down each aisle like a terrified rabbit, I finally ran smack into a pair of grey slacks. I bounced off of them to the hard, linoleum-tiled floor. Looking up, I saw a tall man with glasses bending down to help me to my feet.

"I'm lost. Help me," I said.

"Are you here with your mother?" he asked. I nodded. He took me by the hand and we walked to the front of the store. He disappeared into a partitioned area and I heard a thundering voice announce over the store's PA system, "There is a lost child at Register Two. Would the mother of a lost child, please come to Register Two." He emerged a moment later and again held my hand. I couldn't keep my mind from running wild with new-found terror and paranoia.

"What if my mom…" I began to ask. But he squeezed my little hand and gazed at something behind me. It was my mom. I'll never forget the feeling of the weight of the world being lifted all at once from my shoulders. I never wanted to stop hugging her. The soft warmth of her hug erased the terrible feeling that had so rapidly overcome me. Also erased was any desire to have a pet baby chick of any color. Everything was going to be alright. My world had been restored. The fearsome world that so frightened a little boy would not consume him today. And I knew that my mom would always be there for me. No matter what.

Twenty-five years later, I was sitting in an office in Edison, New Jersey pouring over piping and instrumentation diagrams for a plastic manufacturing process my company was designing. It was a long, slow, process of specifying a million details and then going back to check that all the details were correct. Each line on the page, and there were many, had its own number. The number contained information about the material of construction, size, and location in the facility. In my mind I would create a 3-D picture of how the pipes all hooked together and if I concentrated hard enough, I could see where there were two pieces of pipe with different specifications bolted together. This could be a problem that had to be fixed. Tedious stuff. But, being a nerdy engineer, this was what I did.

Then the phone rang. It was my mom. She sounded tired and like she had been crying. This was not good. She and my dad lived about two hours north of me in suburban Connecticut. My dad was an oil executive who traveled extensively. He was out of the country.

"Steven, this is Mom. I don't want you to worry, but I am having a problem with my eyes." Mom's eyes were aging and her retinas were becoming detached. She described the condition and told me that she had begun to see "floaters" all the time. Her vision would come and go. This had been going on since my dad had left for his trip a week ago. This morning she had awoken with vision in only her left eye. She was scared, but trying not to show it. She bravely told me that she could barely see at all at this point. She had called her doctor to tell him what was going on. He sent an ambulance to bring her to the hospital. She would need surgery. And she was all alone.

Few things terrify me like the thought of going blind. I had seen a few poor souls, mostly in cities, making their way along, their white canes tapping the pavement, feeling ahead of them for curbs. It seemed so incredible to me that they were not immediately hit by cars or robbed or just overwhelmed by the noise and made to collapse and cry out for help. This is what I would do, I was sure. I would not allow myself to imagine such a fate for my mom.

"Mom, don't worry. I will be right there."

She protested weakly. She mentioned my job and my wife and how my dad would be home soon. I could hear her trying to be so brave. But I could hear the fear in her voice too. As awful as the specter of sudden blindness was with the love of her life, my dad, at her side, it was a million times worse because she was alone. I got the address of the hospital and raced to my car.

I don't remember if I told my boss. I don't remember if I called my wife. I barely remember the trip. I shaved half an hour off what was usually a two-hour drive.

"Mom, I'm here," I said as I slowed my mad dash to a walk and entered her hospital room. She looked so vulnerable laying there. I sat down beside her bed and held her soft hand. The doctors had scheduled treatments for her and were telling her that her sight would return. But eye surgery is as delicate as it sounds and there is no doctor who can guarantee an outcome.

As I sat there, we talked quietly about our ups and downs over the years for what seemed like hours. We talked about the time I cut my hand the day we were moving into a new house in Houston and I had to get stitches. We talked about all the times I had tonsillitis growing up, always at Christmas. And we talked about that magic year before kindergarten that I got to stay home with her and how she would play the piano just for me before my sisters would come home from school. Before long the power of our love and our connection had pushed back the fear.

By the time my dad arrived, my mom was calm and we had convinced each other that, come what may, she was going to get better and we would look back at this all someday and laugh. Everything was going to be alright. Our world was restored. The darkness that so frightened us both would not win today. And just as I knew that my mom would always be there for me, this was the day I learned that I would always be there for her. No matter what.

Eulogy

I'm not sure why I felt the need to write a eulogy for my dad. I've written about him several times before. I think it's because it makes me feel a little closer to him.

My dad was the apple of his parents' eye in post-Depression-era Louisiana. What little they had, they showered on their golden boy. Not so much material things as attention and love and the knowledge that he had, and should embrace, certain responsibilities. He grew up tall and hard-working. He enjoyed the attention of being an only child, then doted on his sister when she came along ten years later. He was a Boy Scout, an athlete, a church member, a trombonist, a fisherman and a student. Few things came to him by any means except hard work. He struggled to work his way from equipment manager to twelfth man on his high school basketball team. He fell in love with his high school sweetheart and was true to her for the rest of his life. He was the first in his family to go to college. He moved his young wife and infant daughter to one of the most inhospitable parts of the earth because that's where his employer sent him. He rose in that company from 'summer help' to Senior Executive Vice-President and would have been President had he not been betrayed by his body.

Digression - My dad was the most careful, patient, thorough, thoughtful person I have ever met. The word "meticulous" sums up a lot of who he was. He kept a detailed diary of every mile he ever traveled on business. I still have it. As he was reviewing his retirement package toward the end of his time at Texaco, he noticed that the number of years of service was wrong. They had neglected to include in the calculation two years that he was due, based on the two summers he had spent between semesters in college. He pointed this out to the accountant who was putting the package together.

"I'm very sorry, Mr. Yates," the accountant said, "We can't include those years without documentation."

"No problem," Dad said. "I have the pay stubs."

"You have pay stubs from forty years ago?" asked the accountant incredulously.

"Oh, yes. I've got all of my pay stubs. Shall I send you a copy?"

This tells you all you need to know about my dad. - End of digression.

With my mom, he raised three kids, all of whom graduated from college. He took care of his parents and visited them as often as he could. He respected his elders and mentored those who came after him. He was polite, careful, detail-oriented, endlessly patient and didn't care for the spotlight. He manicured his lawn and kept his power tools in the original boxes, neatly arranged in the workbench he built himself. He never got so much as a traffic ticket. I never heard him use any curse words or any racial epithets. He drank only rarely and never to excess. He was honest, trustworthy, fair and kind. He loved animals, children, and nature.

He was injured once when he ran into a burning garage to save a neighbor he barely knew. He negotiated with Saudi sheiks, Indonesian oil ministers, met the king of Spain and the President of the United States. He traveled the world staying in the best places and was feted with the finest cuisine, but he preferred to flip through his stamp catalogs in his recliner, next to Mom in hers. And he was happier eating a bowl of cereal for dinner with Mom than he was eating filet mignon with business associates and heads of state. He loved to laugh at Tim Conway and Don Knotts. He liked the sound of brass bands.

I have never met anyone who had a negative thing to say about my dad. My mom might tell you that it wasn't always easy to live with a perfectionist, but she wouldn't have had it any other way. My wife would tell you how she was struck by how affectionate my parents always were to each other, holding hands and sharing pecks on the cheek frequently whenever they were together.

Even the cruelest of diseases could not rob him of his dignity and pride. I never saw him cry or even complain about slowly losing control of his body. As his faculties deserted him, he simply tried harder or adapted to make the best of what he had left. And as the end drew near, he even told us where to find a church bulletin from a memorial service he had attended decades before and directed that the same hymns and readings be sang and read for him when the time came.

And now, years later, I can't think of a thing he left undone or unattended to. He was the finest man I ever knew. I only wish that every child could have as fine a father as I did.

And I wish that all my friends could have known him. And that my kids could have known him better, for longer. I could write a thousand pages, but I could never fully convey what a wonderful man he was. He is the example that I'll never live up to. But he taught me that I shouldn't try to be him, but rather to be myself the best way I can. I miss you, Dad. Rest in peace.

And the Rest...

Odd Job

WHEN our kids graduated from kindergarten, the school held a ceremony. Each child lit the "lamp of learning" (really a candle) and each received a "diploma". The diploma said that they were now officially a "lifetime learner". I guess whether we have lit the "lamp of learning" or not, we are all "lifetime learners". Some of the lessons come in the classroom, of course. But lots of others happen in places like the playground, on dates, and in the workplace.

My parents gave my two sisters and me a weekly allowance. I know not all kids get an allowance, and I don't want to seem ungrateful, but it never seemed very generous to me. There was a formula for the amount that each of us received. When I was in second grade, the amount was twenty cents. My sister Michele was in fourth grade, she got forty cents. My sister Sherlyn was sixth grade and got sixty cents. In return we were supposed to do certain chores, but they were loosely specified and completion of the chores was neither monitored nor enforced. I think my parents determined that it was more work for them to try to manage three sub-minimum wage workers than the work was really worth, so they just paid us.

Once I became old enough to want comic books, baseball cards, and candy, I became aware that my allowance would not be sufficient to cover such purchases. So I began doing odd jobs for neighbors, yard work mostly. Now that I think about it, this must have seemed like a bit of a slap in the face to my parents, who did plenty of work in our yard. I think Dad must have seen that I was learning the value of work and money and that the lesson might somehow be better if it was done for someone besides Mom and Dad.

I had a paper route. And I also did a little babysitting. That paid really well and was so much easier than yard work. I caddied at the local country club. I was something of a junior tycoon. I opened a savings account and watched my small fortune grow. By the time we moved away to London I had a few hundred dollars! However, for the two years we lived overseas, I was cut off from my "on-shore" bank account. I was unemployed and lived off of an allowance that my parents gave me. I was never comfortable with that arrangement after having earned my own money. For one thing the amount, while generous, wasn't enough to pay for all the shows, movies, and food I wanted. And for another, I felt guilty about spending my parents' money in ways I knew they wouldn't approve of like buying beer in pubs and paying my girlfriend's way.

We moved back to New Canaan, Connecticut after two years in London. I wasn't thrilled to be back. I was planning to graduate early and head off to sunny California and live happily ever after with the girlfriend I had found in London. So since I was going to be in Connecticut for a few months, I figured I would try to make the best of it. Maybe I would find a part-time job and make some "seed money" for California.

One day my mom and I walked into the local TV store. As we entered the owner was exclaiming, "Where are all these high school kids that need jobs I keep hearing about?" My mom all but shoved me at him and just like that I had a job. It was late August and Wally Olds was my new boss.

Ten minutes later I was carrying Wally's tool box out to his station wagon and we were off to make house calls. This began what was, for most of a year, a happy and interesting business relationship. Wally was a talker. So riding with him on house calls was just a matter of listening to him tell stories. New Canaan is a very affluent town and many of the homes we went to were mansions. We would inevitably have to take the TVs back to the shop for service, so my job was carrying tools and lugging TVs. Wally told me I would be learning every phase of the operation and that as I learned I would receive pay raises, but I'd be starting out at minimum wage.

It was early in my time with Wally that he seemed to take a liking to me. I think I was a good listener and would occasionally make him laugh. One day he said to me, "Do you know Darryl Winters?"

I told him I did not.

"Darryl is a great kid, a couple of years older than you. He worked here two years. He was smart like you, a fast learner like you, worked hard like you, funny like you. He was a pleasure to work with. You know it's strange, after he graduated and went off to college, he never came back, not once, not even to say hello. His family still lives in town and they never come in either. That's just so strange. I kinda miss that kid."

I nodded and didn't give it a second thought.

When I wasn't out on calls with Wally, I was working in the shop with Eddie. Eddie was a genuine WWII veteran, a marine who had fought on Iwo Jima. He had the most amazing stories of those times and he would entertain me as he taught me how to troubleshoot electronic problems and make simple repairs. Before long I was changing picture tubes on big console TV sets.

Digression - All of what I learned working for Wally is now so obsolete it might as well be chariot repair. But it did help me become handy with tools and a better problem solver. - End of digression

I also found myself occasionally assigned to work at the Main Street sales location. Ralph was the store manager, also an ex-marine. And he was as kind to me as anyone has ever been. There was a lot of standing around and waiting for customers to come in during the day, so Ralph and I would talk, watch TV and generally have a good time. Ralph would use the latest technology in the store to tape-record TV shows from the night before and we would watch them the next day. One day the store received a shipment of new-fangled home video game consoles! This was the latest thing in 1977. Ralph and I set up the demonstration model in the store and proceeded to log many, many hours playing video soccer, drag racing and bowling. Although these games were primitive by today's standards, they were a blast to me at the time and to play for hours while getting paid, albeit minimum wage, seemed like the best deal a young man could ask for. Ralph would send me across the street to the variety store for little ten-ounce bottles of Coca-Cola. He seemed to like his job and had a great way with customers. He taught me a simple, low-pressure sales technique that worked well with the affluent folks who came into the shop. Many of them would come in fifty times to "shop" before one day walking in and buying a set in five minutes. So, I learned to be patient and courteous.

Wally Olds catered to some of the very wealthy folks in town. He would tell me to load the truck with our top-end stereo set and go with him to install it, unsolicited, at the home of some business tycoon, or, more often, at the home of the son of some business tycoon. I learned about a class of idle rich folk who apparently did little all day but enjoy themselves between trips to Europe or the Caribbean. Some of them drank too much. I'm sure some had other vices that were not as apparent. Sometimes they would call us and tell us to retrieve the stereos or TVs that Wally had sent them. Usually, they would just pay the bill and keep whatever we had installed.

I visited homes of celebrities, artists, musicians, art collectors and regular folks too. There was a lady who was the ex-wife of a Rockefeller. There was the fellow who collected original paintings by Salvador Dali and a lady who had dozens of original works by Andrew Wyeth.

Digression - One day I was told to go to an address way out in a part of town where there were some very big, very nice, very expensive homes. I later learned that David Letterman lived out there. I knocked on the door of the beautiful home. A moment later I was face to face with Jack Paar. For those of you too young to remember Mr. Paar, he was Johnny Carson, before Johnny Carson was Johnny Carson. He hosted *The Tonight Show* on NBC. He was famous for the stars and politicians he interviewed including JFK, for his sometimes fragile emotions, and for the many careers he helped launch. He was also famous for quitting at the height of his fame in 1962 and appearing only sporadically on TV thereafter. I was star-struck.

"You're Jack Paar!" I said.

"You're too young to know who I am!" he replied.

He invited me in and showed me the TV set that needed

repair. I loaded it into the truck and came back to give him a receipt. He asked me to sit down, if I had a moment. He was curious what an 18-year-old in 1978 knew about him. We walked to a very comfortable, expansive "conversation pit" and I recounted what I knew of his career and my memories of the specials he had done after he left *The Tonight Show*.

He seemed pleased to have a young fan come to his door. We chatted about some of the people he had interviewed and about the many personal objects that decorated his home. One was a portrait of him dressed in armor like a medieval knight. He was interested in me and asked about my childhood growing up in Texas and my recent time in London. Eventually, there was a pause.

"Do you ever miss doing *The Tonight Show*?" I asked him.

"I'll tell you a secret very few people know, Steven. I never stopped doing *The Tonight Show*. I do it several nights a week right here where we are sitting. Sometimes my guests are heads of state, sometimes show business royalty, sometimes it's old friends you may or may not have heard of, and sometimes it's the mailman or my next-door neighbor. And it's as fascinating and funny and interesting as it used to be when we did it at NBC in front of cameras, only there are no cameras. I never stopped. That's my secret."

Jack Paar smiled at me and I stood to leave. He said he hoped I'd come back and see him again some time. I told him I hoped I'd get to deliver his TV back to him after it was repaired. He shook my hand and saw me to the door.

I only ever saw him again when he would buzz past on Elm Street in his little, white Porsche. We made eye contact once and his face lit up and he gave me a mock salute as he sped past. Nice man. - End of digression.

One day I met a fellow in the shop called Norm and was informed that I was to help him install rooftop TV antennas. On nice days, this could be fun, athletic work. It was exhilarating to be outside, up high working with a nice guy like Norm. He showed me how to install and wire a system and we were often welcomed into the nice homes for refreshments and were often tipped, sometimes generously, for our work. On rainy days, it was miserable work. On snowy days it was downright dangerous. One house, the last I ever worked on, had a very steep roof and a three-story drop. We had no safety gear and worked with old, wooden ladders that attached to one another like Tinker Toys to reach whatever heights we had to scale. I guess I'm lucky I never fell.

By Christmas, I had broken up with my London girlfriend. California and happily ever after with her was out. But I had a new girlfriend. Christmas week I worked into the night after school, wrapping and delivering TVs and stereos and putting them under people's trees. That was fun. Looking back, that was about the last of my good times working for Wally.

One day, in particular, I remember going out with Norm. It was January. Freezing cold. On the rooftop, the wind was unchecked. Our fingers would stop working after a few minutes and we would swap out sitting in the truck with the heat on while the other was doing the work, which could not be done with gloves on. It was an old slate roof covered in ice. It was treacherous. It was a huge job and it took from 8am to 4pm without a break to finish. When we got back to the shop, Wally said he couldn't believe we had completed the job under the conditions. He slapped Norm on the back and pulled two twenties out of the cash register and handed them to Norm and told him to go home and fill in his timesheet as if he had worked until 8pm. Wally looked at me and told me there was sweeping to be done back at the repair shop. To say I was disappointed would be an understatement. I was beginning to see how Wally worked.

I was what is called in Old English a "dog's body", the servant of the servant, the low man on the totem pole. I was only there for the money, but slowly, I began to resent the treatment. And once one becomes aware of such treatment, one becomes sensitized to it. Before long I could see I was being given every dirty job that came along. And the raises I had been promised when I was first hired, never materialized even though I had mastered all but the most complex electronic repair tasks. I resolved to mention this to Wally. I told Ralph what I was planning to say. Without changing his genial expression he told me I would find it hard to have that conversation for the next few weeks. I asked him why. Ralph told me that this was the time of year when Wally would disappear for a few weeks and not be seen or heard from. He was dodging creditors. Ralph didn't share many other details other than to say that this happened every year and we'd get our checks from Wally's wife, who was an "off-the-books" employee. And sure enough, three weeks passed without a peep or any sign from Wally. Then, like magic, he reappeared and nothing was said about it. A week later a huge shipment of merchandise arrived at the sales location and it seemed that the business was doing great.

Wally even hired a friend of mine to assist from time to time when Norm was out or when we were moving things too big for me to handle on my own. That was fun. And my buddy Stan seemed to immediately see what kind of business Wally really ran.

"This guy is a BS artist. Haven't you heard about him? It's all over town! He overcharges, double bills, pays creditors late, borrows from hoodlums, the works. He's an 'operator'," Stan told me.

All at once, a number of things snapped into focus for me. I recalled many of the tall tales Wally had told me as we drove around town on calls. He said he had been part of New York City high society in the 50s. He dated debutantes and got written up in Walter Winchell's society page. He said he had a big ten-cylinder automobile that had an automatic oil-changing feature. It all seems like harmless bragging with a healthy dollop of embellishment to me. And what did I care? It was entertaining. But now I saw that Wally thought I was a gullible sap!

Yes, I had dealt with unhappy customers, but I assumed they were just upset that their TVs or stereos had broken. Now I began to suspect they had been ripped off. I started paying closer attention as I worked. I saw that Eddie never wrote the number of hours he spent on a repair on the billing ticket. He had a code of little x's and dashes that represented his time. He never saw what the customers were actually charged. I followed a few billing tickets through the system and saw how Wally would inflate many of them by charging for hours of work beyond what Eddie had indicated in code. And every repair had a bogus "clean and lubricate controls" line item and a charge for it that varied. There were certain repairs that I did where a simple ten-cent fuse had to be replaced to bring a totally dead unit back to life. It took fifteen minutes of my minimum-wage time. And Wally would charge for hours of labor at Eddie's rate and for parts that were never installed.

Wally would install a "lightning arrestor" on every TV

that came into the shop, telling people it would protect their set from catastrophic damage should the house be hit by lightning. Eddie told me that if lightning hit a house, it would fry not only the "arrestor" but the rest of the TV's electronics as well. It was a scam.

And what I eventually realized was that Wally would adjust what he charged to fit what he knew about the wealth of the customer. In other words, he charged as much as he thought he could get away with charging! Most people were so ignorant of what made a TV work and what went into a repair, they would just pay, or never come pick up the set. After thirty days Wally could and did sell unclaimed sets as "used".

After almost a year working there, I went out on a service call with Wally. We were redelivering a set that had been repaired after several attempts and several charges. Apparently, Wally had chosen the wrong lady to rip off. We were in the front doorway, ready to leave, when Wally presented this woman with the bill. She reached behind the front door and produced a .22 rifle, cocked it and fired a round between Wally and me that flew out the door. I was frozen with fear. The woman levered the handle and pointed the rifle squarely at my chest.

Wally said, "Go ahead and shoot! I'll take you to court!"

Easy for him to say when the rifle was pointed at me! She turned to look at Wally and I ran. I ran as fast as I have ever run. I went next-door and asked to use the phone to call the police. They let me in and showed me the phone.

I dialed "zero".

"Operator, get me the police. This is an emergency." A moment later the police answered.

"I'd like to report a shooting," I said gravely.

"With a gun?" the officer asked.

"Yes, with a gun!" I gave him the address and he told me not to go back to the scene of the shooting. He didn't have to tell me twice. I made my way back to the service truck and cowered behind it until the police arrived.

They took the rifle from the woman, verified it had been fired and then gave it back to her! In the ensuing "investigation", to which I was not privy, I think Wally's reputation caught up to him. The lady kept her TV. Wally and I drove back to the shop. I was shaken. For a minute, Wally seemed to appreciate that I had almost been killed because I worked for him. Then the moment passed and he handed me a broom and told me to use it.

A week or so later, I graduated from high school and expected to begin working longer hours, making more money. Summer had begun and all my classmates had found summer jobs in town. It looked like it would be a fun summer of after-work pizza and beer with my buddies. That first Monday, around 9am Wally found me fixing radios and told me I wouldn't be needed. Not that day. Not that week. Maybe not ever again. He'd call and let me know. I was devastated. I had been saving up for a trip back to London. That wouldn't be happening. Now I had the whole summer ahead of me and no prospects as all the summer jobs in town had been claimed.

I walked out into the street past the sales location. I saw Ralph inside and decided to go get a coke from the variety store out of some sort of Pavlovian response and self-pity. In the variety store I recognized Denny Desmond. Denny had been a sixth-grade playground nemesis of mine. I don't think I had spoken to him since then, having managed to avoid him for most of the intervening years.

"Hey, Steve! How's it going?" Denny greeted me warmly.

I answered, "Not great. I just lost my summer job on the first day of the summer."

"Are you looking for work? I manage this place. You can work here if you want to. What do you say?" Denny asked.

And before I knew it, my summer was saved. I guess Denny had forgotten all about our sixth-grade playground squabbling. And I worked there until I went off to college.

But I had one loose end to tie up. I still had keys to Wally's repair and sales locations. I'd have to go back and turn them in. Now, what I'm about to confess is wrong. It's a sin and a crime and I should never have done it. One of the tasks I had been given was to inventory "non-serial number items" in the sales location. This included records, accessories, batteries, small items. Wally ran a pretty loose ship when it came to these sorts of items. And he wanted to get a handle on how much money he had tied up in that stuff. He may have had purchase records of some of it. Knowing him, some of it may have come from sources that weren't exactly legitimate. I had not completed the inventory. And I didn't exactly work for Wally any more.

So I used my keys one more time before I dropped them off with Ralph. All I'll say is that I left for school that fall with a much, much larger record collection than I had started the summer with.

As I walked out of the shop where Wally had first asked out loud where the students were who wanted jobs and I had stepped forward, I thought about what he had told me about Darryl Winters. Maybe I was like him. I was a great kid, now a year older. I was smart, funny, a fast learner, and I worked hard. To Wally, I was probably a pleasure to work with. And like Darryl, once I graduated and went off to college, I never went back to Wally's shop, not once, not even to say hello. My family still lived in town and they never did either. I totally understood now. And I've never missed Wally. But I did learn from him.

THE FAR-OUT CLUB AND MR. RUSZCZYK

One reason that I look back upon my childhood with such affection, is that was the time when I saw so many wonderful things for the first time. Everything from rainbows to department store Santa Clauses were a source of wonder. My first visit to a circus was almost overwhelming. Trapeze acts, fire-eaters, a lion tamer. The fantastic just kept coming! It all seemed like magic. For a child, magic is a real thing that pops up, usually unexpectedly, all over the place. There was literal magic in the fairytales we were told. Technology was often presented to us as magic. The automatic door at the supermarket was magic.

But as we get older, we gradually develop an understanding of how the world works, or at least how parts of it work. And knowledge begins to supplant magic. We come to understand that through natural talent, specialized knowledge, and endless practice the trapeze, fire-eating, and even lion taming are simply skills that one can acquire. We realize that fairytales are made-up stories for small children. And we may even come to understand that the supermarket door opens because of the weight-sensitive switch in the rubber mat that we step on, not any imagined hocus-pocus.

But many of us don't entirely give up on magic. Books,

movies, and TV shows on the unexplained mysteries of nature or history abound. Just because magic isn't present in our neighborhood, doesn't mean it's not hiding in some exotic corner of a distant land, or that it didn't permeate ancient, long-forgotten cultures. Perhaps it is all around us and one simply has to know where to look. This fleeting promise to restore to us some of the long-lost wonder of childhood is appealing.

*****

In junior high, we had a "modern" block schedule. Classes met four times a week at different times on different days. Keeping track of it all just made an already confusing time in our young lives that much more stressful. A curious artifact of this schedule was a free period of 45 minutes that fell on Friday morning. This was the so-called "multi-choice" period.

The "multi-choice" period was very much a relic of the mid 1970s. There seemed to be a cultural need to break away from the highly regimented way of life that had served us so well through World War Two and the fifties and encourage freedom and self-expression in the children, up to a point, of course. Every teacher was asked to offer some talent, skill, or interest that could be shared with a small group of students during the 'multi-choice" period. As I scanned the list of choices, one fairly leapt out at me. It was cryptically entitled "The Far-Out Club" and was offered by Mr. Morrow, a math teacher I had never met.

That first Friday, Mr. Morrow explained that the purpose of the club was to explore the realm of the unexplained. Topics like ESP, telekinesis, mind-reading and the Loch Ness Monster were fair game for the club. He would bring some information on a topic each Friday and he invited us to bring in information or questions. We would discuss the topic or conduct our own experiments. I remember sitting opposite one of my classmates trying to transmit numbers, names, or images to him via telepathy with very limited success.

I also remember Mr. Morrow telling us tales of the occult and supernatural, what amounted to ghost stories. He presented them all as being "possibly" true and he was a good storyteller. Despite the fact that were in a classroom with fluorescent lighting and linoleum-tiled floors, he had the ability to transport us to a virtual campfire in imaginary woods and send a chill up our spines when he would get to the 'clincher' ending of his tales.

Sometimes Mr. Morrow would tell a long, involved story. Other times they were just little "snippets". One snippet was about a lady, absent-mindedly looking for a person's name in the phone book by finding their phone number first. Since phone numbers aren't listed in any particular order it seemed impossible that she could quickly and easily find the number first and then read the name associated with it, especially in a huge big-city phonebook. Was it the "latent unharnessed power of the mind" breaking through? Oh, wow, man!

Later, though, I became skeptical. After all, there was no real evidence that this event even happened. Then it occurred to me that all of the stories Mr. Morrow and my fellow students had brought to the club were most likely just made-up. They could all just be tall tales! And I had yet to see anyone demonstrate any ESP or other inexplicable talent. I concluded that this was all nonsense! A week later I transferred to the "Current Events Club".

My failure to witness inexplicable psychic phenomena in

the Far-Out Club did not kill my desire to do so. And so it was late one evening that I stumbled across a TV show called *The Amazing World of Kreskin*. It was a half-hour Canadian production showcasing the performances of the "mentalist" who would rack up a large number of appearances on *The Tonight Show* with Johnny Carson. I had never heard of Kreskin before and I was mesmerized. In a slick, carefully-worded presentation, Kreskin appeared to read minds and predict the future. He did not claim to have supernatural powers. Rather he said that he had simply harnessed the power of the mind that each of us has, but few of us develop. I was enthralled.

In the weeks that followed, I witnessed Kreskin performing his feats in a many different ways. Over time, however, I noticed certain patterns to the way he operated. Having been a fan of magicians for years, I saw similarities in the way Kreskin operated. Once I started watching him with a skeptical eye I began to detect how his demonstrations could be done through sleight of hand versus 'mental powers' and the show became much less interesting. Shortly thereafter I discovered *Monty Python's Flying Circus* on another channel and never looked back.

I remember reading Henri Charriere's book *Papillon*. It's a great book filled with the supposedly true adventures of Charriere as a petty criminal wrongful-convicted of murder and sentenced to serve his life sentence in the "Devil's Island" penal colony of French Guiana. It tells of his hardships, perils, and ultimate escape from the inescapable isle. The story was made into a great movie starring Steve McQueen and Dustin Hoffman. As soon as I finished reading *Papillon*, I started the sequel volume, *Banco*. This was written after the success of the first book. It tells of Charriere's further adventures after escaping from Devil's Island, but is not quite as compelling. Only a chapter or two into *Banco*, I began to doubt that it was a true story. Charriere was the hero of every incident he retold. His life was a series of heart-pounding adventures and he always came out on top. It was unbelievable. And so I stopped believing. And I stopped reading. I even began to retroactively doubt if anything in *Papillon* was true!

*****

I had a lot of good teachers. They helped give me a real "leg up" in life. Some of them taught me skills like sounding out words, performing mathematical operations quickly and accurately, and speaking Spanish. Some of them taught me about life by being sweet, kind, accepting, tough, or strict. But one of them stands out because he taught me how to learn, reason, question and discover. His name was Ed Ruszczyk (pronounced RUZ-ick).

My mother was skeptical of the "bearded, blue-jeaned" teachers at New Canaan High School in Connecticut. She substituted there on a couple of occasions. She had been a high school math and English teacher ten years before in rural Texas back when the male teachers were clean-shaven and wore suits and ties and everyone said "sir" and "ma'am". It was a shock to her to see the new generation of teachers and students whose vocabularies included "sucks", "ass", and "damn".

I don't think she ever saw Mr. Ruszczyk in action, but she would have been put off seeing the diminutive teacher with his beard and jeans standing on top of the lab tables lecturing the class, drawing sloppy diagrams on the chalkboard, describing "blobs" of warm air, and generally setting a relaxed, undisciplined tone for his classes.

I had Mr. Ruszczyk for Earth Science. I had always done well in math and science, and most of my other classes for that matter. I paid attention and had a good memory. And in most classes, that practically guaranteed an "A". History, Science, Literature, Psychology and other "survey" classes presented information to the student and simply asked the student to memorize and then regurgitate the information on exercises, quizzes and tests. The more accurately one could do so, the better the grade one got. Other classes taught a skill like speaking a foreign language, building things out of metal or wood, writing an essay, or performing mathematical operations to solve different kinds of problems, or proving theorems. These classes were more challenging because simply memorizing facts would not give you the skill that you had to demonstrate to be successful. But until I walked into Mr. Ruszczyk's Earth Science class, science had been all about playing "pitch and catch" with factual information. Consume and regurgitate.

Mr. Ruszczyk didn't answer questions with answers. He answered questions with more questions. Almost like a toddler who just keeps asking "why?" in response to everything you say to them. Mr. Ruszczyk would draw a "blob of air" on the chalkboard and ask, "What happens if I heat this blob of air?"

I raised my hand and said, "It expands." Nailed it.

"Why?" Mr. Ruszczyk snapped back, unconvinced.

Silence. Why? What kind of answer was that?

"How do you know air expands when you heat it?" he asked me. "I'm not saying it does or it doesn't, but how would you show me?"

I felt confronted like I sometimes was by bullies in the hallway or on the playground. And I wanted to push back. I thought.

"You could heat up a container of air and watch it expand," I said.

Mr. Ruszczyk jumped down from the lab table on which he had been sitting and dashed to the back of the room. He took an empty metal container, screwed the cap on and sat it in a water bath on a hot plate. After a few minutes, the container began to deform. It blew up like a balloon.

"OK, Yates, you've convinced me that hot air expands. Now tell me why? Or was that just a lucky guess?" Mr. Ruszczyk asked.

The class laughed. I thought hard. I was in a battle of wits with this guy. No other teacher had ever treated me like this. Most teachers were happy to have a student raise his hand with an answer. This guy was antagonizing me for participating!

"What's air made of?" he asked.

"Oxygen and nitrogen molecules," I snapped back.

"I don't know what that is. Here's a tiny blob of air." He drew a little circle on the board. "Tell me what heat does to it that makes it expand."

I was stumped and frustrated. The whole class was looking at me. Mr. Ruszczyk had pity.

"If you heat something up, what are you putting into it?" he asked. More questions.

"Energy?" I ventured.

"Are you asking me or telling me?" he snarked back.

"Telling you," I said.

"And does the energy make stuff go faster or slower?"

"Faster," I said with a bit more confidence.

"Yeah, so?" he asked.

"The faster moving molecule hits the side of the container harder and makes it expand."

"OK, so what else does hot air do?" Mr. Ruszczyk moved on. No pat on the head for getting the right answer.

"Hot air rises," I said trying not to sound frustrated. There didn't seem to be an end to this.

"Why?" he snapped back way too fast.

My brain hurt. I sat and thought. Mr. Ruszczyk didn't want to lose me.

"If hot air rises, what does it rise through?" he asked.

"Cooler air?" I heard the question in my voice and caught myself. "Cooler air."

"And so what happens to the cooler air?" he asked.

"It sinks." I shot back.

"Why?" he fired back.

I was stumped again. Mr. Ruszczyk didn't betray his enjoyment of this with so much as a smirk. He held out the piece of chalk he had been using and dropped it.

"Gravity?" I caught myself again. "I mean, gravity." I said.

"Why does gravity attract cool air more than warm air?" he asked.

"It's more dense," I replied.

"Hm. Makes sense," he said. And that was it. Mr. Ruszczyk moved on to another topic and motioned for me to let the other students have a chance. This may sound conceited, but most of them had a much harder go of it adapting to Mr. Ruszczyk's style and many of them got frustrated not wanting to play his game.

For the next year, Mr. Ruszczyk challenged me again and again forcing me to think and to experiment and to question the pat facts I had stored in my brain, gleaned from books, TV and other "pitch and catch" courses I had taken. About halfway through the year, I stayed after class to ask about an assignment and he finally let me peek behind his facade.

"You know why I hassle you in class, don't you, Yates?" he asked. I shook my head.

"You are a student. I only get one or two students a year. The rest of the kids in my classes just want a grade. You want to learn. And that's good because I want to teach. I can't shove science into your head, you have to go get it and work to shove it in there yourself. That's why I give you a hard time."

And that was all he ever said about it. I came to enjoy "being hassled" by Mr. Ruszczyk and found that I could use the methods he taught me, or made me teach myself, in other classes and in life. He was helping me build my scientific mind. By simply asking why, like a child, he forced me to actually understand the world, broken down into such simple component parts that I could explain to others, and to defend my ideas against their attacks. And I figured out somewhere along the way that a scientist, a real scientist, was just a student, who must always be ready to answer the endless "whys" and defend those answers by explaining in understandable terms how you got them. And if you couldn't explain something, then you really didn't "know" it, you just "believed" it. And you probably had some more learning to do.

The most interesting lesson Mr. Ruszczyk's taught me involved him showing a videotape of an episode of the series *In Search Of…*. *In Search Of…* was a popular half-hour syndicated show narrated by Leonard Nimoy (Mr. Spock of *Star Trek* fame) in which some phenomenon or event would be presented as an unexplainable mystery. The topics ranged from

UFOs to Bigfoot to the Bermuda Triangle to the Loch Ness Monster. I had been an avid watcher of *In Search Of…* and often concluded, after watching an episode, that the subject unexplainable mystery actually existed outside the ability of science to explain.

Mr. Ruszczyk showed the class an episode of the show about Stonehenge and assigned the class to write an essay on what we thought about the topic. The episode had questioned the ability of ancient people to build the huge stone structure in such a way that it functioned as an accurate calendar and astronomical observatory. It suggested that some occult knowledge must have been employed, possibly gifted to the Druids by visitors from outer space. I was excited to take on this assignment.

My first draft was a regurgitation of the facts shown in the episode and the suggested other-worldly explanations for them. I was actually pretty happy with my essay and went on to do my other homework. As my head hit the pillow that night, a nagging thought crossed my mind. This was Mr. Ruszczyk's class. He didn't show us an episode of *In Search Of…* for us to enjoy and recite back to him. That wasn't his style. So why had he shown it? I got out of bed, snapped on my desk light and began to think.

Building huge stone structures was mostly a matter of raw power or strength. It didn't take much imagination to picture hundreds or even thousands of ancient people pushing or pulling gigantic stones across the English plains. Maybe they used rollers or greased the path with animal fat. They could use simple levers to multiply their efforts. So, building the structure could be explained logically without suggesting ETs mystically levitating boulders. But what about aligning the stones with the ever-changing stars, the movements of the planets, sun and moon?

I began to draw pictures of the solar system and saw that since Stonehenge didn't have any moving parts it was really just a matter of using one stone to set a spot from which to view and then aligning the other stones to create "windows" that would point to the mid-summer sunrise, for instance. It might take many years to figure out where to position each stone and to fine tune the alignment, but there was a repetitive order to movements of the stars, planets, moon and sun, so no ET was needed show the Druids "the answers".

The last question was why. Why would ancient man have cared so much about knowing when summer or winter would start or end? And the answer to that was as simple as The Olde Farmer's Almanac that Mr. Ruszczyk had asked us all to bring to class the next day! Farmers need to know when to plant and harvest crops. It would have been a matter of survival to ancient farmers. And I completely revised my essay.

As I drifted off to sleep, I wondered if all the other *In Search Of...* mysteries were as explainable as this one. And like a shot it hit me. If smart scientific minds thought that the Loch Ness Monster and Bigfoot might actually exist, they wouldn't be the subject of syndicated TV shows, they'd be the subject of university studies, experiments and expeditions. If a real-world phenomenon was presented as too fantastic to be explained by science, it was likely that more facts and some well-grounded thought was called for. That was what Mr. Ruszczyk really taught me. It was intellectual self-reliance. If you can think for yourself, you don't have to accept what someone else tells you at face value. Maybe they are just trying to entertain you. Or maybe they're trying to sell you something.

*****

The summer after my freshman year in college I was looking for work to provide a little cash until I went back to UConn in the fall. Richard Cromwell, a friend from my dorm, lived a few towns over and he called me to say he was going to a "job fair" near where I lived. I met him in a big room over a pizza parlor with about fifty other young people. A fat, balding, middle-aged man started talking to the group about how every kitchen had a junk drawer like the one he held up. It contained a bunch of broken, mismatched knives. He held up a piece of shoe leather and asked the biggest guy in the room, who looked like a pro wrestler, to choose one of the knives and cut through the piece of leather.

The big guy grabbed a knife and began sawing through the leather while the older guy counted the strokes. When he got to twenty, he told the big guy to sit down. The leather was cut about halfway through.

"I'm Dick Broomer of SliceCo Knives. And I want to show you something amazing," said the older man.

He invited the smallest gal in the room to come up to the front. He handed her a small SliceCo knife and gave her another piece of leather, telling her to cut through it. She pushed the knife across the leather slicing it cleanly on the first stroke. Then he had her slice the piece that the big guy had struggled with. One stroke and it was done.

"How many of you think you could do the demonstration I just did?"

Fifty hands shot up.

"How many of you think your mom would be impressed by a demonstration like that?"

Fifty hands remained raised.

Dick Broomer went into his pitch for SliceCo knives. They did seem to be very good knives. A set of ten cost $100. We could make $20 selling one set. We could sell to our parents, their friends, our neighbors, folks from church, and anyone else we cared to do the demonstration for. We could travel anywhere we wanted to and sell and sell. The possibilities for profits were endless. All we had to do was buy a set of SliceCo knives to use in our demonstrations (for $80). And those would be ours to keep even after we retired from the knife-selling business. After all, they were guaranteed for life! He urged us to buy our "sales set" there and then. Most of us didn't have the cash or a check on us right then, so Dick Broomer took our names, addresses and phone numbers, promising to call us so we could get started as soon as we had the money. Richard and I left the demonstration eager to get our $80 so we could buy our "sales set" and get started on our path to riches.

On my way home, I kept remembering what I had seen. Dick Broomer had shown us how the handle of SliceCo knives couldn't be broken, even with hammer blows! SliceCo scissors could easily cut through a penny! The set even came in a case that would keep them all organized and handy in a drawer or hung on a wall! Gee whiz! I had the same excitement that I remembered from seeing the circus, or Kreskin, or *In Search Of....* And for some reason, right then, I remembered Mr. Ruszczyk.

I had $80 dollars, but that was a lot of money. I'd have to sell four sets just to break even. Would my mom shell out $100? Is she even interested in new knives? And how would I feel knocking on the doors of our family friends and the doors of strangers who might not be in the market for knives either.

I remembered that several of the young people at the demonstration were from my high school class. They'd be selling in the same area I would. Our families knew the same people. How many sets of knives would the people of our little town buy?

And I thought about Dick Broomer. From what he told us, we'd be buying our stock of knives from him for $80 a set. By charging our customers $100, we made our $20. But how much did he make? If he bought a set of his knives from SliceCo for $50, he made $30 a set. And he'd be selling 25 or 30 sets just to the "new recruits" before they had sold a single set to anyone else!

I was sitting at our kitchen table when I remembered the term "pyramid scheme" and realized that this was how SliceCo was operating. Thinking about the full picture I was much less impressed with the slick demonstration I had witnessed two hours before. And then the phone rang.

"Steve, this is Dick Broomer from SliceCo. When are you coming in to get your "sales set"?

I struggled to stay calm. "I'm not sure I'll be coming in. I'm considering other work for this summer?" I bluffed.

"Oh really, what other work is that?" he asked.

"I really don't think that's any of your business," I said as forcefully as I could.

"Steve, come on, it's me, Dick!"

"Look, I don't know you and I don't have to talk to you!" I was almost shaking.

"Steve, Steve, it's me Dick CROMWELL! Richard. From UConn. I was goofing on you."

I nearly collapsed in relief. We talked for a bit. He had second thoughts on his ride home just as I had. It seems that Dick Broomer's magic spell wore off if you had time to actually think about the practical realities of sales. We wondered about the people who paid $80 on the spot and whether they regretted it once they got home. Or were they shills, "plants" who worked with Dick Broomer? Maybe it was a more elaborate scheme than it appeared!

I found temp work that summer working in local warehouses. Both Richard and I found that a couple of people we knew had tried selling SliceCo knives and none of them had made back the $80 cost of their "sales set". Thanks, Mr. Ruszczyk.

*****

Magic and wonder aren't reserved solely for young children. But I think that the magic and wonder that appeals to us older children is different. It's a little more refined. I can still marvel at the skill and nerve of a trapeze artist or lion tamer. Their magic is in their dedication and training. And even if I know how "sleight of hand" works, there's still magic in the way a skilled practitioner can fool my eye every time. I love the feeling of magic and wonder. It draws me to the shore to look at the endless expanse of the sea. And it makes me look skyward on clear nights. Understanding oceanography or astronomy doesn't rob the sea and sky of magic and mystery. Knowing how much more we don't understand leaves plenty of room for awe and wonder and makes us all children again.

Different and the Same

Early in the time I lived in London, I was chatting with my American History teacher. He asked what had impressed me most about the English. I told him it was all the little differences. The different names they had for certain candy bars, the funny accents, the English celebrities who were unknown in the States, and the odd fashions that some of the English kids wore. He smiled and nodded. He told me that everyone tended to focus on the superficial differences at first, but that he hoped I would come to see how much more we were alike than different. I wouldn't understand the important lesson he was trying to teach me until many years later.

The playground of my elementary school seemed vast. I felt like I could run as fast as I could for a very long time without escaping its confines. My classmates and I played tag and "ring around the rosy" and "duck, duck, goose" for what seemed like hours in the warm Texas sun. I can still see the pretty Mexican girl with the flashing smile and laughing eyes whose name I didn't even know. I chased but never caught her in the first blush of childish infatuation.

And far across the enormous playground, there were other kids, off in a corner by themselves. I remember the first time I saw them. They were not part of the swirling mass of kids I was a part of. They seemed to be different. I remember moving over closer to where they were. There was a very tall boy with glasses and a very chubby boy next to him. The group of them were holding hands as they came out to their corner of the playground. There were girls in the group and two teachers, one at the front and one at the back of the line of students. They stayed close to the school building, kind of in its shadow. They sat in a circle and I thought they must be playing some game. As I drew nearer, I saw that some of them swayed and moved constantly, as if they were dancing to unheard music. It must have been a strange, frantic music because they jerked and moved like I had never seen kids do. And I remember that very tall boy with the glasses. I locked eyes with him for a moment. I saw him smile a big smile and then nod his head vigorously and raise one arm in a serpentine motion.

I smiled reflexively and started to wave back, but something stopped me. As I continued to watch him, his gaze seemed to drift and his head turned away from me. His smile twisted and became a grimace and I felt that something must be wrong. He looked down at the chubby boy next to him and his arm moved to half hug and half pat him on the shoulder. As I looked around the circle of kids in the shadow of the school building I could see that some of them, maybe most of them, had their heads bowed and were staring at their own laps or at the ground. They seemed to be in a trance or in another world. As I got as close as I would get that day, I could hear them talking, but I couldn't understand what they were saying. It seemed they were calling out urgently, then almost singing, and then quiet. The smile on my face slowly faded but I could not look away. I wanted to know what is was about these kids that was so different.

The bell rang ending recess and as I walked back to my classroom, I asked one of my friends about the kids I had seen, the kids in the shadows. He didn't know who they were. I couldn't stop thinking about them. In the classroom I went straight to Miss Drumgool's desk and asked her who these kids were. She smiled and told me to go to my desk.

Once everyone was back in place, she started to speak.

"Children, some of you have noticed that there is a special

group of students on the playground. These children are in a special class where they are taught by Mrs. Greene and Mrs. Harris. Some of these children may look different or may act differently. They cannot help it. It is just the way they are. They eat lunch and take music and art in their own classroom. When you see any of these children, please be kind and do not stare at them. Don't be afraid of them. They are just children who need special care at school."

For the rest of the day, I thought about the very tall boy with the glasses. I did not want to be unkind. I didn't mean to stare. I was just curious about who he was, who all those children were. It didn't occur to me to be afraid of them. But then, why did Miss Drumgool even mention that? The more I thought about those kids, the more sinister it seemed to me that they were kept apart from the rest of the students. They didn't get to go to the art room with all the paint and clay or the music room with the drums and the autoharp. And they were never in the assemblies. They didn't get to see the puppet show when it came to the school or the fire engine when it parked in front by the flagpole. Why?

That night, I asked my mother about the very tall boy with the glasses and the other children in what I started to call "the special class". She smiled and told me that I was a very lucky little boy. I was healthy and smart and could enjoy everything the school had to offer. She said that some children were not so lucky. "The special class" was for some of these children. Some of them had trouble seeing or walking. Some of them couldn't learn the way I did. They might be in school for years and not learn to read like I could. I tried to hide the fear that swept over me, but Mom could see it on my face. She told me not to worry myself about them. They were getting the special help they needed.

"Will they get better?" I asked.

"I don't know," she said.

"What will happen to them if they don't get better?" I asked.

"There are people who care for special children like them. They need extra love and care.

Don't be afraid," she said.

After that I tried to stay away from the "special class" during recess. Out of sight, out of mind. But whenever I glanced over, I could see them there in the shadow of the building. And I could see the very tall boy with the glasses. I tried not to think of them. And I tried not to be afraid. But the fear would not leave me. Why were these children different and not me? What if I was one of them? How would I deal with being isolated, with being different, with being set apart? Did they do something to deserve being different? Had they done something wrong? How was it that I was so lucky to be "not different"? Was it right for me to just try not to think about them, to wish them out of existence?

Over the weeks that followed, I would ask my mother about them again several times. She tried to comfort me. Then one day, she kept me out of school. She took me to a nice home not far from our church. Inside there was a lady from our church, Mrs. Williams, and a half dozen other ladies. They were having coffee and donuts. I had a donut and they made smalltalk with me, asking me what grade I was in and how I liked school. Then they cleared the large table and put a mat on it. I went into the next room to see what was on the TV. After a few minutes, I glanced back into the kitchen and saw the ladies all standing around the table. I slowly walked over and saw a large young man lying face down on the table. The ladies each had a hold on one of his arms or legs. Mrs. Williams held his head in her hands. She counted out loud and the ladies moved the young man's limbs in a coordinated way. It looked like he was swimming. Again and again, Mrs. Williams counted and the ladies moved the young man's arms and legs. I saw my mother moving his right arm. She moved it out and around in an arc like he was doing the breast stroke. This went on for a half hour. I stood staring at it all.

After they were finished, some of the ladies left right away. Mrs. Williams and some of the other ladies helped the young man into a wheelchair. Mrs. Williams asked me to come over and meet her son, Charlie. I said hello. Charlie did not seem to know I was there. Mrs. Williams said he was tired after "his patterning exercise". She offered me another donut. I watched Charlie slump in his wheelchair. He was strapped into it so that he could not fall out. He must have been 17 or 18. He was easily six feet tall. He was the size of my dad. In time, Charlie looked up at me and smiled. Mrs. Williams told me that he liked me. I smiled. I was trying so hard not to be afraid. But the whole thing was so unlike anything I had ever seen before. I whispered to my mom that I wanted to leave. She finished her tea and said goodbye to the other ladies, Mrs. Williams and Charlie. I was so relieved to be in our car driving away.

Mom explained that Mrs. Williams was doing all she could to help Charlie and that the ladies from the church met several times a week to help "pattern" Charlie so that someday he might be able to walk. I shuddered involuntarily. All of the the questions flooded my brain again. Why was Charlie like this?

Was he born that way or had something terrible happened to him? Why wasn't I like Charlie? What was the sense of it? Where was the justice? Mom could see how upset I was and said that I should pray for Charlie and his mother and for the ladies who were trying to help him. I did.

Over the years that followed, as we moved from town to town, each of the schools I went to had "special classes". As I got older, I could hear my classmates talk about the students in the "special class". They sometimes gave the kids in the "special class" cruel nicknames and laughed and imitated their movements and the sounds they made. I knew it was mean. And I knew that the casual cruelty was just a smokescreen to hide their fear. And, God help me, sometimes I joined in with it. Maybe it was out of my weakness or fear. And I would take my cruelty back if I could, but it's too late. All I have left is the guilt.

*****

I love to think back to my happy childhood. I was raised in Texas by two loving parents with two older sisters. We were solidly middle-class and I don't remember ever wanting for anything. Our home was warm and safe and familiar. I thought everyone had a home like ours, lived like we did, and believed what we believed. Most of the kids in my first grade class were just like me. They went to a church like mine, watched the same TV shows I watched, talked like I did and looked pretty much like me. Except for two of my classmates.

One was Pablo. He was a quiet boy. English was his second language and he sometimes had trouble expressing himself to the teacher. Pablo didn't get the best grades. At recess, he would join in group games like kickball, but he wasn't part of our circle of boys who would talk about last night's TV shows or Sunday's football games. Pablo's clothes were always clean, but looked worn and old. Most of the other kids, including me, were taken shopping by our moms to get new "school clothes" each fall. Last year's "school clothes" became our "play clothes" or were handed down to younger siblings or donated to Goodwill. Pablo didn't have new "school clothes". And most of us boys, in 1966, had short haircuts groomed with Vitalis or Brylcream. Pablo's hair was a bit longer and always seemed to be in his eyes. No one ever said any of these things, but I think we all saw that Pablo was different.

The other classmate who wasn't quite like the others was Annette. Annette was a tall African-American girl. She was the only black child in our class, maybe the only one in first grade. I don't remember if there were any other black kids in Louise Hutchens Elementary School. Annette was quiet and smart. She got good grades. I remember her always wearing pretty dresses. Her skin was very dark and her hair was always done in little braids. She wore little white socks and shiny patent leather shoes. She was a pretty girl who had a beautiful smile that she rarely flashed. The boys and girls tended to separate at recess, so I don't know if Annette had friends among the other girls, but my sense was that she was a solitary soul. I thought that Annette seemed a little sad.

Like most six year old boys, I was pretty self-involved and enjoyed playing with the other boys who were most like me. I remember going to birthday parties that most of the boys in my class would attend. Pablo was never at those parties. I don't think I ever even wondered if he had been invited. Since I didn't go to "girl's parties", I didn't know whether Annette was invited or if she attended. At the time, I don't recall spending much time thinking about Pablo and Annette. I wasn't ignoring them out of malice, I was just in my own world that they didn't seem to be part of. Until Valentine's Day.

I think they still sell those boxes of twenty or so Valentine cards. They were just single-sided cut-out shapes with silly cartoons and Valentine puns. There might be a bee with the message "BEE MY HONEY!" or some such verbiage. We were given a list of all the children in our class, presumably so we would spell their names correctly and not forget anyone. We spent our art class making and decorating a "mail box" to hold the Valentine cards we each would be getting.

The night before Valentine's Day, I recall opening my box of cards and selecting the best ones for my guy friends and a few of the girls who I thought were cute. I filled out the back of each with "Your friend, Steven". I slipped each card into the little white envelopes that came with the cards and put my classmates names on the outside of each. "To Michael", read one. "To Mary Kay", read another. And I filled out cards for Pablo and Annette as I did for all of my classmates.

The next day, at the appointed hour, the teacher told us it was time to deliver our cards. There were a few minutes of controlled mayhem as twenty-five kids walked up and down the rows of desks depositing cards in the decorated "mail boxes". I sorted through my cards and began to deliver them. I delivered Michael's and Mary Kay's and Benny's and Isaac's. But when I came to Pablo's, I shuffled it to the bottom of the deck. I went on and delivered Cliff's and Bruce's and Cindy's and Ann's. When I came to Annette's, I paused a long moment. Then I shuffled it to the bottom of the deck too. Finally, I was left with only those two cards undelivered. I returned to my desk and stashed those two cards in my book bag.

After everyone was in their seat, the teacher gave us permission to open our Valentine's cards. I had gotten one from every kid in the class, including Pablo and Annette. Most of the cards were from store-bought packages just like the one I had. On the back of most of them it read "Your friend, So-and-so" with the name of the child who had sent it. I can still see Pablo's name on the card he gave me and Annette's too. I suddenly knew I had done something terribly wrong. I looked up and saw Pablo at his desk and Annette at hers, going through their Valentine cards. I told myself that with so many kids in the class, they wouldn't miss a card from me. Maybe they didn't. But, in my guilt, I knew that they knew that I had not given them a Valentine card. And I felt terrible. Part of me wanted to get up and give them their card, but I didn't. Waves of shame and guilt washed over me.

If you had asked the six year old me why I had withheld my cards from Pablo and Annette, I would have told you, "I don't know." At age six, I was aware that Pablo and Annette were different from me and my friends. Maybe I was afraid to "be seen" expressing to them that I was "Your friend, Steven" on a "BE MY HONEY" card. Be seen by whom?

Sometimes, when this memory resurfaces, I imagine meeting Pablo and Annette now and apologizing to them. In my mind, as grown-ups, they might brush it off as nothing. But I really do want to tell them how I don't now (and never did) hold any ill will toward them or anyone based on ethnicity or race. I want to recount for them the friendships I have had over the years with people from every background, of every race who were so different from me and how that diversity enriched me and educated me and changed me. And maybe that was it. Maybe the six year old me just hadn't been exposed to enough different kinds of people and gotten to know them as people. Maybe all I could see were the "skin-deep" differences and not how, in a much more profound sense, they were just the same as me.

When I think of this sad moment, I imagine doing the one thing I could have done that would erase it. I roll back the years, reach into my book bag and pull out those two Valentine cards. I walk over to Pablo and to Annette and take each of their hands and put my cards in them and say, "Happy Valentine's Day from your friend, Steven". Each of them smiles at me and I go back to my seat smiling too.

I used to hate thinking about the "special class", about Charlie, and about the Valentines' cards I didn't give to Pablo and Annette. I learned to stifle the fear and shame and regret that would suddenly wash over me when I would see someone who was different. And I have eventually figured out what my American History teacher was trying to teach me that day. There is so much more to be gained by seeing how much the same we all are than by focusing on the differences.

Of course I do not equate race and ethnicity with physical and intellectual disability. As a child I saw my world as so homogenized that my reaction to any kind of difference was fear and confusion, followed by shame and guilt. I am thankful that I have grown beyond that fear and confusion, for the most part, and that I can better see past the superficial differences in people.

My faith has helped me to keep this lesson in mind. Every week in church we say a prayer that begins with the words, "Our Father…". If He's really OUR Father, then that makes us ALL brothers and sisters. And when I think about the kids in the "special class", Charlie, Pablo, and Annette as my brothers and sisters, I can finally begin to forgive myself for the childish way I thought and acted and to channel the shame and guilt into love for all of God's children.

LUIGI

The only way I can tell this story is to tell it backwards. Our little ball of fur, Luigi, beloved 12 year old Maltese, died last night. He had been losing weight for a couple of months, small as he was to start with. He'd had a couple of "episodes" in the past few weeks. Last Sunday, he didn't bolt out of his crate and gallop up the stairs to his dish and water bowl as he normally did. His walk outside was slow and I carried him to his customary lounging spot on the sofa. He rallied during the week, but then succumbed.

It's been a little over two years that I have been working from home. That made me Luigi's primary care-giver and it made me his friend. We developed a morning routine. The little, white fur-ball woke up crying in his crate in the basement around 5am every morning. I would leave my warm, comfy bed to let him out. He scooted up the stairs and attacked his water and food bowls. As I began my coffee-making process, Luigi would wait by the kitchen door. We walked outside in the dark. He patrolled the front and sometimes the side and backyards. He would find the perfect spot to do his business. We usually made two excursions: one for pee and one for poo. Then Luigi trotted jauntily back inside, his tags jingling from his collar, received his treat from me, jumped up on the sofa and stretched out for a snooze.

Throughout our days together, Luigi typically got a nice petting session or two from me before my wife and son got back from work and school, respectively. I kept his bowls from running empty and gave him a nice bath as needed. He let me know when he needed to go out, or when his water bowl was low. Sometimes the little, white fur-ball would come up to me just to make sure I hadn't forgotten him. No chance of that. But he really perked up when my wife came home. She's the Superstar. I never got the Superstar reception, the tail wags, the dog-smiles, but I didn't mind.

When I worked in Hartford, Luigi and I weren't that close. My wife did it all for him. That's when she became his Superstar. For the first ten years of Luigi's life, she did all the baths, all the feeding, all the vet visits, all the everything. She learned all his moods. They became friends. He spent long, cold winter nights as her living blanket, warming her lap. She made sure the little, white fur-ball never lacked food or treats. As the kids grew up and went off to college and jobs, Mom, the Superstar, remained Luigi's best friend, constant confidant and care-giver.

Back when the kids were little, Luigi was a big part of their lives too. He was the happy, yelping reception at the end of every school-day. He never cared how they did on that quiz or what the popular kids were saying. He loved them both for the petting and treats that they traded for unlimited, unconditional little, white fur-ball love.

Luigi was supposed to be our son's dog. But there was just so much love in that little, white fur-ball that he really owned the whole family. Our son didn't make friends easily, but Luigi was more friend than anyone could ever want. He had love and joy and loyalty in limitless supply. And our son was the best little master he could be. The two of them were inseparable.

When Luigi was a little pup, just after we got him, he was seriously ill. Our beautiful daughter sang songs to him until he got better. When our son would come home from a bad day, we would tell him to go pet his dog. There were times when we would find them both cuddled together in Luigi's dog crate, our son folded up like a pretzel, the two of them comforting and loving each other.

Experts tell you to buy your dog from a reputable breeder or to rescue a dog from a bad situation. Do anything but buy one from the mall pet store, who probably sourced the dog from a midwestern puppy mill. Sorry, but that's exactly where we got Luigi. And I am so glad we did.

I had to tell this story backwards, so that it would end with a tiny, white fur-ball, full of puppy joy and love and energy. And with a family who didn't know that pup was just what they needed to be complete. This story ends with twelve years of non-stop puppy love still to come. It ends before my heart was won over by my first pet ever, the little white fur-ball, and then broken when he left us to go play in heaven.

FINDING THE ABBEY

I have been very lucky all my life. Blessed really. In 1975, following my freshman year as a nerd way before it was cool, my social prospects could not have been dimmer. My lowly status in the high school crowd in the affluent bedroom community in Fairfield County, Connecticut made me feel that loneliness and virginity would become terminal conditions for me. I was aching to spread my wings, to reinvent myself. But that was simply not going happen…until one day.

It was early August when my dad came home from work

and, as he had seven times before in my life, he told us that he had been promoted and we were moving. To London. England. The news could not have been better for me.

There are many stories that I could tell about my halcyon days in London, but they are for another time. This one spans decades. In brief, my parents and I moved to London and lived in a flat on Hyde Park. I made many great friends, reinvented myself, found what I thought to be true love, lost my dreaded "v-card" and developed as many bad habits as I could. Amongst those was a taste for English bitter ale. The American School in London was, and still is, located in St. John's Wood in north London not far from the venerable Lord's Cricket Ground and closer still to Abbey Road and the Abbey Road Studios, where the Beatles made rock and roll history. My friend Mike used to walk across that iconic crosswalk, an image of which adorns the cover of the "Abbey Road" album, just to get to school and back. And a number of us would stroll a block or two from school to the Abbey Pub to enjoy a lunchtime pint and a ploughman's lunch, which was a hunk of crusty bread, a block of Cheddar cheese and a few pickled onions.

Of course, The Abbey wasn't the only pub we went to. There was the Princess Royale, the Heroes of Alma, the Bunch of Grapes, the Prince of Wales, Paxton's Head, and many, many more. And it seemed very special to me and my friends back then. It was more than just drinking beer and getting sloshed. It was the place where we rubbed elbows with the locals. Going to an American school, we saw mostly American kids and American teachers. The pubs were where we met and chatted with Brits. They were mostly friendly. Some were curious about the US. Others wanted to know what we thought of the UK. This was the age of punk rock and disco, of Monty Python and *Fawlty Towers*. Older Brits taught us about soccer and tried in vain to explain cricket and politics. They were friendly and funny. It was a unique experience I feel privileged to have had.

I was initially fascinated by all the little differences between the US and London in 1975. Many products were identical, but had different names. Even movies were often given different titles over there. It seemed to me that they were ahead of us in a few things, mostly cultural, and lagged behind us in others, like good food. But as I met a few Brits in the pubs, I came to see that they were really pretty much like me and my friends. They wanted the same things out of life and enjoyed a laugh as much as we did.

It's impossible to explain to someone who's never experienced it, the special charm of a great English pub. Yes, it has a lot in common with every corner bar in the world, but it has a unique magic too. The relative darkness inside takes a moment to adjust to. The dark wooden bar is often adorned with carvings and gaslights. The shiny brass rail beckons you to the bar, not to sit, but to stand next to the banker or laborer or group of friends discussing anything from music to astronomy. And it's hard not to get pulled into the easy chat of such groups. Maybe it's the beer, or maybe it's magic that makes these strangers quickly seem like old friends. The English sense of humor, sarcasm, wordplay, and fun is infectious.

Most pubs had a jukebox and "fruit machine". Some had a TV, usually only turned on for special sporting events. And if you didn't feel like standing, there were usually cozy tables tucked in dark corners where anyone was free to join a lone patron or group. Over the course of an hour or three it was not unusual to move between groups as they came and went. Your chat with a plumber about why the soccer isn't more popular in the US might morph into a discussion with a pair WWII veterans about how the Germans aren't such bad people. And when you had to leave, it was a friendly farewell from one and all and you went out into the street, leaving the magic behind until next time. It's hard to explain. I guess you had to be there.

By the way, it was not strictly legal for we sixteen and seventeen year olds to imbibe. Contrary to a common belief, England had a drinking age of eighteen in those days. But the local pubs didn't have much business on weekdays at lunchtime and they conveniently never asked me or my friends for proof of age. And so it was a frequent occurrence that a group of us would go off to eat and drink and play darts and feed the "fruit machine" (aka slot machine) in hopes of paying for it all. Afternoon classes were a bit easier to take after a pint or two. Although I was surprised once when, on a warm spring afternoon, I found my chemistry class sitting outside taking a quiz as we made our way back to school. I got an "A" in chemistry, so there wasn't any real damage done.

But, after two years, I moved back to the States. Back to Connecticut. Back to the same school in the same town I had left two years before. I returned a different person. I made friends and enjoyed my remaining year there. Then I left for college and life just kept happening to me. I got married. We had two great kids. Work took me to New Jersey and, eventually, back to Connecticut. Not snooty Fairfield County where I had lived before, but quiet, rural, central Connecticut. In what seemed like no time, it had been twenty years since my London days. Then the dreams began.

On those rare occasions when I would wake and remember my dreams of the night before, I had been having dreams about London. I'm not sure exactly when they began. But they did begin and they continued to come to me, off and on, and then more frequently. They came so regularly, in fact, that I began to remember them. They were almost always the same. In my dream, I had returned to London to revisit my old haunts. I walked by our old flat that faced Hyde Park. I walked past Paxton's Head and took the double-decker bus or the tube to St. John's Wood. I easily found my old school. But as I walked from its familiar grounds in my dream, the streets became unfamiliar. Try as I might, I couldn't find my way to the Abbey. In my dream I wanted desperately to revisit that old pub where I had watched the 1976 Olympics and played endless games of darts. I wanted to see if the ploughman's lunch could still be bought with a pint for under a pound. I walked and ran and then I woke up. Every time it was the same.

I even told people about my dream. I told my patient wife who listened dutifully and then got on with raising our kids and keeping our house. I decided I needed to go back. I was telling a friend at work about my dream and he told me that it might be important for me to go back. Maybe my dream meant something. Maybe I would find something there.

It was not cheap to fly to London and to stay for a handful of days, but in the dead of winter, it was as cheap as it was ever going to be. I bundled up and boarded my flight. It was an overnighter to Heathrow. As I groggily emerged from customs and found the van that would take me to my hotel, it was as if I was Dorothy awakening in Oz. There were all those funny, different names for everything from candy bars to soda pop. There was the newspaper that had topless girls pictured on Page 3. And all around me were those crisp accents. Cockney. North Country. Irish. Scottish. Posh newsreader. I was home again. Five time zones from my wife and kids and car and job, this was as familiar as my favorite pair of jeans. After twenty years. What joy!

Once I got to my hotel, I slept a few hours of jet lag away and headed outside. I walked to my old flat on Hyde Park. I had a pint at Paxton's Head. I bought some groceries for my room and had a Cuban cigar as I walked through Picadilly Circus. And I never looked at a map. I didn't need one. Many of the shops had changed. Some restaurants I remembered had been turned into stylish boutiques. There were new, garish tourist traps. But many of the old shops and pubs and restaurants were right where I had left them twenty years before. I had dinner and returned to my hotel to sleep. I wanted to be fresh for the next morning. I was going looking for the Abbey. I was going to "solve" the mystery of my dream.

Morning came with bright sunshine and cool temperatures. I bundled up and headed to the tube. I chose the Underground over the bus because that was the way I first went to St. John's Woods all those years ago. Only later, did I become a regular rider of the famous double-decker buses. The long escalator carried me up to the surface streets and I walked directly to my old school. It was closed on Sunday, but it looked the same as it had when I was a sophomore. I walked all the way around it and got my bearings. I knew that Abbey Road was only a block or so over. I found the Beatles famous crosswalk and the studios. The wall there was covered with graffiti, mostly extolling the group, some memorializing John. I walked along until the road became unfamiliar. No matter. I would start from the school again. This time I walked directly up the road we had always trod when we were going to the Abbey. I had thought it was just a block, but seeing nothing familiar, I walked another and then one more. I was at a corner that felt right. I turned to walk into the old pub, but found instead an architect's office.

I was confused and a bit upset. I stalked up and down the block. It was just like my dream. I was there. But "there" wasn't "there" anymore. I took a long look into the windows of the architect's office. It was modern and new-ish looking. I tried to picture the way the Abbey had looked. It had a "public bar" on the left and a "saloon bar" on the right. We kids always hung out in the public bar. I couldn't remember if I had ever stuck my head in the saloon bar. But the office was divided up into little cubicles and meeting rooms. It was not the same at all. And the front was totally different. I looked for someone to ask. Early on a Sunday, there was no one around. No one to ask. The other pubs were closed. They wouldn't open for hours. I turned back to the tube station. On a whim, I decided to take the bus.

I rode the bus around central London. Knowing some of the bus routes, I used the big double-deckers like my own personal sightseeing vehicles. Baker Street. Oxford Street. Picadilly. Leicester Square. I got out and walked, bought a roll and a bottle of water and enjoyed them as I strolled. So much was so familiar. I felt as comfortable as I was in my living room as I walked the downtown streets of a city of millions. I found myself in Great Portland Square, near my hotel. It was after noon and I knew there would be a soccer match on. I figured the pubs would have TVs on and I felt like a pint. I wandered into a friendly neighborhood pub with a delightful name, "The Queen's Head and Artichoke".

I watched the game and enjoyed my beer. I struck up a casual conversation about the game with three chaps sitting next to me. It's funny how easily that happens in a London pub. I have been to lots of bars all across America and left without a word to anyone but the bartender. But English pubs are friendlier places. And it's strange how quickly you can start to feel a real kinship with total strangers. Before long I was laughing and joking with these three guys like we were old friends. It turned out one of the guys was a postman. A thought occurred to me. Was he familiar with St. John's Wood? Yes! His daily route covered St. John's Wood! Did he know the Abbey Pub? Yes! My heart was racing. Somehow, over thousands of miles, from dream to reality, I found myself tipping pints with a man who could solve the riddle of my dream.

"I know the Abbey," he said. "It's not there anymore. It was converted to an office a few years ago. An accountant or something."

"An architect?" I ventured.

"Yes! You know my route better than I do!" he chortled.

And there it was. The answer. I couldn't find The Abbey because it wasn't there anymore. Maybe the pub closing had somehow triggered my dreams. And even though I couldn't walk through those old wooden doors and belly up to that old oaken bar and order a pint and a ploughman's lunch, I had come as close to that as twenty years later would let me. And I had my memories of the old times. Memory adds such a rich patina to things. It edits out the rough edges and cloudy days and replaces them with luster and sunshine.

I told my new "pub friends" about my dream and they

listened attentively. We finished our beers and I wished them well. That's part of the deal with "pub friends", there's no expectation of a lasting relationship. It's a casual friendship, but a real and deep one that lasts only as long as the "session" in the pub. Then you go your separate ways until the next time.

Memories can be wonderful things. All we have are memories, the fleeting present moment, and wishful plans and dreams for the future. I have wondered why there were times when I felt the need to go back to a place and retrace my steps. Since you can never recapture a moment or relive an experience, maybe going back is an attempt to confirm that it really happened and that it wasn't just a dream. Maybe going back separates the ghosts of things that were from the dreams of what may come.

A Miracle at St. Barbara

In my book, *Getting My First Hug*, I tell the story of our son passing the driver's test written exam. It took a few tries and a lot of study. I am proud to say I helped with some of the study part. It's great to bask in the happy ending of that story, but I'd be lying if I said I didn't have moments of doubt, especially after one "near miss". But our family finds strength in our Orthodox Christian faith. And I made a special trip to our church to pray for our son and his efforts to pass this test.

Those of you who have never been in a Greek Orthodox church may not know that the walls and ceiling are typically covered with beautiful icons of saints, angels, scenes from the Bible, and Jesus Christ. The Byzantine style of the iconography of our church depicts the saints looking directly at the observer, as one sees one's self in a mirror.

At church the Sunday after he had passed the test, I lit candles as I had the week before. I prayed prayers of thanks for the success our son had in passing the driver's test. Having a driver's license would open doors for him and change his life for the better in so many ways. I recalled my recent bout of sadness and doubt following his last unsuccessful attempt and heaved a sigh of relief.

I returned to my place in the congregation and looked up at the beautiful icons of our church, as I so often do during the Divine Liturgy. I began to notice that there was a strange quality to the appearance of these once-familiar icons. As I looked more carefully, focusing my admittedly no-longer sharp eyes, I saw that the frames of each icon had become like windows and the images of the saints appeared, not as stylized representations, but as real, live people! I was stunned by these apparitions. I looked from one to the next. Some were larger than others, each in scale to his icon. I marveled at the living, human forms of these holy people. I could see them moving! They were looking right at me! And I heard each saint saying to me, "Where was your faith? Why did you fear so much? Why did you ever doubt that your prayers would be answered?" They lovingly chastised me, almost teasing me about my foolish doubt that God would answer my prayers. And I became ashamed of my weak faith. I believe. Forgive my unbelief. (Mark 9:24) I finally knew what those words meant. I get it. Message received.

I must admit that the emotion of the moment literally boggled my mind. It was an amazing site to see the icons of our church, so familiar to all our parishioners, suddenly come to life! What were once painted images, were now humans living in the walls of our Sanctuary! Even the small figures of the Stilite saints, now alive, looked down upon me with love. And I cry when I remember the Panagia, the large icon of the Virgin Mary presenting her son to the world, as it appeared to me then, a symbol of a mother's love and of God's love and forgiveness toward all mankind. I knew my sin of doubt could be forgiven if I could strengthen my faith. And here I was, surrounded by role models. As I have taught others, I still had to learn that the Church does not send us into battle unarmed. A wave of warmth, like the embrace of the mother of Our Lord enfolded me.

Looking up a moment later, the icons were once again painted images as they had always been. And they were no less wondrous to me then or now. This entire episode took place over a period of a minute or two. I do not think that anyone else in attendance saw what I saw. I am not accustomed to swearing as to the truth of things, but I swear the above written words are the truth. Miracles are real. God talks to His people. Amen.

Scary Stories

I have never been one who cared much for horror movies. It's never made sense to me that intentionally scaring one's self should be entertaining. I should clarify that when I say horror movies, I am referring to the modern shock and gore type, not the classic Universal monster movies of the 1940s. Karloff as Frankenstein's monster, Lugosi's Dracula, Claude Rains' Invisible Man and Lon Chaney's Wolfman are, to me, wonderfully entertaining fantasy stories. Perhaps that's inconsistent or illogical but the difference is clear and makes sense to me.

Perhaps horror is a more complex concept than we think.

Consider ghost stories. They are often presented in the way that urban legends are, as being true accounts of events that actually happened to "a friend of a friend". I think I am made uneasy by the way that such stories are told to children. No caring person would regale a child with detailed accounts of an actual violent, grisly crime. But to artfully suck them in to a fictional account, presented as factual, of fantastically gruesome stories is considered good, clean fun? That does not compute.

When I was a boy, growing up in east Texas, the world seemed like a very safe place. My parents were wise and caring and capable of shielding my sisters and me from any harm beyond a skinned knee or hurt feelings. I often think back on my childhood as a golden time and I feel so sorry when I hear others talk about abusive parents or cold, unloving homes. I never knew how lucky I was back then and I took it for granted. I understand now and I am eternally thankful.

Our family's religious faith was a sort of generic Protestant one. I was baptized in a Methodist church. But as we moved every few years, we attended Presbyterian churches. When we lived in Houston, when I was about eight, we attended St. Andrew's where our family was very close to that of the minister, Dr. Douglas Harper. That church had an affiliation with a camp in Livingston, Texas called Camp Cho-Yeh. It is still in operation as a Christian retreat and conference center. Camp Cho-Yeh had, and probably still has, acres of forest, meadows, a lake, a swimming pool, rustic meeting houses, and little A-frame cabins. It was an idyllic setting for a weekend of fellowship, nature study, and general R&R. It was run by a family called the Hagermeyers. They made sure that the camp was kept tidy and that the rustic amenities were all in order.

They acted as guides and advisors to the families who visited and they were friends to many of us as well. The Hagermeyers had a daughter who was friends with my sisters and a son named Blue, who was a bit younger than me, but was a good companion on hikes and fishing trips.

My dad loved Camp Cho-Yeh. He was busy working his way up the corporate ladder for a big oil company. He was an engineer, complete with a flat-top crew cut and glasses. My dad was tall and slim and I always picture him smiling down at me and quietly explaining the world to me in terms I could understand. He and I took long walks at Camp Cho-Yeh and he would find real Indian arrowheads and spear tips made of flint. We did crafts where you would spray lacquer on a spiderweb held against a piece of construction paper. My dad was a geologist and at Camp Cho-Yeh he collected rocks for his collection and to make crafts out of. He glued many small flint pieces to small, varnished pieces of plywood like a mosaic and made the shape of an arrowhead on one and a tomahawk on another. Those plaques adorned my bedroom walls until I moved away to college.

I have happy memories of Camp Cho-Yeh, but I also have two memories that were not so happy. One of these is the memory of a chat I had with Mr. Hagermeyer. I think I was discussing the realism of a particular cartoon and I found myself telling Blue that it was impossible for a person to be squashed as flat as a pancake as Huckleberry Hound had been in the cartoon. Blue disagreed. We appealed to Mr. Hagermeyer to settle the question. Without much hesitation, Mr. Hagermeyer quietly said that it was indeed possible for a person's body to be squashed flat as he had seen this happen in Korea, during the war. He said a tank had rolled over an unfortunate soldier and its great weight had rendered his body as flat as could be. It was stunning to me to hear of such a thing, told in such a matter-of-fact way by a man who was so genial and soft-spoken. Being so young, I did not dwell on this though. I had fish to catch and trails to explore.

The other less-than-happy memory I took away from Camp Cho-Yeh troubled me for years. It was the fall of the year and Halloween was coming. So one night, by the light of the campfire and several Coleman lanterns, the adults took turns telling ghost stories. I must have been preoccupied with something else because I don't remember any of them, except one. Mrs. Hagermeyer, a pretty lady about the same age as my mom, told the story of Britt Bailey.

She wove a spell-binding tale, but the part that stuck with me was this. Britt Bailey was a man who hunted and drank whiskey. And he wanted to be buried with his hunting rifle and a jug of whiskey when he died. But when that time came, his wife, thinking that whiskey was inappropriate for a Christian burial, buried him with only his rifle. From that day to this, the ghost of Britt Bailey, surrounded by an eerie glow, roamed the countryside looking for his jug of whiskey. Some folks would leave a jug outside their home to keep the malevolent spirit away, as kind of an "80-proof Passover". And this was not simply a scary story, it was true. Mrs. Hagermeyer told us to look on any map of Texas and we would see Bailey's Prairie, Texas, where the haunting began. And she was right. There is such a town, not far south of Houston.

For years afterward, when I had trouble getting to sleep, and the headlights of a car would pass my closed curtains, I would imagine that the glowing ghost of Britt Bailey was coming to get me, armed with his hunting rifle, seeking a jug of whiskey, that I could not provide. He was my personal boogeyman. I don't remember when I stopped thinking about Britt Bailey. I guess the years and the events of growing up just displaced those fears. And I wouldn't be writing this now except that I was listening to a story on a podcast not long ago by the actor and storyteller Stephen Tobolowsky. He was telling about a report he gave as a schoolboy in Texas about Moses Austin, father of Stephen F. Austin, the first President of the Republic of Texas. It so happens that Moses Austin was born in Durham, Connecticut, not far from where I live. I was looking this up on Wikipedia. One link led to another and I stumbled upon the Wikipedia article about Bailey's Prairie, Texas. It told about Britt Bailey's conflicts with Stephen F. Austin. It also contained the legend that Mrs. Hagermeyer had told all those years ago including a reference to Bailey's Light, a mysterious white ball of floating light reported by the locals. A retroactive shudder ran down my fifty-one year old spine.

I've been richly blessed throughout my life from my golden childhood to my thirty-plus year marriage to the girl of my dreams. The one great tragedy I have experienced was my dad's passing. After fainting out of the blue one day, he underwent a battery of testing that eventually revealed he had Shy-Drager Syndrome, a degenerative condition of the autonomic nervous system. Over the next few years he became weaker and weaker and he died at sixty-four. I remember when the realization of what was happening to him and what was to come hit me. It was senseless that a man who had never done anything but good for others and had never smoked, drank or abused himself should have this happen to him. And he bravely endured the slow failing of his body as one faculty after another betrayed him. My mother, his one and only love, likewise bravely held his hand through the cruel decline and end. It was as random and horrible a fate as there could be. I miss him every day and still cry about it, more than ten years later.

Maybe we tell ghost stories and watch horror movies to distract ourselves from our fear of the real horror and sadness that life can hold. Maybe if we can instill in ourselves such over-the-top fear of the fantastic, then the fear of our own mortality will seem less frightening. I prefer other distractions to keep me from dwelling on the finite nature of our time on earth. I have a faith that helps me deal with it. But I have not perfected it to the point that I have no fear or sadness.

I recently converted our family's slides to digital images to share with Mom and my sisters. They are a treasure trove of images of times long ago when Dad was happy and healthy and with us. And I've begun digitizing my own family's VHS tapes. Yesterday I saw a scene of my dad smiling and doting on my son. And then there are the three of us, Dad, my son and me, all smiling, sitting on the sofa in my house watching something on TV. I don't remember what it was. But maybe it was Lon Chaney or Boris Karloff, giving us an entertaining little scare so that we would hug each other close and maybe shield ourselves and each other from some of the bigger ones.

WALTER SCHALK SCHOOL OF THE DANCE

Beauty and grace are ideals that we all admire and aspire to. Even if we are not fans of ballet, seeing the delicate and athletic moves of a trained dancer has universal appeal. And even if one would prefer not to dance at all, no one wants to dance poorly. Most of the dance I've seen in the popular media in the last quarter century is a jerky, rhythmic, explosive brand that is linked to rap and hip-hop and other "club" or "house" music that came about after my musical tastes were mostly locked down. I can admire Madonna or Beyonce and the rest, but thankfully, I'm rarely if ever called on to perform any of their maneuvers.

Yet even today there are those rare occasions when almost everyone is expected to dance. I'm thinking of wedding receptions when a band, or more likely a DJ, plays one of those songs with wide appeal and a basic, primal rhythm that even I can follow or a slow, romantic number that overrides my knowledge of my limitations with my desire to hold my partner close and sway to soulful words and languid melody. And knowing how to dance is one of those skills that, like being able to start a fire without matches, is rarely needed but is impressive if not essential when it is.

Of course, in generations past, dancing was considered a skill that every young man and woman should possess. Before video games, karaoke, beer pong and trivia nights, dancing was one of the few entertainment options for couples on a night out. And before TV and movies, it was almost all there was outside of taffy pulls and bear baiting exhibitions. I'm not sure where my parents learned to dance, but when I was thirteen, they informed me that I was to attend the Walter Schalk School of the Dance to learn "ballroom dancing". Whether I liked it or not. We lived in Fairfield County, Connecticut, a fairly well-to-do area. I like to say we were some of the poorest people in the one of the richest towns in the country, which was pretty close to the truth. And Walter Schalk dance lessons weren't cheap. They must have thought it was pretty important for me to learn to cha-cha because there was no discussion of whether I wanted to learn.

Now, at thirteen, I was at the zenith of my awkwardness. I had braces on my teeth, mild to moderate acne, and was, at least in my mind, one of the least popular kids in the junior high. I got really good grades. Strike one. I was good enough in sports to compete, but not good enough to win. Strike two. And I was a relatively new arrival in town. Strike three. At an age when the coolest boys were starting to pair off with the cutest girls and attended "couples' parties", I was happy to get through a school-day without being punched or having my sexuality openly questioned in the lunchroom.

Digression - A year or so earlier, there was a universal belief among boys that girls carried cooties and should be fled from whenever possible. Classroom activities were gender-segregated when they were not "boys versus girls". Thus had it been since kindergarten. Without any warning, the rules abruptly changed, possibly on a day when I had been out sick. Suddenly, boys yearned for nothing so much as to get close to the prettiest girls in the class. Those of us who had been deeply emotionally-invested in the "boys versus girls" mentality were caught out like partisans of an unsuccessful *coup d'etat*. Nobody likes pretty girls more than I do, but I had not been informed that the cure for cooties had been found and distributed seemingly over night. I had to play a desperate game of catch-up. - End of digression.

So there I was, one October Tuesday evening in my church clothes being dropped off at one of the town's four elementary schools and walking into the cafeteria, now cleared of tables, with chairs lining the opposing walls, boys on one side, girls on the other. I took my place on the boys' side well away from the popular boys from the junior high, pushed to the margins near the home-schooled and parochial-schooled boys.

Enter the sauve, angular figure of Mr. Walter Schalk, flanked by a young man and a very pretty young lady, both about eighteen years old. Mr. Schalk had the young couple demonstrate several dances for us. I recall the cha-cha, the foxtrot, the jitterbug, and the coolest of the dances, "the fad". From time to time in the demonstration, Mr. Schalk would smoothly cut in on the young man and take the young lady in his arms and spin her around like Fred Astaire or Gene Kelly would do in those old movies. Then he would simply turn away and the young man would move back in without missing a beat. It was very slick.

Then Mr. Schalk demonstrated how the boys should walk across the expanse of floor to where the girls were sitting and bow and ask one of the girls if she would care to dance with us. She would consent and we were to take her offered hand and walk to a vacant spot on the dance floor. Again, slick. However, when Mr. Schalk directed the boys to select partners, there ensued a scene reminiscent of the Great Oklahoma Land Rush of 1889. Those of us with poor reflexes were unprepared for the speed of our classmates. And when we arrived across the floor, the girls that remained displayed, at least in my mind, a mixture of dismay at having not been selected by the first wave of boys and disappointment at the appearance of us in the second.

Looking back, it was a strangely beautiful moment of innocence. The girl I asked to dance was one I had never met before. I didn't know her name and would never learn it. We smiled awkwardly at each other. She couldn't have been as uncoordinated and untalented as I was, but she did not betray any expression of chagrin at having me across from her as we tried out the slowed-down steps of the cha-cha, then the fad. (The fad was the "coolest" of the dances Schalk would teach us. It was accompanied by a very watered-down, public-domain, generic "rock" instrumental.) These two dances were performed, at least that evening, without any physical contact between the partners.

Then came the waltz and the jitterbug. These involved my left hand holding her right and my right hand being placed on the left side of her waist. Thankfully she, like all the girls, was wearing white cotton gloves so that my sweaty palms were not as obvious as they would otherwise have been. We stuttered and moved through the first pass of these dances and then returned to our seats as instructed. It was over.

I began breathing normally again and was ready to leave, but there was one more ritual to perform before we were dismissed. The door prize. Mr. Schalk would quickly walk up the row of chairs in which we were all seated throwing little numbered paper tickets at us. If you caught your ticket on the fly, which was almost impossible, he would throw you a second. Then he would call out one number for the boys and one for the girls. The winners got some item of sporting goods from the store in which I believe Mr. Schalk held a financial interest. And then we were dismissed.

Each Tuesday this was repeated for the course of the school year. I got a little more confident in asking a girl to dance with me. My reflexes improved to the point where, from time to time, I made it over to some of the most popular girls in the class and asked them to dance. And I actually learned how to dance! As awkward and artificial as the whole thing was, it kind of worked. I became a little more at ease around my classmates, especially the girls. I learned some of the girls' names and some of them seemed to know mine. A few of them even seemed to not hate having to dance with me.

The last class of the year was Parents' Night. This meant that the parents of the students attended the class to watch their offspring show off what they had learned. Mr. Schalk had paired us up before that night so that the selection of partners would appear less manic and would result in pairings of appropriate height. My partner was a lovely young lady with long, fine blondish hair. She smiled at me as we danced. That was nice. We made it through the cha-cha and fad. Then we did the waltz with its two points of contact. Finally, we began the jitterbug, which involved a spin of her under my arm. It went well until her lovely hair became entangled with the buttons on my blazer's cuff. It was one of those moments in life when time slows down. I panicked, of course. My first reaction was to run, but attached as we were, that was out of the question. After her initial reaction to having her hair pulled, albeit accidentally, she smiled and patiently waited for me to untangle our linkage. Seeing her smile made me feel nicely different than I had ever felt before. It was calming. I relaxed and took a close look at the knot and undid it. We finished our jitterbug. Maybe it was just me, but it seemed like we were a little closer somehow. We smiled at each other as we went back to our respective row of seats for the door prize ritual.

Many years later, at a class reunion, I was chatting with a lovely female classmate who I did not recognize. It turned out that she was my Parents' Night dance partner of so many years before! I reminded her of our "temporary connection" and that same sweet smile from so many years before returned. Don't get me wrong, I don't think this was any romantic spark or attraction on either side. It was just a sweet moment of innocent youth shared between two people. And like dance lessons, it may seem old-fashioned, but it was nice.

Before Mr. Schalk dismissed everyone from the Parents' Night finale, he mentioned that the Walter Schalk revue was being held in six weeks. Those wishing to "take the next step" (get it?) could sign up to participate. Of course his words were not aimed at the students, but at the parents, many of whom were, at that moment, experiencing great pride in seeing their son or daughter demonstrating new-found grace and skill. Many, if not most, signed up on the spot.

Digression - Regarding the business model of a dance school, it is something to behold, a pinnacle of capitalist perfection. I'm sure not all dance schools are successful, but Mr. Schalk's sure was. And I know that he did not invent the business model, but he surely executed it with practiced efficiency. First, there was the not-insignificant tuition for the ballroom dance lessons that each student (or rather their parents) paid. Then, remember the door prizes? The sporting goods that were the prizes were things like baseball shoes that might not fit the lucky winner. So they and their parents had to visit Mr. Schalk's store to trade them for ones that did. And while they were there, it was not unlikely that some further purchase might be made. Cha-ching.

Then there was the tuition for the summer session that was required to participate in the revue. Then there was the rental price of the costume to be worn for the revue performance. Or rather costumes, if one was "lucky" enough to be in more than one number. Most were. Then there were tickets to be purchased for family and friends to watch one's own children dance in one of several performances of the revue. And photographs (later videotapes) of your child dancing in the revue? Those were available for purchase. (Photography by individuals was prohibited. Too distracting for the dancers.) And none of these items was bargain-priced.

And consider the psychology involved. As a parent would you want your child to be part of this process and its high-profile events, or be a wall-flower? And once your child had participated for one year, would you want them to continue on to another, or be a quitter? And if your first-born child had been a part of all this joy, don't your second- and third-born deserve to also, or do you play favorites?

And a chosen few students of the dance, who had paid for years of instruction and might continue to pay to be in the "advanced modern jazz show troupe", might be tapped to work as instructors as the young man and woman who demonstrated the dance steps to our ballroom class had. Even if they were paid, they had likely paid more to get to that point than they would ever recoup.

None of this is illegal. But it is shrewd. And highly profitable. At least I assume it was for Mr. Schalk. In fairness, kids did learn to dance. And I don't think the parents felt bad about the money they spent. But it seemed to be a bit of a racket. - End of digression.

I did two years of ballroom dance with Mr. Schalk and participated in one revue. I can still do a rough approximation of the jitterbug I learned there. In the forty years since then, I have yet to have the opportunity to perform my cha-cha or waltz. But on certain nights, when I do find myself on a dance floor opposite my lovely wife, beware, I will break out "the fad".

Happy Birthday to Me

There are few things a child anticipates more than his or her birthday. And, according to every circus ringmaster, there are children of all ages. So, it's not so crazy that I am still very enthusiastic about my birthday. My birthday falls on December 30, the second-to-last day of the year. It's a day before New Year's Eve, the night EVERYBODY parties. It's less than a week after Christmas, the day when EVERYONE is feeling festive. It's smack-dab in the middle of the cold and flu season and usually among the worst weather days of the year. In short, it's a terrible day to have a birthday.

It's terrible for presents. You've heard of the old "Christmas/Birthday-Combo Present Scam", right? That's when Cousin So-and-so gives you a pen and pencil set with a Christmas card on which he has written in "and Happy Birthday". Oh, and did I mention that my sister's birthday is December 29? Yeah, that's right. You've heard of the old "Double Birthday-Combo Cake Scam", right? That's when you get the supermarket bakery sheet cake that has a diagonal border of yellow frosting between your sister's pink frosting and your chocolate frosting. It's kind of like when they partitioned Korea or Vietnam or Berlin. What could be more festive?

Oh, and remember in grade school when they would announce that it was this boy's or that girl's birthday? The whole class would sing "Happy Birthday" to them. In some schools, they would put it on the class calendar. The birthday celebrity's mom would bring in cake or cookies or both along with Hi-C or Hawaiian Punch. Sometime they would invite the whole class to their home for the "real" party. Well, guess what? School is always out on December 30, so that never happened for me. But, I got over it. Well, sort of. OK, it still bugs me. A lot. There. I said it. Boo hoo.

My earliest birthday memories are happy ones. Just the family was gathered and I got the toys I wanted and I got to blow out candles. I was too young to notice or care that the gifts were wrapped in Christmas wrapping paper or that the candles were the ones my sister had wished on and blown out the day before. And did I mention that I was always sick? From birth to age twenty, I was sick with flu or tonsillitis almost every year in the period from Christmas to my birthday.

I was probably eight or nine when I organized my own first real birthday party. I had an idea of what a real birthday party should be like and invited a dozen of so of my classmates, neighborhood chums, Cub Scout comrades, and Little League teammates to a party that would feature games, food, candy, presents (for me) and cool take-home gift bags (for the gang). We even sent out supercool Batman-themed invitations! I thought it was a classy touch.

When the big day arrived, I remember decorating the house with balloons and some of the Batman pictures from the leftover invitations for thematic continuity. We laid out the snacks, potato chips AND fritos. No expense was spared. The Cokes, Fanta orange sodas and Grape Nehis were properly chilled. And we waited. And waited. Out of fifteen invited guests, zero showed up. And there were no RSVPs. In fairness, I don't think any of those kids or I for that matter, knew what an RSVP was, but it stung like hell to be sitting there an hour after the appointed time coming to the realization that not one of them was coming. Not even the kid from next-door! Next-door! And, on top of the party that didn't happen, were all the presents that I didn't get. I'm not saying I was counting on getting a Major Matt Mason spaceman set or Mattel Thingmaker Creepy Crawlers set, but I wouldn't have minded.

I learned my lesson. After that disaster I basically gave up on my birthday. It remained a family-only thing. It was about getting the presents I had wanted, but didn't get for Christmas. Often, I would get the "base model" toy for Christmas half-knowing that the accessories were coming in five days. And there were usually the gifts from relatives that had been mailed, usually with the Christmas gifts. One or two of them inevitably got opened on Christmas by mistake. But since those were often pajamas or underwear, it was no great tragedy. (Underwear? For a child's birthday present? Really?)

As a disclaimer, I should say that I know much of this sounds like (and is) the rantings of a spoiled, white, suburban kid. I was blessed with a functional, two-parent, middle-class household. I thought everyone was. My bedroom, yes, I had my own bedroom, had a great collection of the latest toys. I thought everyone else's did too. In my defense, I went to a lot of other kids' birthday parties. And they were what I dreamed mine should be like. They weren't expensive affairs. We're not talking about pony rides, clowns and blow-up bounce-houses here. But there were ten to twenty kids in attendance, each with a gift for the birthday boy. There were games of bingo, pin-the-tail-on-the-donkey and the occasional piñata. That's all I wanted, my fair share of the birthday bounty. Is that so wrong?

And TV and movies glorified the birthday party too.

Usually, these fictional parties were surprise parties with all the added hi-jinx and merriment. They looked like so much fun. What did I have to do to deserve a party like that? I behaved. I got good grades. I went to church. There just wasn't a way to make it happen.

As I got older, the importance of the birthday party among my peers faded, mercifully. Our family celebrations became dinner out at a nice restaurant, sometimes a place of my choosing. That was nice. And I remember 1980, when mandatory registration for the selective service draft was reinstated under Ronald Reagan. It seemed that he was itching to go to war with the Soviets. My college classmates and I had an exaggerated and unrealistic sense that we'd end up dead in some far-flung corner of the world. But unlike them I was born before January 1, 1960, twenty-six hours before, to be precise, and so I was not required to register! Whew! My birthday had actually worked for me! Maybe that was the great balancing of the karmic birthday scales. Not getting a set of Jarts when I was eleven was a pretty good trade-off for not dying in Afghanistan at age twenty.

And I eventually grew up and got married and we had a family of our own. My wife indulged me on my birthday, even though I know she thought it was silly. And you really can't beat the homemade cards and gifts from your own kids. My daughter made some labels that turned a little shampoo sample into "Dad Shampoo - Special Formula for Dads!". And my son, who was just learning about music celebrated my favorite rock group with a homemade card that designated me as "Steely Dad"! Those things more than made up for the birthday disappointments of my childhood. I was at peace over the whole thing.

I never made much of the "milestone birthdays". I turned 20, 30, 40 and 50 without any special fanfare. It was more than enough to get kisses from my wife and kids, the gifts I had bought myself and some from them, and a dinner out. And I thought they felt pretty much the same.

Five days after my 50th birthday there was a blizzard in Connecticut. We were all hunkered down with fires in the wood stove and fireplace. There was a college football bowl game on. It was the perfect night to stay in. It was 5pm or so when my wife reminded me that we were supposed to go to a party. We had a friend who sang professionally. Her choir was having a holiday party at one of my favorite restaurants and we were invited. Looking back, it made no sense that we would be invited to such a party, but I knew the food would be good, so why not? Now, however, the wind was howling, snow was piling up and I was feeling very lazy. I suggested we blow the party off. My wife was having none of that. She marched me into the shower and had clothes laid out for me by the time I had toweled off.

And so it was that I found myself scaling the steps of the restaurant up to their private banquet room. As I approached the top of the stairs, I saw our beloved family priest, Father Peter, chatting with the brother of my college roommate. How odd that they should be here! An instant later, sixty people shouted "Surprise!" at me and I nearly died from the shock!

And this was not just any old surprise birthday party. Oh, no. This one outdid all the old TV and movie surprise parties put together. People had come from two states away, driving for hours through a fierce winter storm. There were friends from my work and from jobs I had years before. My closest friends from college were there. My wife's family was there.

People I had not seen in years were there. The foul weather had put the event into question, but they had all come. There was a spread of sumptuous food the likes of which I had rarely seen. There was an open bar. There were decorations! Everyone had name tags that identified them and their relationship to me! On the wall hung a huge poster of me in my Sunday best taken when I was four, about the time of my earliest birthday memories. There was an endless soundtrack of my favorite songs playing. My wife had put together several hundred pictures into a slideshow of my life that ran continuously on a big screen.

After the shock and joy had sunk in a little, my wife stopped the music and slideshow to play a video she had made that told my life story in pictures and narration by her, our daughter, and our son. It showed what a wonderful life I had been blessed with from the beginning right up to that wonderful, stormy, blustery night. My wife's narration was funny, our daughter's was sweet, and our son called me his hero. I smiled and cried and felt ten feet tall. Finally, a huge, delicious cake was brought out with fifty blazing candles that I blew out. I didn't need to make a wish. I had already gotten everything I could wish for and had ever wanted out of a birthday.

That big roomful of friends and family cheered for me and shouted for me to make a speech. But for once in my life, I was truly speechless. I wanted to say something important, or funny, or sweet, or loving. But no words came, only more joyful tears. If I hadn't been so overwhelmed I would have just said thank you to them all for being there that night and being in my life. Thanks and love were all I would have wanted to express. I hope my tears did that.

After a wonderful evening, we went back out into the subsiding storm carrying presents and leftover food. Our kids helped load all the stuff into the car. I gave my wife a huge hug and kiss and thanked her for the best evening of my life. I told her that everything I had ever wanted from my birthday, I had gotten that night. She smiled and told me she was happy to hear me say that because she was never going to try to top it. It would be back to little birthday celebrations after this. And that was fine with me.

Memory and the Blessing of Forgetting

After years of feeling very much to the contrary, I don't think I was bullied very much growing up. While bullying is sadly a reality for many, I think I was just a worrier. If there hadn't been big kids, tough kids, kids who smoked, or kids who did anything that could be perceived as threatening by a nerdy, goodie-two-shoes like I was, I think I would have found something else to be afraid of and worry about. But there were such kids, with longer hair than I had, who wore torn jeans and leather jackets with fringe and smoked Marlboros. And I fretted endlessly over the occasional random profanities casually directed my way by them.

Looking back, I'm sure they didn't spend a fraction of the time thinking about me that I spent obsessing over them. Maybe it was all karmic payback. Only years later would I recall an incident where I was the bully. It is significant that I didn't remember it for many years. It meant so little to me. But it meant a great deal to my victim.

Fifth grade in Houston may have been the first time I was

aware of some sort of omnipresent, low-grade threat potential from boys in the class who were tougher and bigger. I was taller than most, but not tougher or bigger really. Let me be clear. I was never threatened directly by any of these guys. They were just there. Big. Tough. There. My awareness of them didn't really alter my behavior in any way. It was sort of like the Cold War. I was aware that nuclear annihilation could be minutes away at any given time, but I didn't let it affect my day.

I think it might have been in response to this low-level dread, of potential bullies, not nuclear destruction, that it dawned on me that there were geekier, smaller, weaker boys than me, who might potentially be made to feel the same way about me as I felt about those bigger, tougher boys. Or maybe I just wanted to see what it would feel like. Or maybe I was just bored. But I one day, out of nowhere, for absolutely no reason, I laid out an elaborate ambush and beat-down plan to a kid in my class who had heretofore been an absolute nonentity in my life. Let's call him Alvin. I told him how I knew his route to school and I could pop out at him and beat him up and no one would help him. Based on movie and cop-show bad guys I had seen, I laid out this threat in detail, just to see him react with understandable fear. And then, just as quickly as the stupid notion to do this awful thing had occurred to me, I dropped it and forgot all about it and went back to being the same nerdy kid I had been five minutes earlier.

And I never gave it another thought. That is, I would never have given it another thought, except that Alvin had taken what I had said in that stupid moment seriously, as one would. For a day or two he apparently lived in fear of me. His walk to school was a tortuous paranoid odyssey. He ran and dodged and hid and varied his route hoping to avoid me. He sat in class sweating bullets wondering when the attack would come. By the way, his reaction was perfectly reasonable based on the crazy, stupid, unprovoked, violent threat I had made to him. Finally, he could take it no more and he went to the teacher.

I was asked to stay after school for the first and only time ever. Our teacher sat between us and asked me if I had terrorized Alvin. I actually had to think about it.

"Ooooohhhhhh. Yes. I did that. But I never meant a word of it. Sorry. I don't know why I did that. I had no intention of ever harming you. Why would I? You've never done anything to me," I said.

"So, why did you say those things?" Alvin reasonably wanted to know.

"Darned if I know. But I promise I won't do it again," I said.

And that ended the whole thing. It was so weird and out of character. But I did it. And thinking about it, all these years later, it dawned on me that I may have been doing just what Alvin did, living in fear throughout junior high constantly anticipating attack by dark forces. Maybe I was taking to heart with literal, melodramatic seriousness, something that one of my torn-jean-wearing, Marlboro-smoking classmates said in a moment and never gave another thought to.

I so clearly remember one moment in eighth grade when Tommy Henrick stared into my eyes and said he would kill me. He swore it. I thought I saw blind rage and deadly seriousness. All the murderous passion a "bad kid" in a rich, upper-class suburb in Fairfield County, Connecticut could muster, he directed at me. I had trained myself not to react and I stared dead-faced as he repeated how he would kill me some day, when I least expected it. And I never turned my back on him again. I lived the next year looking over my shoulder. And when I happily moved to London at the end of that year, I never expected to see him again. And I didn't.

That is, I didn't see him until our twenty-year class reunion. My wife and I were making idle chit-chat with my now-grown classmates and we had been talking to this one chap for several minutes when I asked his name. It was Tommy Henrick. It was clear from his friendly small-talk and easy smile that he had no more memory of me or his death threat to me than I had years before of my threat to Alvin. And what did my former would-be assassin end up doing with his life? Was he a mob enforcer? A Navy SEAL? No. He was a distributor for Highlights children's magazine.

It's funny how two people can be part of an event and for one of them it is life-changing, rarely leaving his consciousness, a moment they remember every detail of and will never forget. For the other, the moment passes and is forgotten like last week's newspaper.

When I was in college, I drove three of my friends to a Jerry Garcia / Bob Weir concert at the Cape Cod Coliseum. As you might expect, there were mind-altering substances present at the show and stupidly, I sampled some. On the way home, I fell asleep at the wheel and rolled my car onto its roof. By some miracle, no other cars were involved and neither I nor any of my three passengers was seriously hurt. Of course, we were all shaken up pretty badly. This event fit into a sad pattern of bad decisions I was locked into for a few years mostly involving substance abuse of one kind or another. Eventually, I am happy to say, I pulled out of this pattern and got my life back together. I became ashamed of who I had been and many of the things I had done. I tried to forget them and tried to hide my past from anyone who didn't know about that time in my life.

But I would think back to that terrible night and the sound of the impact and the shattering glass and crunching metal. Sometimes the memories came unbidden into my mind as I drifted off to sleep or woke up in the middle of the night. It had been years since I had seen any of those three friends. I wondered if they had the kind of PTSD that I did. I felt guilty for what I could have done to them. But I was too ashamed and afraid to reach out to them and say so. So I let the years pass and tried to forget. Of course, the one thing you can never run away from is yourself. And guilt weighs on one's mind until amends are finally made.

Eventually, I bumped into two of my passengers at a festival in Hartford. After some small talk I blurted out my shame and begged forgiveness for almost killing them so many years before. They hugged me and told me not to worry. They forgave me and told me that they had never held any ill will toward me. If it hadn't been me driving, it might have been one of them and the results could have been worse. I was relieved and my burden of guilt was lighter, but not gone.

Finally, at another friend's fiftieth birthday party, I faced my third passenger. I couldn't remember if I had ever seen him after that awful night. In my mind I imagined that he had nursed a grudge against me for nearly thirty years. Had he been hurt? Did he have some nagging injury that flared up when the weather changed reminding him of the careless fool who almost killed him, whose negligence caused him nightmares and pain?

I approached him and reintroduced myself. It took several moments and a few hints before he gave me any look of recognition at all. Then I recounted the tale of the car accident we were both in that I caused. And I waited for his venom to be spat upon me. I braced for the sting of his righteous, vitriolic anger.

"Are you sure I was there?" he asked with a laugh.

"Oh yes, man. Don't you remember? I rolled the car! The firemen took us all back to the station. Your father came and got you," I reminded him.

"Nope. Doesn't ring a bell. I'd remember something like that. Jerry Garcia? I don't think I've ever seen Jerry Garcia play live. I don't even like the Grateful Dead," he persisted.

"Come on, man. You were riding shotgun! Doesn't ANY of this ring a bell?" I pleaded.

"Steve, I don't remember any of this. If you say I was there, ok. There's lots of things from those years I don't remember. It was a long time ago. I'm married with kids now. I've had a career. If I was there, then there was no damage done, at least not to me. Forget it," he said with another laugh. He patted me on the back and disappeared into the party.

And it was over. I could finally say goodbye to the ghosts of that horrible night. I hadn't been arrested. I didn't even get a ticket! My parents quickly forgave me and were just happy I was alive. I got another car and have never been that stupid behind the wheel since. So, after thirty years it seems I got a hell of a free pass on that one.

Memory is a blessing and a curse, I suppose. I'm thankful for most of what I remember. Seeing my wife in her wedding dress as she walked up the aisle toward me. Holding out my hands to each of my children they took their first steps. Sunsets in Hawaii. And I'm thankful for a lot of what I've forgotten and for what others have forgotten about me. Maybe having a sin forgotten is the next best thing to having it forgiven.

Why I Hate Bob Guccione

Everyone has their own story about learning the "facts of life". Some people get "the talk" from Mom or Dad. Some people have an older sibling or friend who clues them in. Some people learn about sex "on the street", whatever that means.

My early sex education consisted of a book I found one day in the magazine rack in our living room. I was ten and I stumbled upon this volume that I can only assume my parents had planted there for me to find. It didn't have much text. There were several pictures of animals in pairs, a grown animal with a baby animal. On one page, for instance, was a mother duck with a downy, little duckling. On another, there was a full-grown dog with a puppy. And on the last page, there was a picture of a Nordic-looking woman holding a baby to her breast! I stared at that picture for a long time and then put the book aside. My parents and I never spoke about this book, which had been borrowed from the library and disappeared as mysteriously as it had appeared.

My real sex education had started a few years earlier. I noticed that certain women I would see on TV or in the movies made me "feel funny". Barbara Eden, Tina Louise, Julie Newmar, Yvonne Craig, and others gave me this "funny feeling". It was vague and I didn't dwell on it. Perhaps I mentioned it to Brent Tuttle, who lived next-door. Maybe that was how we got on the subject of Playboy magazine one day in his backyard tree fort. He disappeared inside his house and returned with an issue of the magazine. I vaguely remember looking at the models and feeling odd about sharing this with another guy.

Fast forward to seventh grade where our junior high actually had sex education as a unit of science class. Mr. Sutton gave us all anatomical diagrams of cut-away sections of the male and female reproductive organs in the frontal and profile views. These were drawings that might have been useful to a urological or gynecological surgeon, but the crucial information about the mechanics that made sex actually happen were vague, to put it kindly.

This called for further research and independent study. Another friend of mine had a father who had collected "men's magazines". Among these were copies of a periodical called Penthouse, published by a Mr. Bob Guccione. A regular feature at the front of each issue was the Penthouse Forum. These were "letters" to the editor purported to be from readers, mostly male readers. Some of them discussed articles from previous issues, interviews with prominent cultural figures and politicians. But others recounted readers' experiences with members of the opposite sex. The letters indicated that such experiences were generally reserved for underclassmen at small, mid-western colleges.

An odd thing about these letters was that these young collegians seemed to be practically tripping over females craving their company. In each and every one of them, there was a willing, if not aggressively pushy, young woman who seemed desperate to have sex. If she hadn't happened upon the writer of the letter, it would have been with the next hapless fellow to walk by. These small, mid-western colleges were a virtual minefield of sex! I assumed that most of these hot-blooded ladies were, of course, from the nearby mid-western states.

There must be something in the water, I reasoned. Either that, or there was some incredible metamorphosis that occurred between matriculation and the first day of classes. I would have to bide my time.

Eventually, I found myself off at college. My roommate and I often discussed the available co-eds in our dorm and around campus. We would go "combing", his hometown's term for cruising bars, parties and other gathering places for eligible ladies. To be honest, we had an abysmal record. I can't imagine what was wrong with our technique. We'd go to a bar, buy a beer, stand off to the side, and stare at any unattached ladies the way a hungry lion stares at a wounded gazelle. And yet, the ladies didn't flock to us. Baffling.

But they say that repetition is the key to success. So we repeated this unsuccessful strategy for the next several years, still amazingly (to us), without success. They also say that doing the same thing over and over and expecting different results is the definition of insanity. "They" say a lot of conflicting things, don't "they"? I wonder who "they" are and if any of "them" are freshmen at small, mid-western colleges? Looking back, perhaps my crucial error had been my choice of college. The University of Connecticut isn't a small, mid-western college. Argh!

There's kind of a happy ending to my story, however. Even though I never did end up writing to the Penthouse Forum about any crazy experiences, I did end up happy. "Combing" aside, I met a bunch of nice girls at college in the dorms, in classes, and elsewhere. I became friends with several of them and one of those friendships blossomed into love and eventually a marriage that has lasted thirty years and counting. The Forum letters never mentioned love. They never really described how all the wild sex fit into a real life like the one I was living. They didn't mention STDs or pregnancy or "the morning after" either. I wonder if any freshmen from small, mid-western colleges ever sued over the consequences of their Forum-worthy escapades? Or at least wrote cautionary letters to Penthouse Forum that never got printed?

The "other shoe dropped" when an upperclassman laughed at a group of us freshmen who were discussing the latest month's issue of Penthouse and it's batch of Forum letters one day.

"You don't actually think those are real letters from readers, you do? Those are all written by the same writers that write the rest of the magazine, you dopes! Don't they all seem the same to you? Can't you see the format they all follow? Frosh!" he scoffed and walked away.

We looked at each other sheepishly and it was suddenly as obvious as our "combing" strategy had been unsuccessful, that is to say completely. We'd been had. It was embarrassing and infuriating. Mr. Guccione had whipped us into a frenzy by showing us pictures of the undraped female form, and then snookered us with fiction disguised as fact into thinking we had easy access to the same. The charlatan! How many others had been duped? Countless of our college freshman brethren were out there making fools of themselves and striking out repeatedly in pursuit of an X-rated Brigadoon, a licentious mirage. What could be done to save them?

With the kind of sudden wisdom that a mouse has after the trap snaps shut on its tail, we agreed that it was in the everyone's best interest to let our comrades learn the lesson for themselves. It would spare us further embarrassment and thin out the competition for eligible ladies when we began employing our new, breakthrough dating strategy, code-name: Sincerity.

And so to you, Mr. Bob Guccione (who passed away in 2010), I say, "Shame, sir! Shame on you! A portion of a generation of young men are wise to you! And while, thanks might be in order for your having taught us skepticism and wariness when, in the future we are baited by the 'too good to be true', scorn also is your due for your duplicity and literary prevarication. Good day, sir! I said GOOD DAY!"

The End of Gone Forever

I take you to a time that feels like long ago. Kids played Little League baseball, Pop Warner football, maybe some sport at the YMCA. There were Boy Scouts and Girl Scouts. And beyond that, kids just played. Cops and robbers. Cowboys and Indians. Tag, hide-and-go-seek, maybe shoot some baskets, or play in the woods.

For adults there was golf or bowling or bridge games. And lots of time with the family. All of these simple pleasures were of the moment. Aside from a few snapshots, they were here and gone with only the memories remaining. And it was a fact of life that you would miss out on things.

Only books and old magazines had any permanence. And magazines were meant to be disposable. Nonetheless, most families kept stacks of old Life, National Geographic and Sport Illustrated mags around for kids to cut up for school projects and because "they might be valuable some day". Libraries, even though they were the depositories of the civilization's accumulated knowledge, were not exactly the liveliest places in town either.

And so it was for a very long time. Nostalgia was a much

smaller thing when there was no media to experience again. The span of human memory was pretty much all we had.

One of the things that makes life so precious is that it is finite. Once-in-a-lifetime events come along, well, once in a lifetime. Therein lies their unique value. Civilization began when mankind began keeping records, writing things down. On clay tablets, then papyrus, then parchment, paper, film, magnetic tape, and now digital media. And as much as has been gained by recording events and accumulated knowledge for posterity, something has also been lost.

In a previous career, I worked at a large metropolitan solid waste depot. This is where garbage trucks dumped their contents when they got full. The depot fed a municipal waste combustion facility that burned the trash to make electricity. Several times a year a panicked member of the public would show up at the depot. They had thrown away something valuable and hoped to retrieve it from the literal mountains of garbage that moved through the place every day.

The superintendent of the depot was a kind man. He would listen to their stories and sympathize with them about their lost wedding ring or other priceless, irreplaceable heirloom that they believed had ended up in the trash. He would walk them back to the enormous "tipping hall", a room the size of a football field with a ceiling forty feet high. Depending on the time of day, the garbage could be piled up almost to the ceiling across the whole of that expansive, cavernous room. Often they were undaunted by the prospect of finding their "needle" in the gargantuan, smelly "haystack". It says a lot about the power of sentiment, regret, or fear that these folks would don gloves and poke about in the trash until either they realized the futility of what they were trying to do or the superintendent told them that they had to leave. That was when they were faced with "gone forever".

When I was young, we lived in a small Texas town that had one movie theater. That theater had one screen. For thirty-five cents, I could watch whatever movie was playing there for the week or two that it would run. Then, the name of another movie would appear on the marquee and the last one would be "gone forever". True, it might end up on the late, late show on one of the three TV channels we had back then. But most movies didn't. They were simply gone.

TV was the same. I was part of one of the first generations of kids who grew up with TV. I watched sit-coms, westerns, cartoons, sci-fi and variety shows, whatever was on. There were a small number of syndicated shows like *I Love Lucy* that always seemed to be on in the afternoon or early morning hours. But the prime time shows were ephemeral. If, like me, you became a loyal watcher of a particular show and missed an episode, you might have one more chance to catch it as a "summer rerun", but if not, it was gone forever. When your favorite show was cancelled, it meant you would likely never see it again.

Even music seemed to be like that, perhaps to a lesser extent. I remember taking a long car trip, just my dad and me, when I was very young, perhaps three or four. We listened to the radio and one or two songs stuck in my memory. I couldn't remember the words, just the sound of them. But when they ended, they were gone. If I had been a little older, I might have remembered the name of the song and might have bought the single or the album. But even those would only be available for sale at the local record store for a few weeks or maybe months and then they would be, for all practical purposes, gone forever.

Even our friends and family were like that. There was a time when moving away from the town in which you were born and raised was a virtual cutting of ties forever. Oh sure, there might be letters mailed or phone calls made to stay in touch, but over the years, the number and frequency of these diminished and most, if not all, of the connections were lost. In time, some of those you left behind would move themselves so that even if you reached out with a letter or call, you might not find them. The post office would only forward mail to a new address for so long. College friends, work colleagues, comrades in arms, all were often gone forever even after being closer to you than family for a time. I moved over half a dozen times in my elementary and high school years and at least that many times in my professional years. My memory is filled with names and faces of people I shared time, experiences and emotions with. Most are gone forever.

No one called it "pop culture" back then. To a lot of adults, movies, TV and the music on the radio were frivolous. They shed no tears that much of it was quickly gone forever. Old celluloid films were stored in warehouses in Hollywood and the volatile celluloid degraded to unwatchability over time or melted in the un-air-conditioned spaces, or, worse yet, burned. It's a sad fact that many, if not most, of the movies from Hollywood's Golden Age are lost to time.

The same is true of old TV shows. So little value was placed on the content of many of the shows of the 50's, 60's and 70's that the tape on which they were recorded was seen as being more valuable than the shows recorded on it and new shows were recorded over old ones again and again. Most of the Golden Age of Television? Gone forever.

Music suffered the same fate, as 78's gave way to 45's and LP's. Stacks of them were sent to dumps as record players to play them on became scarce collectors items. And as 45's and LP's gave way to cassettes and cassettes gave way to digital, some, if not most, of that content was not deemed worth transferring.

Like the "disposable" culture I grew up in, I gave little thought to what was left behind or what was lost along the way as I grew from grade school to high school and college and into the work force. There was always something new to replace the stuff that was gone forever. Growing up meant moving on from one thing to the next big thing that was always touted as being "new and improved". Looking back wasn't something people did. The past was prologue. We were going to spend the rest of our lives in "the future". It seemed wise not to be loaded down with too many artifacts of the past. Who cared that so much was gone forever? Life goes on. The old was cleared away to make space for the new. It was the order of things. Ever had it been. Ever would it be.

I was watching TV in 1972 when I first heard the word nostalgia. It was a commercial for a record, not of new music from the hottest new group, but of music from the "fabulous Fifties". These songs that were popular before I was born were being brought back from "gone forever". Oldies radio became a thing. Perhaps there had been a few people who had not moved on, but they were outliers. Now, looking back became a mainstream thing to do. And as time crept forward into the 80's and 90's, nostalgia for the 60's and 70's became a thing. Cable TV channels devoted to "classics" popped up.

Meanwhile I had my head down and my nose to the grindstone trying to make a career to support myself, my wife, and family. Even as I was aware of the culture of the 80's and 90's, I distanced myself from it by clinging to the music of my late teen years, rather than troubling myself to explore the new sounds. I was "aging out" of the demographic that new music, movies and TV were targeting as my children were growing into it.

I think I had some kind of breakdown as I began to experience career burnout in my late 40s. It was my "mid-life crisis". I thought back on my life, particularly my childhood. It seemed so happy compared to what I was going through. I had to find out why. Perhaps if I could put my finger on the key to this happiness that seemed gone forever, I could find my way back there. Maybe I could undo "gone forever".

Without realizing I was doing it, I had already started down that path. In my 30's I had begun again to collect comic books and baseball cards, not as financial investments, but as touchstones of my youth. When I found, in a town hall basement comic book show, a copy of the very first Batman comic book I ever bought, back when I was six, a wave of inexplicable giddiness washed over me. My mom had thrown the first one away, but now I had another. And holding in my hands a Joe Morgan rookie card took me back to my days as a ten-year-old member of the Astro Buddies Fan Club in Houston.

And at some point, with the coming of the internet and niche cable TV channels I began to discover other pathways to things that I had thought were gone forever. I found a dealer who sold me bootleg DVD copies of the old *Batman* and *Green Hornet* TV series. The pain of seeing them cancelled and being gone forever (except for unpredictable glimpses over the years here and there) was wiped away. In one of my first forays "surfing the internet" I found the 1961 Vincent Price movie *Master of the World* that had been a vague memory from some second-run movie matinee deep in my childhood years. I've plugged partial lyrics from some of the songs from that long-ago road trip with my dad into search engines and recaptured the songs they came from. And by searching on the name of the first friend I made in 1971 when we moved from Texas to New England, I reconnected with him after thirty-eight years.

And it doesn't seem like it will end. Somehow, through a combination of a few stubborn hoarders of old TV, movies and music mixed with digital technology, "gone forever" seems to be going away. Online I've found bits of information I never knew about my father, who passed away in 1999. Is the loss of gone forever a good thing? If gone forever made the finite more precious, does its demise cheapen our experiences? I don't think so.

As anyone who's ever seen the sea of smartphones raised to record a concert, fireworks display or piano recital knows, you can either record an event or experience it. You can't do both. Real-life human connection can't be recorded, even if aspects of it can. Even if a baby knows its mothers face from a recording of it on a screen, you still can't hold hands with a YouTube clip. And no Google search can hold a candle to a first kiss. Maybe the end of gone forever will actually make the things that can't be recorded even more precious. Maybe if we allow ourselves to miss out on the the movie, the TV show, or the song, because they'll never really be gone forever, we'll focus more on the precious things that someday will.

A Natural Supply of Things to Use

I had a typical public school education. For most of it we were not taught to, nor asked to, think critically. We accepted and learned the lessons we were being taught as the truth, the state-of-the-art, the consensus view of the world. I don't recall any moment in any class when a teacher would pause and say, "Not everyone agrees with what I just taught you. Here is a dissenting view. It is up to you weigh all the facts and formulate your own opinions."

I was in third grade when they taught us the term "natural resource" in science class. The teacher wrote the definition on the chalkboard, "A natural supply of things to use." In 1970, this was the accepted way of thinking. The world and all that was in it was a supply of things for mankind to use to create civilization. This seemed to make sense to me. It was in keeping with all the other things I had been taught.

A condensed version of the then-accepted narrative I was taught began with the Big Bang and the creation of the earth. Earth begat life, which evolved into man. Man populated the earth until Europeans came to North America and founded the United States of America, which institutionalized liberty and justice for all. Technology that began with fire and the wheel had likewise evolved to the atom bomb and the transistor. The US was in the early stages of a process using that technology that would take men to the planets in our solar system and beyond. That may seem naive and politically-insensitive today.

Yes, we were using, and even using up, our planet, but there were an unlimited number of worlds with unlimited resources "out there". Earth was, in a sense, the first of an endless number of stepping stones to the stars. That seemed OK to me, even natural.

At some point after that day in third grade, I began to become aware that this straight-forward, onward-and-upward line of reasoning might be a bit of an over-simplification and might even be deeply flawed. As I grew older, I came to find out that the simplistic version of history I had been taught was one-dimensional. Thanks to TV, I couldn't miss or ignore the racial upheaval in the US, the unrest in the Middle East, Southeast Asia and elsewhere. Even the industrial revolution, with all its benefits, came at a price of environmental damage, species extinctions, and social injustice. Shortly after the moon landing, America would limit its manned space exploration program and indefinitely postpone its reach for the planets and stars.

I began to hear another narrative that was emerging that challenged everything I had been taught. It was troubling and confusing. Mankind was reframed as a disease infecting the previously healthy ecosystem of the earth. The beautiful Disney-produced "true life" nature stories of animal families thriving in the pristine wilderness were replaced by "Silent Spring" warnings that man had irreparably destroyed the natural world through his greed and stupidity. Even the bald eagle, symbol of American greatness, was being driven to extinction by the chemical pollution with which mankind poisoned nature.

The revision extended to history as well. Much of what I had been taught was apparently a lie. It was all war, conquest, tyranny, and slavery. And the worst of all these warring groups was the Europeans, who would become the Americans. And America had despoiled and ruined everything it touched. It was a corrupt, imperial bully who trampled the poor, installed evil dictators around the world to do our bidding, and enslaved Africans. When Lincoln dared to free them, he was killed and the maltreatment was reframed under Jim Crow, whose legacy taints race relations in America to this day.

And science and technology were not tools of progress lifting us to the stars, they were the sure means of our own destruction. Over-population and nuclear annihilation were coming with the promise of mass starvation and irradiation.

From sexism to racism to imperialism to rampant corporate greed and control of the world's economies, doom was imminent. The gloomy chorus drowned out the Pollyanna version of life I had once believed. Everyone hated everyone else. Race against race. Country against country. Ideology against ideology. Our world was a poisoned powder keg and the fuse had been lit. The doomsday clock was at 11:59:59. Over and out.

Now I don't want to spoil anyone's apocalypse. And for you doomsayers out there, know that before you finish reading this sentence you may well be blinded by the flash of multiple thermonuclear devices vaporizing us all to atoms. If so, congratulations, you were right. I was wrong. Boy, is my face red! Or it would be except it's melted off like that guy at the end of *Raiders of the Lost Ark*. Enjoy the oblivion!

In the event that we are all still here, allow me to suggest that there may yet be hope for mankind's survival in the longer term here and perhaps even beyond the surly bounds of earth. It's true that there is much to fear in the future, much to be ashamed of in the past, and plenty of serious problems in the here and now. But I still believe in man's capacity to reason and solve problems and I believe in the earth's capacity to heal itself. Neither capacity is limitless, but if we apply the former to assist the latter, then I believe there is hope.

First all the news is not bad. History is filled with startling positive advances that may begin to balance with the mistakes made and the damage done. As Carl Sagan pointed out in *Cosmos,* slavery, common for millennia and widely accepted as a normal practice, had been largely eliminated. (Sadly, it is making a come-back. Two steps forward, one step back.) And that change was relatively rapid when compared to the ages that scourge existed. Human rights, especially for women, while perhaps far from fully won, are on the table for discussion, especially in the most developed nations. Diseases that commonly wiped out great swaths of populations have been all but eradicated in most of the world. Literacy and communication technology are proliferating in the most developed nations and beyond.

Environmental devastation continues in some regions, but significant environmental progress has been made elsewhere. Air and water quality in the United States is better today than it has been in decades and continues to improve. The most developed countries have recognized that sustainable methods of production are not only possible, but vital if there is to be long-term prosperity. While wealth is held disproportionately by the relative few, many of them are setting the example of using that wealth for the betterment of mankind. Philanthropy is alive and well and these wealthy individuals may be able to do what governments seem unable to.

Violent crime is a fraction of what it was in the US a hundred years ago. The struggle for civil rights has been extended to include not just race and gender, but also sexual orientation. Forms of abuse that thrived in the shadows since ancient times are being dragged into the sunlight of public discourse and relegated to the shrinking margins of society.

True, many of these blessings are not global yet, but the seeds exist and the problems now become logistical ones of proliferating them more widely. These challenges are herculean, no doubt, but so was the challenge of sending a man to the moon.

*****

One of the saddest aspects of today's society is the decline of civil discourse. Having a polite conversation about anything beyond the weather can mean traversing the minefield of socio-political sensitivities. Everyone has a "hot button" that they are just waiting to have pushed. And the most widespread addiction seems to be to outrage. Everyone is being injured by someone or something. We are all victims and as such entitled to have our grievances heard and reparations made. When did we all become so intolerant, so polarized, so sure that we are right and that others are wrong? Our nation has always been divided in some ways, but the divisions seem to be getting deeper and wider and more infused with anger. How will we meet the challenges that lie before us if we can't stand each other?

Somewhere way in the back of my brain, I can hear my mother's voice saying,

"There are two sides to every story."

"Not everything is black or white."

"You don't have to take everything to extremes."

"Be reasonable."

"You learn more from listening than from speaking."

We must step outside the echo-chamber that so many of us inhabit. Many of us have, innocently enough, fallen into the habit of reading only the words with which we agree, watching only the network that expresses our firmly-held beliefs, and listening only to the talk-radio personalities who reinforce our preconceived notions. This is how brain-washing works. Where is the loyal opposition? Where is progress through compromise? Whatever happened to putting yourself in the shoes of the other guy? We don't even wonder how or why "the other guy" came to believe something other than what we do. We condemn him out of hand. But it's not too late. We are all one calm, reasoned conversation away from building bridges of understanding rather than burning them.

*****

I consider myself to be a scientist, by education and profession. And I have to laugh when I hear people talk about this or that as "settled science". Or that "every mainstream scientist believes this or that". These statements expose an ignorance about the very nature of science. Science is an ever-advancing discussion based on a systematic, cyclical method of hypothesis, experimentation, and conclusion that never ends. Each conclusion simply leads to the next hypothesis. No science is ever settled. And we would do well to remember that countless scientific advances were made in the face of near-unanimous opposition. Galileo, Newton, and Einstein, to name only three, were ridiculed as blasphemers, crackpots and lunatics in their times. But science doesn't vote on the truth, it designs experiments to reveal that which cannot be denied.

Any scientist who doesn't openly share his or her notes,

source code, and methodology with the world is hiding something. Science is about handing everything over to those who may want nothing so much as to disprove your life's work, because you believe it can stand up to their aggressive scrutiny. And even if it cannot, it may be useful in advancing the work of another.

You want "settled science"? Consider gravity. Newton showed mathematically that gravity was a force between two objects. Settled? Centuries later Einstein showed through math, physics and confirmed astronomical predictions that gravity is simply the result of curved space-time. Settled? Scientists today are investigating the existence of gravitrons, particles of gravity, as part of quantum field theory. Others are investigating gravity waves, also predicted by Einstein. Call me a heretic, but it doesn't seem settled.

What we lack so often today is respect for the opposing view. We've been conditioned to try to "win" discussions. But that's absurd. No one "wins" a discussion. That's like the first-chair violinist trying to "win" a symphony. The purpose of debate is not to determine who is "right". It's to get all the pertinent ideas out in the open, to weigh the relative merits of those ideas so that informed decisions can be made. The more ideas that get incorporated into a workable solution, the more comprehensive it's likely to be.

Digression - I have tremendous respect for Vince Lombardi, who coached the Green Bay Packers football team in the 1950s and 1960s. He was a brilliant coach and motivator of men. His most famous quotation is, "Winning isn't the most important thing. Winning is the only thing." That's a powerful motivating sentiment. But it's a terrible life philosophy. It ignores the finest qualities of man. Things like mercy, judgement, moderation, tolerance, compromise, inclusion, brotherhood, hope and love.

Obsession with "winning" can end in, "the village had to be destroyed in order for it to be saved" or the final scene in *Dr. Strangelove* where Major T. J. "King" Kong rides an atom bomb down to its target happily hooting and hollering in "victory". -End of digression.

There was a recent "debate" between Bill Nye (the Science Guy) and Ken Ham, a believer in the "creation science" model of the origin of planet Earth. The hallmark of the exchange was the civility and politeness each man accorded the other. There was precious little agreement between the ideas each presented, but each got to present his ideas! And each got to be heard. How much more progress and understanding could there be if this would become the model for discussions on the whole range of topics that divide our society? True, that moment of "winning" might be lost, but if it meant saving our world and again turning our sights to the stars, maybe something better would be gained.

*****

One more thing. Technology now provides us with an unlimited number of ways to become informed. Through our devices, each of us has at his fingertips the accumulated knowledge of the ages and up-to-the-minute news, speculation, editorial, trivia, tripe and ravings. The task has become how to sort fact from fiction, filter out opinion, and focus on what matters. For ages we have turned to news sources to help us do this. I suggest it now may be time to turn away from them.

It's easy to see how government-sponsored news might be

biased to benefit that government. But it may be less obvious that commercially sponsored "news" is not, has never been, and is not even meant to be, anything more or less than a means for the sponsors to sell their goods and services. As such, broadcasters adhere to practices that are designed to maximize viewership as measured by their ratings. They have an interest in keeping viewers concerned, even worried, about actual events and possible future events.

There was a time when the national news was broadcast in fifteen minutes on the three major television networks. Local news took up another fifteen minutes. And that was it. All the news the nation seemingly needed in half an hour! And the world kept spinning. This expanded to "news hours" and the all-news networks have taken it to around-the-clock. We never close. Is there more news today? Is the increased coverage necessary? Is it helping?

The reporting of weather is a great example. I've lived in the Northeast US since 1971. Even extreme, "dangerous" weather, like an ice storm, used to be fit into the five minutes allotted to the weather in the evening half-hour of local news. Nowadays, every predicted winter storm, no matter how small, even if it never materializes, is named and triggers "extended storm team coverage" for hours on end. Supermarkets sell gallons of milk and bottled water, loaves of bread, and tons of batteries to panicked shoppers. And sometimes not a single flake falls.

The local television stations defend this practice in the name of public safety. They don't mention that they make their largest profits from self-produced programming like… weather coverage. And news outlets run the same scam. The public has a right to know! Responsible citizens must be informed! But take a closer look at how the 24-hour news stations do this.

If an event occurs, they may have two minutes of video footage and an equal amount of text to go with it. But they repeat this footage on a loop for hours, consulting various correspondents who have nothing substantive to add to the two minutes of text that has been read, paraphrased, dissected, parsed, and speculated upon while the video footage replays and replays. And note that they do break for commercials. As vital as is the public's need to know may be, equally vital is the public's need for non-stick cookery, athlete's foot powder, and non-FDA-approved male virility pills.

On 9/11 and the days that followed, almost every TV channel carried repeated images of the planes hitting the Twin Towers, the towers collapsing, and other grim scenes of that terrible day. It is important that those images were captured and for us to have seen them. But what purpose was served after we had seen them once or twice or more? Was something special supposed to happen after the twelfth viewing? No. We were being inured to the horrifying event. Was the intention to make us more sensitive to the loss of life, or less? For many of us the effect was simply to disturb us emotionally more and more. The Red Cross recognized this and aired public service announcements (PSAs) advising people to avoid repeated viewings of disturbing scenes. I think these PSAs should still be running. Many of us are not under-informed, we are over-saturated with "news" that does not serve us, does not affect us, and that we do not need to know.

The question is how to "tune out" and how much. When I supervised a largely discontented union workgroup I heard a steady chorus of grumbling and complaints. I was tempted to ignore and avoid the people I supervised because of the nearly constant drone of anger and bile. But I couldn't because buried in amongst the idle chatter were a few legitimate facts that I needed to know about and act on to keep the workplace as safe and productive as I could make it.

So seek a news source that you can control, such as a website that you can access on your own terms, when you want, as needed. And avoid casual exposure to the non-stop flood of pessimism and doom. Replace the reflexive desire to check the headlines with a thoughtful decision to listen to your favorite music, inspirational talk, guided meditation, or other uplifting content. It's out there. Or unplug entirely, at least for a while, take a walk, smell the roses, listen to the birds. In freeing yourself from the treadmill of negativity, you may find you are more open to new ideas and civil discourse. And if enough of us do this, maybe we can get back to reaching for the stars.

The Honeymooners

I am a very lucky man. On many counts. Chief amongst my blessings is my wonderful wife. I remember being smitten the moment I first laid eyes on her in our freshman dorm at UConn. We became friends long before we ever dated. We enjoyed years of getting to know one another and becoming closer. And once we had both gotten our single lives and careers going, we became engaged and were married. We had a beautiful wedding and a big, fun reception with tons of friends and relatives. We received a bunch of lovely wedding presents. My parents gave us a honeymoon. In Rio. Wow.

I was working at a job I didn't like that much, feeling a great deal of pressure from a tough, unsympathetic management. My wife was going to move out of her comfy Brooklyn apartment to my less comfy New Jersey apartment increasing her commute from an easy 45 minutes each way to a brutal two hours each way. So, a week in paradise was just what the doctor ordered.

The day after our wedding, we had breakfast with a bunch of our Connecticut friends who had made the trip to New Jersey and stayed over. We were all a little hung over. We bid them farewell and headed back to *our*, formerly *my*, apartment to pack for our big trip. My dad was a top executive with Texaco and had made all the arrangements. He had handed me an envelope with two airline tickets and a voucher for a limo ride to and from JFK. The airline tickets were part of a package tour of Rio.

At the appointed time that afternoon, a black town car picked us up and whisked us to the big airport. We waited in the terminal until our flight boarded and settled into our snug coach seats for the 10 hour flight to Rio. We were excited and a little tired after the whirlwind of events of the past 48 hours. The plane's cabin doors closed and the crew readied for takeoff. Then we heard this announcement.

"Will passenger Mr. Steven Yates please come to the front of the plane and see the head flight attendant."

My wife shot me a look of panic. I quickly got up and walked up to the front of the plane. I couldn't imagine what could possibly have gone wrong.

"Mr. Yates?" the flight attendant asked.

"Yes, I'm Steven Yates. What's the matter?" I asked, concerned.

"Varig Airlines wishes to congratulate you on your wedding and invites you and your wife to travel with us upstairs in the first class cabin," she said with a smile. She handed me a note from my dad that said that this was part of our wedding present.

A wave of relief came over me, followed by almost giddy excitement. I turned and looked for my wife who was leaning out into the aisle two dozen rows back wondering if we were being thrown off the plane. I motioned frantically for her to join me. She had no idea what I was trying to tell her.

I walked half-way back to her and yelled, "Grab our carry-on and follow me!" I had that funny feeling that if we hesitated for an instant the opportunity would evaporate.

I turned and followed the stewardess up a spiral staircase into the spacious, beautiful first class cabin. This was a 747. I had never even seen what was in that bulge at the top of the jumbo jet, much less imagined flying up there. As I was shown to our seats, I looked back and my poor wife was struggling up the twisted staircase carrying her carry-on bag and mine. She was a little angry and more than a little confused. The stewardess took our bags from her. I apologized and whispered to her that we had been upgraded to first class as I eased her into the large, comfortable leather seat and took my place next to her.

Neither of us had never flown first class before. I've only had the pleasure a few times since and I have flown a lot over the years. And while I have seen videos of ultra-first class "apartments" with showers and butler service on some high-end carriers and private jets today, the service we received then was a dream.

Before we had fully settled into our cushy seats, a lovely Brazilian flight attendant was offering us champagne. Not a glass each. A bottle to share. We accepted of course. Naturally, it came with a large pineapple onto which were skewered two dozen large cocktail shrimp. She gave us each a perfect rose and a box of chocolates. And this was all before the plane had left the ground.

My wife had forgiven me for making her haul our bags up to the first-class cabin by the time we had polished off the shrimp and champagne. Her mind was occupied on other things, like ordering dinner from the menu we were given and enjoying a cocktail with a nice, warm nut assortment.

The level of service was amazing. There were twelve seats in the luxurious cabin, only half of them occupied. And I never laid eyes on any of the other passengers such was the space between the rows and the arrangement of the seats. And every few minutes the lovely stewardess was back presenting us with little gifts and treats. Little velvet slippers? Check. Personal "comfort kit"? Check. (Not familiar with the personal "comfort kit"? It contains a sleep mask, nail clippers and file, hand lotion, cologne, earphones, etc.)

And the spacious tray table in front of each of us had its linen table cloth, placemat and napkins changed more quickly than we could soil them! Glassware, silverware, and dishes were whisked in and out and this was before we had even ordered dinner! Eventually, we made our selections, surf and turf for two accompanied by a nice, dry red wine. Of course, soup and salad came first, with a sorbet between courses to cleanse the palate. It would have been one the best meals I had ever eaten even if it had not been served at 30,000 feet.

By the time the Baked Alaska was served, I could tell my wife was getting sleepy. We kissed and she drifted off to sleep. I was surveying the selection of movies and wondered what other treats might be available. I asked my new best friend, the stewardess, if there was any beer to be had. Of course, there was. She recommended Brahma, a Brazilian brand that came in an enormous one-liter can. It was delicious. I imbibed as I watched my movie. As I got to the bottom of the can, it was miraculously replaced with a frosty-cold full one. I'm not sure how many times that miracle occurred because I, too, drifted off to sleep in this airborne nirvana.

When my wife and I awoke, a hot towel and a delicious hot breakfast was already set before us. We enjoyed slowly rousing and nibbling at the tropical fruits, eggs, bacon, sausage, and french toast. We reluctantly prepared for arrival in Rio and the movable feast wound down. Pulling ourselves together we awaited our ever-present flight attendant to cue us to disembark. But she never came. We luxuriated for a while longer, but eventually we got a bit restless. Standing up, we became aware that we were alone in our penthouse. I ventured down the spiral stairs and saw that the plane was empty. Completely empty.

We carried our things downstairs and exited the plane. We still did not see a soul. When we got to the concourse, there were only a few people purposefully walking by. All the signs were in Portuguese, but most of the arrows pointed in one direction and so we walked that way. Eventually we came to a counter at which stood serious-looking uniformed men with sidearms. It was passport control, we realized. We dug out our passports and showed them to the men, who spoke to us in Portuguese, a language neither my wife nor I understand. We smiled weakly at them and they spoke more Portuguese to us. We smiled again, shrugging and pointing to our passports. The men were now lecturing us in Portuguese about who-knows-what. They seemed to want something, but we had no idea what it was. It couldn't have been too important because after fifteen minutes, they simply gave us back our passports and waved us on. A bit dazed, and more than a little afraid, we made our way to the baggage area where our two suitcases stood out in the open by themselves. Odd. Now what?

We suddenly became aware that we were in a foreign country where we did not know a single person. We couldn't speak the language nor read any signs. We didn't know where our hotel was and even if we did, we had no idea how to get there. Oh, and we didn't have any local currency. "Helpless" sums it up nicely.

Out of nowhere stepped a woman who exclaimed, "You must be my two lost sheep! You've caused me a lot of trouble and worry! Shame on you! I am Lydia."

Then she laughed. She asked to see our tickets. I showed her the envelope my dad had given me and she dug out a slip of paper that I had overlooked. It was apparently a voucher for transport to our hotel.

I noticed the rather tough-looking man who was silently standing beside our potential savior. He was dressed in black and looked like a limo driver. He was completely bald and had a permanent sneer on his face.

"Give this man one hundred American dollars," Lydia said matter-of-factly.

I tightened up. This must be how the kidnap/mugging/torture/murder plot begins, I thought. My wife and I looked at each other. We had no choice. I handed my likely future murderer $100. He slipped it into his pocket as if he didn't want anyone to see and in the same motion brought out a huge wad of colored paper that he stuffed into my jacket pocket, all the while scanning the area to make sure he wasn't being observed.

"This is Max. He has given you 600,000 cruzados. This is a very good exchange rate, many times what you can get from the banks. Come along!" said Lydia, walking toward the exit.

We followed the woman who, for all we knew, was the only English-speaking person in Brazil, to a tiny van and piled in. She regaled us with information about Rio and warnings to avoid this and that area as Max drove like a maniac across the city. The airport was on the other side of the city from the famous beaches, where our hotel was located. We were not to worry about the dangerous-looking slums we were flying through at 60 miles per hour. But we were not to open the windows either. After forty minutes that seemed like two hours, we arrived at the Sheraton Copacabana. As we piled out of the tiny van, I heard a woman's voice calling my name.

"Mr. Yates! Mr. Yates!", cried a lovely, smartly-dressed woman. "You are Mr. and Mrs. Steven Yates, yes?"

We nodded.

"Oh, thank God. We were so worried. We were about to call the police. You were not with the other passengers from your flight. I was at the airport to greet you. Oh, thank God you are alright! I am so sorry. Please forgive me. I am

Anna-Maria. I am so terribly sorry that this is the way you have arrived in Rio."

Anna-Maria handed my wife a huge bouquet of roses and signaled a man to take all our baggage. Lydia started to get out of the van but Anna-Maria practically shoved her back in and closed the door.

"You will never see this awful woman again!" Anna-Maria said as the van sped off. "I am so sorry you had to meet her at all. I should have been there to greet you, but when you were not there I feared you had missed the flight so I called Texaco and they called New York. Your father must think we are terrible!"

She took us by the hands into the beautiful hotel lobby and sat us down on a sofa. There were suddenly drinks in our hands and a plate of fruit in front of us. Anna-Maria dashed off to call off the nationwide search that was doubtless underway to find the missing American VIPs. She was quickly back at our sides and was smiling warmly.

"Now, let's start again. Welcome to Brazil! Welcome to Rio! I am Anna-Maria and I am at your disposal every minute of the next week you are in our city. I am the secretary of Mr. Tocci, the Vice-President of Texaco Brazil, who sends his warmest regards and welcome."

Anna-Maria handed me a letter, on Texaco letterhead, from Mr. Tocci welcoming us and telling us that the resources of the company were at our disposal to assure that we had the best time possible while we were there. He apologized that the President of Texaco Brazil was out of the country and that he had not been present to meet us at the airport. It seems that Dad had put the "fix" in and the red carpet was being rolled out!

Anna-Maria got us checked into our room. She introduced us to Severino, the man who had taken our bags from the van. He was to be our driver for the week. Not only would we have Anna-Maria as our guide, on-call 24/7, but we would also have exclusive use of a car and driver, on-call 24/7. The only catch was that Severino did not speak a word of English. But we could call Anna-Maria, who would translate. Anna-Maria handed us an itinerary that had fun events mapped out for the week. There was a cruise on the bay with swimming, a trip to Sugarloaf Mountain, a soccer game at the world's largest stadium, and dinner out every night at the best restaurants in town. We could do as much or as little as we liked. She took us up to our room which had a huge fruit basket and more flowers, compliments of Texaco, left us with a phone number to contact her, and was gone. Whew! Welcome to Rio!

Over the next week we had a wonderful time seeing the sights, relaxing on the beautiful beaches and eating sumptuous meals. My wife and I ventured out alone with Severino to the beach each day and for one meal at the famous Hippopotamus Club and some shopping, but we called Anna-Maria to be with us for most of our excursions. I remember seeing the concrete Christ on Corcovado Mountain and taking the cable car up to the breath-taking evening view from Sugarloaf.

Perhaps the most fun was seeing a soccer match between two local teams at Maracaña Stadium. It seemed almost empty even though there were 20,000 fans there. The stadium held 100,000. Anna-Maria warned me not to wear anything resembling "team colors" as fans could be a bit crazy. She wasn't kidding. The fans of each team were separated by a ten-foot high fence topped with razor wire. And the playing field was separated from the stands by a concrete moat twenty feet wide and twenty feet deep. The players emerged onto the field via underground tunnels. And the upper rim of the stadium was a paved road. Constantly circling the crowd looking down for any sign of trouble was a military jeep with a fifty-caliber machine gun mounted in the back! However, the game proceeded without incident. And the passion that the Cariocas (Rio residents) had for their teams was contagious.

Our final night in Rio we went to the apartment of a wealthy friend of Anna-Maria, Isidore. He was an older gentleman who was eager to show off his beautiful home and all of its features from the walk-in fridge to the pile of Persian rugs in his living room. Isidore was very well connected. I think he might have been involved in our getting upgraded to first class on the flight down. He was pleased to hear we had enjoyed the first-class treatment, but dismayed that we might be flying home in coach. He began making calls and assured us that this would not stand.

Our flight out was an evening flight and we had to vacate our hotel room by noon, so we were invited to stay at the home of Mr. Tocci for the day. It was a lovely downtown apartment. Mr. Tocci himself came by at lunchtime to greet us and make sure we had enjoyed Rio. We gave him a glowing report. I said I was sad to have to go back to the States. He asked if we would like to stay and live in Rio. He was serious. He said he could help me find a job there. My wife and I looked at each other, but decided that it was best if we returned to our lives and enjoyed our perfect memories of the Brazilian paradise. That night Isidore was at the airport with us and he apologized profusely for only being able to get us upgraded to Business Class! No apology needed.

I have to say, though, that while we were well-insulated,

it was obvious that Rio is a city of the very rich and the very poor. And we enjoyed, mostly guilt-free, living like the very rich for the week. But, ever-present, in the distance were steep mountainsides rising up surrounding Rio. And clinging to those cliffs were tumble-down shacks, a shantytown, the *favelas*. More like a shanty-city. The poverty in Rio was so profound and such an insoluble problem that the government had actually completed a program of painting the shacks bright colors so that they would appear like gaily-colored bungalows in the distance, rather than the hopeless slums that they were.

It is strange how the mind works. I was aware of the poverty there. Mostly I was afraid of the extreme violence that I had heard it occasionally spawned. As we basked in the Brazilian sun on a nearly deserted Ipanema Beach one hot and sultry weekday afternoon, I saw a vendor selling beer perhaps twenty yards from us. I walked over and used my few newly-acquired words of Portuguese to ask for a "*cerveja*". The man handed me a liter-bottle of ice-cold Brahma Beer. I held out my hand with a few dollars worth of Brazilian coins in it. He picked out about fifty cents worth and thanked me. Fifty cents for a liter of excellent beer on the beach! What a bargain!

I returned to my wife and enjoyed polishing off the delicious brew in a few minutes under the beating sun. I sat the empty bottle off to one side, intending to put it in a trash can when we left. The beer vendor came by a little while later and took back the bottle. I thought that is was very responsible of him to help keep the beach clean in that way. Then he returned and handed me several Brazilian coins. It was the deposit on the bottle. Based on my understanding of the coins, it was about twenty cents. The beer had only cost thirty cents! I had another one and marveled at the value.

Later, I considered the more sober reality of the situation. The beer vendor couldn't have made more than a dollar or two in the several hours we were there. And I was told that beach vendor was a sought-after job and that only a precious few licenses were granted for people to operate on the famed Rio beaches. Such vendors were monitored closely for honesty lest they upset any of the valued tourists. It was likely that this friendly man would spend all day in the sun catering to tourists like me and then return home to one of the shantytown shacks with barely enough profit from his day's work to feed himself, never mind any family he might have.

The Brazil that we saw was beautiful. The people were friendly and celebrated living in such a beautiful, tropical place by dancing the samba of their neighborhoods with pride in contests against dancers from other areas. They were beyond passionate about their local and national soccer teams. And they worshiped the Brazilian racecar drivers who risked death for thrills and fortune. Their lives seemed fueled by the desire to live every moment to the fullest and to find every bit of joy available to them. Perhaps desperation and the drive to escape was behind that desire. Whatever the case, it made for a unique flavor and an unforgettable experience.

LESS IS MORE

I've always said that I can live anywhere. Having moved so much when I was growing up and always being happy, I don't think it's the location that determines happiness. There are happy and miserable people in every town, so it's not the town. Maybe some people aren't suited to big city or small town life, but for me, it doesn't matter. And I also believe that you live on the inside of your home. If you have a room, or a corner of a room, that's yours, that you can make into what you want it to be, then you can be happy there no matter what's just outside of your door.

And maybe the logical extension of that line of reasoning is that you live inside your head. If you can find peace within yourself, then maybe it doesn't matter where your house is, nor if you have a corner in it that's yours. There is a nascent movement that seeks to educate people that happiness comes from within and not from external things, particularly material possessions, and definitely not from having large quantities of excess, disposable, mass-produced, consumer goods that go out of fashion quickly so that they can be replaced with the next new thing. This can be summed up by my wife's favorite phrase, "Less is more."

We lived in a four bedroom, two-and-a-half bath home on 2.3 wooded acres in rural Connecticut for 22 years. The local schools were good. There was virtually no crime. It was an idyllic place to raise our two children. It was a domestic paradise in many ways. The street was quiet with a dozen other homes like ours filled with a dozen other families like ours. It was the only home our children ever knew. It was one town over from my wife's hometown. When we moved there she felt like she was going home. I had a basement "man cave" that I filled with baseball cards, comic books, my music and video collections, and a comfy couch to enjoy them all from.

When I first laid eyes on the house, the deceptively spacious cape was 99% complete. The developer had used it as his model home as he sold the other lots on the street intending to allow the eventual buyer to choose the fixtures and some floor coverings to make it their own. It was at the very top of our price range. My mom and dad lived an hour south and they came house-hunting with us and their experienced eyes could see this was the place for us. Dad took me aside and told me as much. They would help us and make sure we could make the payments. They wanted us in this new house rather than one of the smaller, older colonials they had seen.

And so it was that we moved in in the spring of 1991. It seemed so big and empty, but we quickly filled it with love and in time filled it with stuff. Baby stuff gave way to kid stuff. Kid stuff to adolescent stuff, then teen stuff. The garage, then a garden shed, housed a push mower that gave way to a lawn tractor and a wood chipper, garden cart, chain saw, snow-thrower and every other power tool needed to maintain "the spread". My wife built gardens on every level area of the property. Wooded areas were cleared for more gardens. It was beautiful. We put in a pool and build a deck around it. It was home to birthday parties, holiday gatherings, graduation celebrations, and more. Twenty years passed like an afternoon.

Before our time in that house, I had never lived anywhere more than four years. I moved in an eager young man of 30 and seemingly overnight found myself at 50 wondering where the time had gone. That year my wife's beloved brother passed away suddenly. She became understandably deeply contemplative. One morning she came to me and laid it all out. She had always wanted to live near the water. Long Island Sound, only a few miles away, was calling to her. She had done some research and found a quaint, little neighborhood between a cove off the Connecticut River and the Sound. It was a quick walk to either or both, any time we wanted. And there was a tidy, little cottage that was priced just right. We could swing this. Was I OK with it? Without a moment's hesitation I said yes. The thought of moving hadn't crossed my mind in two decades and I was ready to go in under a minute.

We bought the "beach house" before the realtor could even finish his pitch. We "camped" in it every weekend we could. Our son would be graduating from high school in May, so we wouldn't be moving in until after that. After several "camping weekends", we realized that we would have to downsize our possessions substantially and that the little beach house would need a significant addition/remodel/update. This was going to be a process. But we began the process right away.

The beach house lacked a garage and a master bedroom of sufficient size. We found a great architect who designed the addition. Before it was done, it would include finishing the basement, rewiring the entire house and gutting almost every room in it. The little 1959-era cottage "had good bones", but little else. The architect not only created the design, but he acted as construction manager for the work.

Digression - We had a three-way contract amongst the builder/general contractor, the architect, and ourselves. This ended up being the most important thing we did right in the whole process. All of the work done by the builder or his sub-contractors was subject to inspection, sometimes unannounced inspection, by the architect and his experts. All of the bills submitted by the builder or his sub-contractors were reviewed and approved by the architect before we paid them. The architect was an experienced, trained expert in every aspect of the project. He assisted in the design from the paint color scheme to door knob and drawer pull selection. It was not a free service, but it was worth every penny, many times over.

How do I know it was worth it? Most of the builders

I have talked with HATE the idea. That's how. Now, I'm sure that the vast majority of builders/general contractors are highly-educated, highly-skilled, honest, professionals who strive to provide their clients with high-quality work at an affordable price through constant, open communication that is documented and memorialized as part of fair, legally-binding contracts. But there may be a very few builders/general contractors who don't adhere to the highest ethical and professional standards. Such individuals, if they even exist, don't appreciate having their work checked, their bills questioned, their adherence to agreements monitored, or any oversight at all by knowledgable parties. Such dastardly operators, if they are out there, count on their clients' ignorance, trust, and inability or unwillingness to challenge them once the job has begun because doing so may result in costly delays or "change orders".

Through the use of an architect and the three-way contract we put into practice the policy articulated by President Reagan with regard to the Soviets, "Trust, but verify." - End of digression.

Before work could begin, we had to present the plans to the local Zoning Board of Appeals (ZBA). These individuals, working as volunteers on behalf of the town, are charged with approving or rejecting plans that call for any sort of exception to local building codes. Such exceptions are granted only on the basis of "hardships". Suffice it to say that their work involves some measure of subjective judgement that greatly impacts the lives of property owners of the town. Our architect presented the plans and, after a bit of redesign, they passed. Whew!

The work began in August and would be finished in

mid-December. We had that long to "skinny" our possessions down so they would fit, even into the somewhat expanded beach house. It was at about this time that I experienced a series of revelations.

First, I realized that I had become a collector, an accumulator, not quite a hoarder. I had begun over the years since I left my parent's home collecting music, first records and then CDs. I collected movies and TV shows, taped from the air, then on DVDs. I began collecting comic books and baseball cards in an effort to recapture my childhood. Of course, like many people, I had a personal library of books and magazines. And I had boxes of memorabilia from my past. As a family, we had collected furniture, photographs, artwork, clothes, and family heirlooms of different sorts. Some of this stuff could be compacted. CDs and DVDs came in bulky packaging that could be discarded. The discs fit into notebooks reducing their volume to a fraction of what it had been. Photos could be digitized. Even my beloved t-shirts could simply be photographed. Their specialness was in their graphics which could be preserved forever digitally taking up virtually no space at all. But what of the rest?

This was when the second revelation came to me. Value was ephemeral for the most part. Furniture that my parents had given me, that I imbued with sentimental talismanic value, was simply used furniture to everyone else on earth. It could only be sold for a token amount, and only if a buyer could be found. Even charitable organizations didn't want most of it. Some day, we had envisioned passing these treasures on to our children as if they were dreaming of furnishing their homes with out-of-date, out-of-style relics that weren't even technically antiques. And these things would have to be stored until the time was right for this passing on, should it ever occur. And so much of what we had accumulated was given to Goodwill or simply thrown away. The amazing thing to me was how little I missed most of these things. My beloved comic books, over 20,000 of them, and my complete Topps baseball card sets for twenty consecutive years were donated and I have yet to shed a tear for them. I had gotten my use out of them and now, presumably, it's someone else's turn.

The third revelation was this. Not only did I not miss the things I got rid of, getting rid of them actually made me happier! Karl Marx said that the more you own, the more you are owned. And darned if he wasn't right! Having fewer possessions filling closets and cabinets and boxes made me feel lighter, more nimble, more in control of my life. Instead of a half-dozen boxes of childhood detritus, I have one. Much of what I got rid of were souvenirs of events that weren't worth remembering. Getting rid of old clothes that I never liked in the first place felt wonderful! Once I realized that I could not recover the money I had spent on a pair of ill-fitting acid-washed jeans it felt great to remove them from my life. The drawers of my dresser became half-full, rather than jam-packed. My closet became easy to search through. The junk drawer that was full of stuff that was truly junk was a joy to empty into the trash! And I haven't missed one of those miscellaneous nuts, bolts, widgets, used batteries, or doo-hickies yet. I doubt I ever will.

And the final revelation was that now I had emptied my life of so much stuff that was not important to me, that I didn't want or need, I should try not to simply re-accumulate any more. In the beach house there simply wasn't room for more stuff, so I stopped collecting. A public library is a great way to enjoy every book, CD, and DVD ever made without having to keep and store them all. And the money I have saved by stopping the collecting habit helps offset the money I stopped making when I retired in 2011.

An addendum to all this disgorging of physical items is the analogy we figured out about information. Just as I compulsively collected things, I compulsively collected information, specifically news and opinions. When our cable TV bill topped $250 a month, my wife and I had a talk about it. We weren't watching 90% of the channels we were paying for. And we could still find plenty to watch online thanks to the internet without cable TV. And I realized that the hours of news and opinion that I was passively consuming was a source not of enlightenment, but of depression. And most of that news did not directly affect me. It wasn't useful. And the opinions, the debates, were simply an endless recycling of anger and bias and "hurray for our side". I had had enough. I continue to train myself to turn away from the news and turn toward uplifting art, literature, spirituality, and people. And I tell everyone who will listen to try doing the same. As with the furniture I never sat on, the clothes I never wore, and the nuts and bolts I never found a use for, I have not yet missed the sound and fury of the public forum at all. I did watch a hawk circling in the sky and then land in our oak tree this afternoon and I saw several deer grazing in the wetlands beyond our backyard. They were beautiful.

And so we moved our stripped-down inventory of stuff into our new-old beach cottage. My wife has a few smaller gardens that she enjoys. I write and try to play my guitar. I listen to a wide variety of music. And we enjoy watching our children as they embark on their lives' journeys. We find our happiness in helping others and worshiping at our church. I guess I'm becoming more like my beloved grandparents whose simple lives of pleasant routine seemed so attractive to me when I was a child. The less stuff that clutters my life, the more I can see the rich and wonderful life I've been privileged to live, the more I can remember the people I love, and the more I look forward to what's coming next.

Pseudoscience

I'm too young to have lived through the golden age of patent medicines. In historical documentaries one hears about over-the-counter medicines that were common not so long ago that contained everything from heroin and cocaine to mercury and arsenic. These compounds could be purchased by anyone and used however they saw fit to treat maladies ranging from "dispepsic malaise" to tuberculosis. It doesn't seem like a bad thing that the Food and Drug Administration has taken these products out of the hands of John Q. Public.

As a child, I remember seeing only a few of the weakest remnants of these "medicines". One was Dr. Tichenor's Antiseptic Mouthwash. My grandmother had an ancient bottle of this peppermint-smelling solution in her medicine cabinet. Curiously, I recall it being applied to mosquito bites and never used as a mouthwash. Another was Dickinson's Pure All-Purpose Witch-hazel. I never really knew what it was used for, but because the word "witch" was part of the name I thought it best to steer clear.

These particular products aside, I can imagine a simpler time when folks did not have access to proper modern medical care and would utilize patent medicines, folk remedies, and such to treat conditions, real or imagined, trivial or serious, on their own, a practice that seems potentially fraught with danger. I suspect the literature would confirm this fear. Thankfully those days are mostly behind us, or are they?

I confess to being, or having been, a scientist and chemical engineer by education and vocation. I believe in the scientific method and I like to think I can sniff out hooey, bunkum, and baloney when it's being peddled as science, but it's not always easy. I worked in the solid waste (garbage) and wastewater (sewage) businesses for over fifteen years. As you can imagine, odor and odor control are topics closely allied to these industries. And as you can further imagine, there is an army of salesmen out there ready to provide products and services to address the problems that foul odors can create.

I was working at one trash facility that had a big public relations problem with neighbors who complained about the smell. And so a solicitation to solve this problem was written and made public. And the bids and proposals began to come in. I was tasked with reviewing many of these. I noted that many of these companies tried to differentiate themselves from their competition by claiming that their product did not simply "mask" odors, as did the inferior products on the market, but "eliminated" odors through science! They never provided details about the science. When queried, they would offer to give a demonstration.

We chose two of these companies to provide demonstrations. We had large metal roll-off bins similar in size and shape to those overseas shipping cargo containers you may have seen. The two bins we set aside had been used to hold raw municipal solid waste, aka garbage. They stank. I mean, they wreaked to high heaven. Each odor control company made a presentation. Honestly, they need not have bothered.

Over the years, I've developed something of a distaste for certain kinds of salesmen. I guess as with any profession there are bad ones out there mixed in with the good. But if I have a serious problem, I don't need a smile and a smooth line of patter, I need a solution. I think of it like I think of doctors. I want the best doctor. If he or she has a good bedside manner, that's swell, but the skill matters most.

I sat through two separate presentations each of which was chock full of anecdotal stories and testimonials of companies their products had saved. In particular, one fellow had a story of de-skunk-ifying a Maine Coon Hound that he seemed to think would "wow" me. After most of an hour they would pause and ask for questions. I asked each salesman one question. How does your product work? You'd think that would be a question they would have a ready and understandable answer for. You'd be wrong. I heard an outpouring of buzzwords and scientific sounding phrases. Enzymes. Ionic attraction. Molecular neutralization. Schwanamaker's pairing.

"I'm sorry. I'm just a simple chemical engineer. You're going to have to dumb this down for me. Enzymes act as catalysts to speed up chemical reactions. What's the reaction? Ions are charged particles. What ions are we talking about? What are the charges? And to what are they attracted? Exactly what molecule is neutralizing what? Is it an acid-base neutralization? What is the acid? What is the base? And, forgive my ignorance, but what is Schwanamaker's pairing and how does it eliminate odor?"

These straight-forward questions were met at first with silence, then more buzzwords, and finally some major-league double-talk. I pushed a blank paper and pen across the table.

"Just write down the chemical reactions that eliminate the odor-causing compounds," I said.

One fellow gave me a blank stare for the ages. The other told me that I was asking for proprietary information. I offered to sign a secrecy agreement. He said that his company's lawyers would have to draw something up. This had never been done before. I told him there would be no purchase until I understood the science behind how the product worked. Both salesmen told me that I would be so blown away by their demonstration that I would beg them to sell me their product. I pointed each of them to a roll-off bin. Each one deployed his product inside his respective bin and closed it up. We would reconvene in 24 hours to sniff the results. Each salesman left me with a little bottle of his product. One smelled of lemon and flowers and the other had a mild "fresh linen" smell, kind of like detergent. The salesman called it "the smell of clean". Wow.

The next day only one of the salesmen returned. The other did not respond to phone calls or emails. At the insistence of the salesman who was present, we checked the absent salesman's roll-off bin first. It smelled strongly of garbage with faint notes of lemon and flowers. Not compelling. We closed it up. The salesman who did return proudly opened his roll-off bin. It smelled slightly less strongly of garbage. He claimed victory and asked for the sale. I told him I would get back to him.

As I thought about the demonstration, I recalled the phenomenon of "olfactory fatigue" and realized why the salesman who was present wanted us to smell the other salesman's bin first. My nose had gotten a strong whiff of garbage from that first bin and so was a little desensitized to it when we opened the second. I called one of my colleagues over and had him smell the bins in the reverse order. He concluded that they both still smelled of garbage, but he thought the lemon and flowers bin smelled a little less.

In a follow-up call to the salesman who had claimed victory and asked for the sale, I repeated my request for literature references to "Schwanamaker's pairing". He promised I'd get something soon. He faxed me a third-generation photocopy of an article about weak electrical effects in liquid systems, also known as "surface tension". It was not what I was looking for.

In the end we found that improved processing practices like moving the oldest garbage out first and keeping the facility doors closed on windy days reduced the number of odor complaints from our neighbors more than anything else we tried.

I was reminded of this episode the other day when I was accosted at my gym by a young "bro" who, out of nowhere, in response to no questions, began proselytizing about his vegan lifestyle.

"Are you a vegan, Bro? I am. It's the only way to go. I was 260 lbs. three years ago. I should be dead, but I gave up the meat and look at me," he said lifting up his shirt to show me his abs.

"You gotta give up the meat, Bro. It poisons the enzymes that metabolize your muscle growth. Meat just feeds the parasites in your system, bro. It's the worst. And alcohol is the double-whammy. You have to quit the alcohol. I did. Alcohol nullifies all muscle-growth metabolism, Bro. Reverses it! It's the worst, Bro. I start every day with a green drink to detox. Gotta neutralize the toxins, Bro. Then I mash up five avocados in some quinoa and kale and run that through the juicer, Bro. And look at me," he said, this time showing me his biceps muscle.

"I grow my own parsley and oregano. I'd grow all my food if I could. Hydroponics, Bro. And high-nutrient organic fertilizers, all-natural, Bro. Boosts the anti-oxidants that really crush the toxins. All food should be grown that way. That's how I'd do it if I could grow all my food, Bro. I'd grow something else too, Bro. But that's not legal yet, but soon, am I right? You know it, Bro."

"Hey, Bro, I gotta bounce, but you should totally give up the meat and the alcohol, Bro. They're killing ya, Bro. All the work you're doing here in the gym is wasted, Bro. Hate to tell ya, Bro. But it's true. The meat and the alcohol undo it all and reverse it! Shame, Bro. Think about it. I'm out, Bro."

I hadn't said a word. I don't think I even nodded. Except that I didn't want our "conversation" to last a second more than it had, I would have loved to pick apart the nonsense he was preaching so fervently.

Where did you go to medical school? The University of Mars? And you are a licensed dietician? No? Then you must have an analytical chemistry or biochemistry background, right? No, Bro? And what are the toxins in your body that you are fighting? How did they get there? Do you have any lab test results? And what double-blind, peer-reviewed study confirms any of the baloney you're claiming? And you're telling me I've got *parasites*? Based on what? And by what mechanism does alcohol "nullify" muscle growth? What does that even mean? And you're going to grow your own food? How? Do you have farming experience or a degree in Biology? Botany? Horticulture? And you're saying you want to grow marijuana?

How does that impact your muscle growth metabolism, parasites, and toxins, Bro?

This guy may have been a harmless stoner, but he was preaching the kind of pseudo-science that is everywhere. And we all fall victim to it. No one has time to do all the research on everything. We all rely on friends, family, advisors, and the media to provide us with news and information. But we have to filter all that stuff very carefully. Once you let a bad idea into your mind it's hard to get it out.

And lot of smart people can fall prey to pseudo-science because of a distrust of traditional institutions like the medical profession, big business, the military, or the government. Any time one of our trusted institutions lets us down through ineptitude or corruption, a flood of folks rush in to offer their conspiracy theory and alternative lifestyle solution.

Don't trust the military after Vietnam or the government after Watergate? Then become a self-sufficient, well-armed survivalist.

Don't trust the food supply because of agricultural conglomerates and GMOs? Grow your own super-foods in the basement.

Don't trust your doctor because he has lunch with the pharmaceutical salesman? Self-medicate with native herbs and detoxify with a "cleanse" and enema.

Never mind that you may lack the training to properly convert your home into a fortress, or to safely grow food on a subsistence-level. And a few pamphlets are all you need to fend off diseases and treat serious life-threatening conditions, right? Medical school, schmedical school! What is the medical definition of a cleanse? Who cares? It sounds healthy (or at least clean!).

I'll point out that I am not a doctor, or a farmer, or a military man so please don't listen to me. Just be careful who you *do* listen to. And if you hear yourself giving out advice that you can't back up with facts, maybe say that, so the next person in the chain of mis-information doesn't end up using *your* patent medicine.

Fighting the Last War

There is nothing more comforting than getting good advice from someone you can trust who is "in the know". Each of us has limitations on our knowledge and experience. Being able to take advantage of someone else's knowledge and experiences allows us to reach beyond our limitations. It's like looking through a powerful telescope to reveal what you could not otherwise see. It almost feels like cheating.

Now that the statute of limitations has run out, I can admit that several of my classmates and I "borrowed" the answer book for our Heat, Mass, and Momentum Transfer chemical engineering class. "Transfer" was a key, very difficult class, taught by the author of the text, who was surely brilliant in his day and was equally surely not a great teacher by the time I met him. His class was a "weeding out" class. If you could not pass "Transfer", you were not going to get a chemical engineering degree at UConn. Having the answer book, guaranteed us full points on our homework assignments, which counted for close to half of the final grade in the class.

We borrowed the book with the professor's permission although he may have thought it was a more short-term loan. And we returned the book the day after the term ended. I know that I passed that course on the strength of my homework grades because my exam grades were dismal. Having the advantage of the answer book made all the difference because the professor taught the same course the same way as he had done since he wrote the text many, many years before. His "inertia" meant that the answers that worked in 1969, worked for me in 1980. Life is not always that way.

Long digression - In the spring of 1984, I was in a corporate softball league. Our team was good and we had a blast playing softball and even more fun having pizza and beer afterward. One evening I was driving home after pizza and beer. The car in front of me signaled for and made a right turn. Unbeknownst to me, he then made a u-turn and darted back across the road. I hit him broadside without braking at 35 to 40 miles per hour. I remember seeing the driver directly in front of me as the terrible sound of crushing metal and shattering glass exploded in my ears. I felt the shoulder belt tug violently against my chest. I didn't know it at the time, but it had, in that moment, done two things. First, it saved my life by keeping me from flying into and through my own windshield. Second, it had given me a "green-stick" fracture of the sternum. Fair trade.

My car spun a full three hundred-sixty degrees and came to rest against the curb. My first thought was that I had just killed the driver of the other car. It took me a minute or two to undo my seatbelt and force my driver's side door open. I staggered out onto the road dazed. A good samaritan who had been driving behind me and saw the whole thing approached me and told me to sit down. I leaned on him and asked if the other driver was dead. He sat me on the grass at the side of the road and told me that he had seen the other driver and he looked fine, better than me.

The ambulance arrived and took me to the hospital where

my fractured sternum was diagnosed. I was put in the intensive care unit for observation. A doctor there told me that I was in shock and should rest. He gave me Percocet and I laid back on the bed. I was aware of another patient in the room with me. He was quiet. I assumed he was asleep and I closed my eyes. A moment later, a nurse roused me and took blood from both my arms and took my blood pressure in both arms. She explained that they were concerned about damage to my heart after the impact and chest trauma caused by the seatbelt. She left and I closed my eyes again.

It was hard to relax, but I tried. Just as I began to drift off to sleep another nurse arrived and she took blood from both my arms and took my blood pressure in both arms. This was done hourly for the next twenty-four hours, thus preventing any REM sleep at all. As I settled into this unsettling routine, a loud klaxon sounded and my room quickly filled with people and equipment. The heart of the man in the other bed had stopped. I was groggy, but aware enough to be traumatized by the real-life version of what I had seen on TV a hundred times. The man in the other bed died. As the equipment and personnel exited the room, an ER nurse came over to me and told me that everything was fine and I should relax and rest. Sure. No problem.

Eventually I was transferred to another room that I shared with another man who did not die. The blood-letting and blood pressure-taking frequency decreased. I got some sleep and began to feel better. Except when I sneezed. The doctors go into great detail telling patients suffering from a green-stick fracture of the sternum what that means. The ribcage that protects all your vital organs flexes in a way that is better than if it were to simply shatter, in the same way a green stick bends, but does not break. They don't tell you that if you sneeze, you will involuntarily flex the ribcage again causing a sharp, blinding pain unlike anything you've ever felt before. I guess they want you to figure that out for yourself.

A day or two later, it dawned on me that, because of the way things had happened all I had with me were the clothes I had been wearing after the softball game. I was in a backless hospital gown and my three day old jockey shorts. I got to a phone and called my parents who were out of town. I left a message telling them I was hurt, but recovering in a New Jersey hospital. I called my fiancé and told her the same. Finally, I called a friend at work and asked him to relay information about my status to my boss. He asked if I could receive visitors and I told him I could.

That afternoon, he and several other folks from work (and the softball team) came to see me. It was good to see people that I knew. They brought me flowers. We chatted. Then they had to go. Before they left I told my friend I needed a word with him in private. As the others waited outside the room, I asked him to give me his underwear as the ones I was wearing were days old and rapidly acquiring a life of their own. He refused. Right then I clearly saw that in life there are friends and then there are friends who will give you their underwear. He was one of the former.

I recovered without lasting effects. The driver of the other car, who was not wearing a seatbelt, was found to be at fault. He had neither a license, nor registration, nor insurance. Oh, and he was also found to be intoxicated and he was completely uninjured. Clean living pays off? The point of this digression is that I now needed a new car. - End of long digression.

A few weeks after I was discharged from the hospital, I was shopping for a new car. My dad was with me and helping me through the process. I settled on a 1984 Thunderbird Turbo Coupe in "bright canyon red". It was an awesome-looking sports car with a black interior, power-everything, five-speed stick shift, and a turbo-charged engine that had power to burn. I loved it. Dad took me to lunch before we closed the deal.

My dad was a pretty quiet guy. He didn't just talk to fill the silence. He spoke when he had something to say. He was considered, deliberate, intelligent and insightful. He made careful studies of any decision, especially any decision that involved spending money. I asked his advice. What did he think of the car?

"Steve, I would never buy this car," he said frankly, looking me squarely in the eyes.

I was crushed. I guess we would have to keep shopping. I had already had daydreams about how everyone would envy me in my hot, new wheels. I pictured myself visiting friends and having them come out to the street, whistling and walking around my T-bird in awe.

"Why not, Dad?" I finally asked. I knew he must have seen some fatal flaw in the car's design or had some other sensible reason why this was not the car for me.

"This car is a two-door. I like a four-door. It has a manual transmission. I prefer an automatic. It has a black interior. That could get hot in the summer. It's too sporty and not really a practical car for me," he said.

He could see the crushing disappointment on my face. And so he continued.

"But this car isn't for me. It's for you. I'm 48. You're 24. If you like it, that's all that matters. If you like it, let's buy it!"

And I smiled at him and to this day, it's one of the memories of my dad that is frozen in my mind. He looked so sharp in his suit. He was smart and confident and wise. And he loved me and wanted me to be happy. There just couldn't be a better dad. And he knew that the perfect car for a son might wasn't necessarily the perfect car for his father.

Spoiler alert. That generation of T-Birds were not great cars. They were good-looking, expensive to maintain, and they fell apart within about five years. I enjoyed it while it lasted. I'll wager there are more 1959 Edsels on the road than there are 1984 T-Bird Turbos.

Just a year or two later I found myself at a career crossroads. I had been laid off from my first job shortly after I got the T-Bird. I quickly found work with a competitor of my former employer, but that company turned out to be poorly run and they treated their people even worse. I was ready to jump ship and I asked my dad's advice. He had been, at that point, with the same company for nearly forty years. In that time he had steadily advanced from entry-level to top management. He was well-respected in the company and across the oil industry world-wide. When it came to business, few men were as successful as my dad. What did he think?

"Steve, you should think long and hard before quitting. This will be three jobs in a little over four years for you. You don't want to get a reputation as a "job-hopper". I see many resumes of engineers your age cross my desk. One of the things we look carefully at is if they are committed to their jobs. If we see that they change jobs frequently, it doesn't look good. Maybe you should tough it out for a while longer," he said.

It felt like a body-blow. I was miserable in my job. Each day was a stressful, anxious marathon of angst. Layoffs were talked about constantly. Management found new ways to squeeze more time and effort from every employee. Everyone who could find another job, left. Skilled engineers were not only leaving, some were changing professions to get away. This wasn't me "job-hopping". This was me getting off the Titanic before it slammed into that iceberg. I ended up leaving. And a year later I left *that* new company for yet another job, this time to return to Connecticut so we could raise our kids there.

It turned out that over the years I would change jobs several more times. By the time I retired from engineering, I had, in a little less than thirty years, changed jobs six times. Dad ended up working only for Texaco for forty-five years. But I got my biggest pay increases when I changed jobs. And I was not alone. My colleagues did the same. It was an industry trend that continues to this day. Had Dad been wrong? Was he giving me bad advice?

I don't think Dad was giving me bad advice. He was giving me the benefit of the knowledge and experience he had acquired in his lifetime. But he didn't have experience in changing companies. And much of the knowledge he had was out-of-date. Just like with the T-Bird, he was speaking to me from his perspective, which was what I wanted. But like the T-Bird, I had to make my own decision based on my situation, which I knew better than anyone, even my wise and thoughtful dad.

His insights and opinions were valuable. They were like a telescope that allowed me to see beyond my experience. But there is a funny thing about telescopes. As they peer out into the universe they can see the light of very distant stars. That light, as fast as it travels, may have taken millions of years to get to the lens of the telescope. The star whose light is reaching the telescope today may have, in the course of those millions of years, burned out long ago. It may not even exist any more.

They say that military men are always prepared to fight the last war rather than the next one. The generals are prisoners of their experience. They know what worked before in a life-or-death struggle and are reluctant to abandon that. They don't want to let go of their trusty rifles even if the next enemy may be armed with ray-guns.

I find myself in that same trap. My kids are grown and out in the workforce. Like any good dad, I want to help them if I can. But my knowledge is dated. What I once knew as state-of-the-art, high-tech jargon is now so antiquated that my kids can only learn about it in history books. And yet I squirm in my seat, eager to give them the benefit of my hard-won knowledge and experience even though I know it's useless telling them how to succeed in 1987. Instead I try to listen to them and offer a little common sense and wisdom about human nature. Maybe some day they'll be wondering why they ever listened to their old dad after he had been out of the game for so long. Maybe they'll think of me the way I thought of that chemical engineering professor who taught the same course the same way for twenty-five years.

Like sailors venturing out onto uncharted seas, each of us must make his own way. Once out of sight of land, we have no choice but to proceed. At such times, even if the advice of our aged counsellor may be obsolete, it's comforting to have at least that. It's a milestone of maturation to be able to carefully examine such advice and sort out the timeless wisdom from the dated knowledge. As anyone who has ever used a GPS knows, it pays to keep one's head up and eyes open and sometimes ignore the device and trust your gut.

MAN ABOUT CHURCH

There's a great O. Henry story called "Man About Town". A newspaper reporter is assigned to write a story about the kind of stylish *bon vivant* young men who frequent the best restaurants and clubs and are seen with the best kind of people. He dons his finest clothes so as to fit in and he sets out to find such a fellow. He interviews bartenders, doormen, and waiters. They tell him about such men, but can never name or point out any to him. For weeks he haunts the finest restaurants and the trendiest clubs and befriends the tony upper crust folk who know "men about town". One evening he is hit by a car as he dashes from one club to another. The patented "O. Henry twist ending" comes as he reads about his accident in his own newspaper and sees himself described as a "typical man about town".

This theme is echoed in Woody Allen's film *Zelig* in which Allen plays a "human chameleon" who takes on the characteristics of any group of people he spends time with. This is taken to an extreme in the movie when he hangs out with a group of black jazz musicians and actually becomes one! In the end, his character and the psychologist who is studying him fall in love, which suggests that love may simply be a natural result of similarity and/or familiarity.

When I graduated from high school and went off to college, without much thought, I also kind of graduated from my church. I had been baptized, raised, and confirmed in the Protestant church. My parents took my sisters and me to church most Sundays. As we moved around Texas, the US and even overseas, they sought out Protestant churches to attend and by their example raised three kids who all claimed the Christian faith as their own. My sisters and I sang in church choirs and belonged to church youth groups. My dad worked on church committees and Mom participated in Bible study and took her turn supplying refreshments for the youth groups.

But when I left for college I began a period of more than twenty years during which I attended church services only a handful of times. I still believed in God. I had a Bible that I moved from apartment to apartment with me, although it didn't get much use. I prayed, mostly when I felt troubled or needed help. But I got used to having Sunday mornings free.

I kept pretty busy, maybe so that I wouldn't think about

what was missing from my life. I was focused on my career, my apartment, my hobbies of music, sports, TV, and going to the gym. And I was focused on my girlfriend, who became my fiancé and, ultimately, my wife. It seemed I was constantly driving to and from her place or to and from my friends' places. I easily filled my time with frivolous amusements. There didn't seem to be any harm in it. My time was my own, right?

After eight years away from the church, I got married. My wife insisted it should be in a Greek Orthodox church as that was the faith she had been brought up in. I had no issue with that. One church was as good as another, I'm sure I thought. The kindly priest's only question to me was if I had been baptized in the name of the Holy Trinity. I told him I had and that was that. As our children arrived, they were each baptized in the Greek Orthodox church, again at my wife's insistence and again with no protest from me. It was only after the kids got a bit older that my wife told me that she wanted to start taking them to church. I'm sure I justified my staying home by citing the long, hard hours I worked to support the family. Besides, all the best sports were on Sunday. And when that wasn't on, there were movies and TV shows to watch and comic books to collect and read. I wasn't hurting anyone, was I?

I had been away from the church close to twenty years by then. And strangely, deep inside, I may have heard the smallest, quietest voice calling me back. I'm not even sure if I mentioned it to my wife. But over time, as she visited church after church in our area, sometimes traveling most of an hour to get to a Greek Orthodox church, I began to identify in myself a small but growing feeling as a hunger to be close to God again. One Sunday I surprised her by getting dressed and accompanying her and the kids to a local Episcopal church.

It were a small, historic Episcopal church nestled in the woods. There were a group of priests that took turns officiating at the services there. The congregants were a diverse group, with a vaguely hippie vibe, who had come from many Christian faith backgrounds. They were friendly and welcoming to us and to our kids. It was great to see them in the Sunday School nursery finger-painting with other kids. I thought that this might be our new church home. It was certainly convenient enough being five minutes from our home. But my wife, while acknowledging how pleasant it was and how nice the people were, said that it just didn't feel like church to her. And so she would keep looking and I went back to sleeping in on Sundays.

One Sunday a few weeks later, she and the kids came back from another "church shopping" trip. This time they had gone nearly an hour west to another Greek Orthodox church. I expected to hear her say how far it was and how long the ride had been and what a chore it was to haul the kids there. But that's not what she said.

"Steven, they have the most wonderful young priest there. He really seemed to speak to me in his sermon," she said.

I could see she was impressed, even moved, by the experience, but I just assumed she would keep "shopping". But that's not what she did. She went back to this distant church again and again. Now, I'm not big on long car rides. And giving up a chunk of my weekend wasn't exactly on my "to-do list". But curiosity and that small, but slowly growing, spiritual hunger inside me got me up and dressed early one Sunday to see what this church and this priest were all about.

I had been in Greek Orthodox churches before, but this one seemed to glow inside. The first thing I saw upon entering was a huge icon on the far wall of a woman with her arms spread wide and a little boy standing in front of her. Her face had a stoic beauty to it and an inscrutable expression that I found magnetic. I gazed around the church and saw that most of the walls were covered with icons of saints. I didn't know who they were, but the beauty of them was undeniable.

The choir, unseen, sang from a loft above and behind us. Two chanters intoned responses to the priest's prayers and readings. Even though half of the service was incomprehensible to me, being in Greek, it all seemed to speak to me. At one point a procession of altar boys carrying candles circled the church. Behind them the priest walked carrying a covered tray and chalice. Clouds of incense billowed from a censer. It was a feast for the senses.

I picked up a rhythm to the service as it progressed. I began to recognize certain phrases being repeated again and again. I didn't know what they meant, but the cadence and melody was hypnotic. The congregation stood and sat and stood again. They knelt at one point and arose again. It was clear to me that there was a deep reverence and meaning to these movements, even if it was unknown to me. Finally, the priest, in his white and gold vestments, spoke.

His sermon was brief. He spoke about the Gospel reading of the day and how it related to our lives. His words were plain and easy to understand, yet profound and true. There was an undercurrent of joy and love in his voice. And then he was done. We filed up to the front to receive his blessing and a little piece of bread. And we went home.

I understood what my wife meant when she had said that the little Episcopal service we had gone to didn't "feel like church" to her. If this was what church was, I wasn't sure if I had really ever felt anything like it.

My wife never asked me to go to church with her. She never asked me to go to THIS church at all. She didn't have to. I wanted to go back the following week. And the week after that. Each time I would enter that beautiful Sanctuary, I would feel like I had entered heaven itself. And familiarity with it and with the sights and sounds and smells of the Divine Liturgy only made that feeling grow stronger.

And this priest's brief homilies seemed, almost eerily, to be directed at me. My wife felt the same way. Week after week, he was somehow reading our minds and speaking directly to us. Over the weeks he spoke about

> "the depths of despair" and how faith can provide the way out,
> "a mother's love" and how we never outgrow it, even in our old age after our mothers are gone, and
> "physical disabilities" being a means for God's grace to be made manifest in us.

As I came to know and understand the Divine Liturgy by following along in the service book, which provided an English translation as well as the Greek text, it became apparent to me that there was a purposeful structure to it all. There were prayers, the presentation of the Gospel, the reading of Epistle and Gospel verses, recitation of the Creed (a statement of what we believe), the presentation of the elements of bread and wine, a mystical transformation of the elements into the Body and Blood of Jesus Christ, more prayers and then Holy Communion. Every Divine Liturgy offered a chance for the faithful to be physically united with Jesus Christ. As the Orthodox prayer book said so eloquently, Holy Communion allowed the people to dwell in Him and have Him dwell in them.

Once I had reached this level of understanding, I realized at once that I was starving for Holy Communion. And not just any Holy Communion, but Holy Communion as it was offered here, in this church (and in this Church). I spoke to Father Peter after the service. I told him I wanted to to learn more about the Greek Orthodox faith. We scheduled an appointment to talk further. He recommended a number of books about the history and dogma of the Orthodox Church. I read them all. It struck me that none of the beliefs of the Orthodox Church seemed foreign to me. It was a straightforward belief in God as given to us in the Bible. As I learned about the history of the Orthodox Church, this made sense as the earthly Church was in a sense, although eternal, "born" on Pentecost as described in the Book of Acts in the New Testament.

The Old Testament described the covenant that God made with the people of Israel and how they struggled to keep the covenant. It contained prophecies about the Messiah who was to come and stories of how the prophets were rejected or worse. For the first time I saw how the Old Testament related to the New Testament as the New Testament fulfilled the prophesies in the coming of Christ. The Gospels told Jesus' story and Acts told about the beginnings of the Church, which was the instrument He left for us when He ascended to heaven. The Epistles provided additional information about how the Church and its members should know and understand Christ and His teachings.

I also learned about the Orthodox Church's approach to the worship. First, it was eucharistic, with every Divine Liturgy being a "Little Easter", centered on Holy Communion with Christ. Second, the yearly calendar followed the life, ministry, death and resurrection of Christ as if they were happening now, as if we were active participants and witnesses. Third, prayer and fasting were the disciplines that were required for members of the Church to participate in the life of the Church. Life in the Orthodox Church is not a passive observance. It is an active, working experience. (I'd find out the literal truth of this before long.)

Everything I learned about the Orthodox Church drew me closer to it. I discovered a depth to the experience that included veneration of the Saints, including Mary, the mother of Jesus. I had known that there were saints in the Protestant Church, but I had not learned their stories and they had not been held up as examples and models for daily inspiration. And the beauty of the church itself was a constant inspiration. The "earthly heaven" in which we worshiped kept me in prayerful contemplation of how I was spending my life here on earth in preparation for an eternal life with Christ. The goal of constant prayer was made clear and attainable to me in the church. No matter where I looked, I was inspired. The sights, the sounds, the smells, the tastes surrounded me with holiness.

I think Father Peter saw how sincere I was and how deeply the Church was reaching me. I suspect he had seen others like me awakened by the centuries-old Church with its ancient, unchanged beauty and connection to the eternal God. We selected January of 2000 as the time when I would join the Orthodox Church. With my brother-in-law standing with me and my family looking on, I was chrismated, joining all of them in the Greek Orthodox Church. But this wasn't the end of my journey. It was only the beginning. The following Sunday I received Holy Communion as part of the Saint Barbara Greek Orthodox Church family. And the feeling of belonging, not just to the local church community, but to the world-wide Orthodox family of faith was amazing. And I was energized to learn more and to give back to this well of spiritual riches that was being poured out onto me.

In the sixteen years since that time:

- I was called to teach Sunday School and I sought and earned a Teacher Education Certification from the Greek Orthodox Archdiocese of America. There is no better way to learn something than to try to teach it. It forces you to read, think, and try to express your personal understanding. And if you listen to your students, they will teach you still more through their earnest questions. They will test your knowledge and challenge you to grow and learn more. It's a paradox that every time I try to give back, I end up receiving more.
- I was called to begin and grow the ministry of the Saint John Chrysostom Oratorical Festival at our church encouraging young people to speak about their faith in a program that is part of a nation-wide competition. Few things that I have ever done have been as gratifying to me as working with the young people and their families in this ministry. It's amazing to watch quiet, timid, nervous young speakers grow into confident, energized, powerhouses who lift up

and inspire people who are many years their senior. Parents who see this remarkable growth often credit me, which is flattering. The truth is I am no more responsible for this growth than a gardener is for making flowers bloom. I coach, encourage, and nag, but God's grace makes flowers and young speakers grow.

- I was called to facilitate a pre-marital workshop called "The Journey of Marriage" and travel to churches near and far to speak with couples about the Orthodox Church's view of, and role in, the Sacrament of Marriage. If I am honest, I have to admit that I am not quite a perfect husband. But like teaching Sunday School, delivering the content of this workshop to young couples is as much a benefit and education to me as it is for them. And when I go "off-script", it is often to relate truths that I am only just learning thirty years into my marriage. Looking into all those sincere young faces inspires me to try to apply the lessons I am teaching them in my own marriage.

- I was called to membership in our Parish Council and work on its committees including the parish Safety Committee and the Scholarship Committee. I am not being modest when I say that my talents don't really lie in the area of administration, debate, and decision-making required of Parish Council members. But I have served two two-year terms and found that what I can do, on a good day, is to facilitate those talents in others. I take inspiration for such work from my patron Saint Stephen, who was

chosen to assist with certain functions to free others to focus on the "ministry of the word".
- I joined with many of our church's members in work on fundraising and stewardship, lecturing on topics of faith, working in the kitchen, acting as a Summer Camp Orthodox Life teacher, assisting in the beautification of the church grounds and more. And at every step along the way I have found the brotherly and sisterly love of members of the church family from the youngest pre-schoolers to the most senior members who founded our beloved church and many of its ministries. And I have enjoyed the spiritual guidance and fatherly love of our priests and their wives, the *presvyteras,* who have generously poured out their wisdom, faith, and love on my family and me. It is impossible for me to explain the love, the wonder, and the joy I have felt in the discovery of this larger family I never knew I had. I hope that non-believers read these words and doubt how it can be. And I hope they come and see.

And all of this has come to me without me, for a moment, deciding that I wanted to "do good", "become a churchman", "get involved", or "help others". This all came out of my search for what was missing in my life. I'm like the reporter in O. Henry's "man about town". As you can read in other parts of this book, I have not always done the right thing. I sometimes feel like I have dug myself quite a deep hole and that God has provided His Church as a way to lift me out of it.

If I am seen by people in my church as being an example of someone who has done good things, has gotten involved, and has contributed to others, that was never my intention. Those things happened as by-products of my search for God's grace in myself. And ironically, every time I do think of one of my activities as being benevolent or philanthropic, I quickly find myself receiving more blessings than I can give. In trying to find what was missing in me, I have have become, through God's grace, a better man.

Go Out and Play

From my earliest memories, my mom would often tell me and my sisters to "go out and play". We did live in some pretty small towns, but we also lived in larger cities and her refrain was always the same. "Go out and play!"

When I was very young, and we lived in West Columbia, I wasn't allowed to cross the street. So I explored our small yard and quickly knew every tree, bush, blade of grass and every inch of our sidewalk. My sisters were older than I was and so had little interest in playing with me, although they like to tell stories about dressing me up in their "pretend costumes", mostly some of mom's old clothes and some old Halloween costumes. We did play hopscotch on the sidewalk and jacks on our little porch, but these didn't offer the kind of adventure a little boy was interested in.

Eventually, I would explore beyond our yard. I ventured down the sidewalk. I discovered our neighbor's beautiful roses and, in trying to pick one to take home to mom, discovered that roses have thorns. I quickly determined which houses on our street had dogs and which dogs were "friendly" and which were not. When you are eye-level with dogs, even the "friendly" ones are a bit intimidating. And the ones that bark, snarl and charge at you are down-right terrifying.

Down the street in the other direction was the McCain's house. Mrs. McCain ran a nursery school we called "play-school" out of her home. She had several industrial-strength pieces of playground equipment in her backyard and neighborhood kids would congregate there throughout the day. Sometimes I'd have the place to myself and other times the swings, merry-go-round, seesaws and monkey bars would all be full. You could wait for a spot to open up, but your best bet was to get in line for the big, tall slide. That line moved and you could have a lot of fun in short bursts. Plus you could get to know some of the other kids as you waited in line.

I met Laura Lee Snyder in line waiting to use the slide. Laura Lee was a pretty little blonde girl. She may have been my first female friend and eventually, maybe, my first girlfriend. We sat next to each other at play-school and I even walked her to her house afterward one day. She showed me her yard and the big tree she liked to climb in her front yard.

I had some experience climbing trees. We had a small tree in our backyard. There were two kinds of trees when it came to climbing: good ones and bad ones. Good ones had lots of low, reachable branches and then lots of branches that could be reached from those. The best trees had trunks that you could practically walk up, like a ramp. Bad trees didn't have any reachable branches, but were not unclimbable. You could get a boost from a friend up to the lowest branch. Or you could reach up and grab hold of low-hanging leaves. If the leaves didn't tear off, you could "hand-over-hand" it up the branch toward the trunk, slip a leg up and flip up onto a branch that you couldn't otherwise reach. Climbing up never was too much of a problem, but getting down could be. You had to look down to get down and sometimes you had climbed high enough up that the instinctive fear of falling to one's death would kick in. In minor cases, one would work up the courage to slide down to a jumpable altitude. In extreme cases, an adult or older sibling would be summoned to perform a rescue.

Laura Lee Snyder and I became friends bonded by a shared love of the cartoons *Magilla Gorilla* and *Peter Pottamus*. Even in the days when there were only three channels to choose from, there was plentiful cartoon kiddie fare in the afternoons on weekdays after the soap operas. I think that Laura Lee Snyder and I even talked about getting married during the commercials. Marriage seemed like a good way to ensure that our routine of play-school, tree climbing and cartoon-watching would continue uninterrupted well into the future.

I got it into my five-year-old head that to cement our engagement I should bestow on Laura Lee Snyder a token of my esteem. Flowers seemed like the obvious, if clichéd choice. Roses were out. Too thorny. So, I found some bluebonnets and Indian paintbrushes growing along the railroad tracks behind our house and created a nice little bouquet. Now, how to present them to Laura Lee Snyder with some style? I had it! I'd climb the tree in front of her house with the bouquet in my back pocket. When she came by, I would get her attention and drop the lovely gift down into her hands. Perfect. To get her attention, I would toss down a pebble.

My plan proceeded well until I got to the part where I had to find an attention-getting pebble. Laura Lee Snyder's yard lacked a good selection of pebbles. In fact, it really only had more sizable rocks. I selected the smallest of these, put in in my pocket and climbed up to my perch to await my future bride.

A few minutes later, Laura Lee approached according

to my plan. I tossed down the oversized "pebble" and my plan went awry. Rather than landing at her feet to attract her attention, it landed squarely on the top of her skull causing her to collapse in screaming agony. Her mother dashed to her aid. The two of them looked up at me with shock and horror etched on their faces. Needless to say, this ended our engagement.

*****

Our back yard in Bellaire was bounded by fences on two sides and large bushes in the back. The bushes had a sort of hollow area inside them, meaning that if you could push past a few outer branches you could actually go inside them. These little "rooms" became clubhouses, pretend spaceships, and hiding places, depending on the circumstances. In the heat of a Texas summer, after being told to "go out and play", our little, secret rooms in the bushes offered cool, shady comfort.

One of the neighborhood kids, Curtis, brought some of his treasures to the secret bush-room clubhouse one day. He had a troll doll, a Rat-Fink ring and a glass jar containing live bees. The troll doll had hypnotizing blue eyes and was naked, although not anatomically correct, presumably. And out of his head grew a shock of reddish-brown hair that we all thought was amazing. We had a discussion about where trolls fit into the pantheon of fairies, elves, and gnomes. This discussion led nowhere and was tabled. We turned to the Rat-Fink. The Rat-Fink ring held three actual Rat-Fink figures in blue, red and green. It was the product of an undisclosed amount of investment in a certain gumball machine at the local supermarket. I quickly added acquiring a similar ring to my 'bucket list'. And then we turned to the jar, empty but for three live, buzzing, flying honeybees. Curtis casually mentioned that he was starting a honey manufacturing operation with these three bees. I was desperate to get in on the ground floor. He explained to me the technique for catching the bees and even offered to help me get started. What a friend!

I popped into the house to secure an empty jar with lid which my mother handed over with nary a question. Curtis walked me to the lilies that formed the border between our two front yards. Sure enough, there were bees flitting about the large flowers. Curtis opened the jar and waited for a bee to land on a flower. He positioned the jar under the flower and the lid above the bee. In one smooth motion, he brought the lid down, nipping a bit of the flower off and screwed the lid on as tidy as you please. My only thought was about what I would call my honey company. I was thinking of a play on the word "buzz" or "buzzy".

With my mind more on marketing than production, Curtis handed me the jar and told me to try it. What could be simpler? I waited until a bee landed on a flower petal, unscrewed the lid from the jar and positioned the jar and lid in the approved manner. Then my honey empire plans went awry. The previously imprisoned bee, his prison door now open, simply flew up onto my hand and punished his captor in the only way bees know. He stung me.

Few sensations of childhood are as profound and impactful as the sting of a bee. Perhaps the pain of the needle of a doctor's syringe or the pained screams and accusatory finger-pointing of a former fiancé and her mother. I ran inside seeking the medical attention only a mother can give. An hour later, with much of the pain having subsided, she uttered those words again, "Go outside and play."

*****

In El Campo, a farming town, "going out to play" took on a new meaning. Yes, there were neat rows of track houses with lawns for playing ball on, and trees for climbing, but there were drainage and irrigation canals along which grew wild berries and in which lived water moccasin snakes, which are poisonous. And beyond the few small blocks of our subdivision were vast plowed fields stretching as far as the eye could see.

During the school year, we stayed close to home, playing in the neighborhoods, especially in Brent Tuttle's fort. His dad ran a real estate agency and Brent was an only child. This meant he had some of the coolest toys on the block. One of them was an actual building! It was a pre-fab plywood shed perched atop four five-foot high four-by-fours. It had a window, wooden steps, and a door, which could be locked from the inside. It was great for pretending all kinds of things from war, to pirates, to spies. And it was there that he showed me the first copy of Playboy I ever saw.

During the summer, though, "going out to play" meant carefully stepping through a barbed wire fence and walking out into the fields. I remember walking for hours in cotton fields until, like a ship at sea beyond all sight of land, we would be so far out into the fields we couldn't see our neighborhood or anything but cotton fields stretching out in all directions to the horizon. Sometimes there was a group of five or six of us. As we walked one of us would spin some yarn about the cowboys and Indians that used to live and fight and die right where we were standing. Sometimes someone would find an old, rusty machine part and we'd speculate what kind of weapon or tool it came from. And one day we came upon a gigantic pile of soil that had been baked almost solid by the sun. We broke off chunks and threw them at each other in a game that was part dirt clod fight and part "king of the mountain". I don't remember anyone ever getting more than a scratch or skinned knee.

And somehow, once the sun started to get low, we always headed back in the right direction and always made it back to our neighborhood in time to hear someone's mom calling out that it was dinnertime. Those days seemed to last forever. Maybe someone would have brought an old metal canteen and shared swigs of warm, metallic-tasting water, or maybe we just ignored that we were thirsty. My parents never asked where I was all day. Mom would ask if I had eaten lunch and not seem bothered that I hadn't. They never asked who I was with. There was just an assumption that the neighborhood kids were all good and would look after each other. In 1966 and 1967, while the Summer of Love and psychedelia were happening elsewhere, it might as well have been 1950 or 1930 where we were. Our corner of the world seemed like a safe, unchanging place.

On rainy Saturdays, one of the neighborhood moms would load a bunch of us kids into her station wagon and drop us off at the movies. That's right, just drop us off. We'd each have thirty-five cents in our pocket and that would buy a ticket to whatever was playing on the one screen inside. Sometimes it would be a second-run kiddie picture like *The Three Stooges Go Around the World in a Daze* or a dubbed Italian Hercules movie. Other times it would be a western or a Jerry Lewis or Bob Hope movie. Sometimes it would be a Hammer Pictures horror film! Whatever it was, we watched it. I even remember watching the spaghetti westerns of Sergio Leone starring a young Clint Eastwood. And after the movie, we'd go outside. Sometimes it had gotten dark. It was such a weird feeling to go inside from the bright sunshine and exit hours later into darkness. And we'd somehow find whoever's mom was picking us up parked, sometimes a block or two from the theater. There was never a fear that one of us would wander off or be molested in any way.

And we behaved too, because if you didn't, they wouldn't throw you out, but they would confine you to a small soundproof room with uncomfortable folding chairs within the theater so you wouldn't bother the rest of the audience. (It was also used for crying babies, so it smelled like baby poop.) How do you like that? Even the "bad" kids got taken care of until their parents would come pick them up. It was a simpler time.

*****

In Corpus Christi, we didn't have endless fields to wander, but there was a neighborhood full of kids that all went to the same school. At nine and ten, it was the age when boys played sports. Yes, maybe there was Little League baseball and Pop Warner football, but we played sandlot pick-up games. Oh, the endless hours, the endless days of playing until the sunlight failed or until our parents called us in. Whoever had the biggest, widest, flattest yard hosted the games. And rules were made up on the spot or handed down from dad to older brother to us. If you didn't want to kickoff to start the game or didn't want to punt the ball (because you weren't a good kicker or because you didn't want to break a window) you could "p for k" (pass instead of kick). If you didn't have enough guys to field two teams, you could call "permanent quarterback" or "permanent rusher" and play on both teams. We rarely kept score or if we did, we'd rebalance the teams if things got lop-sided. It was so much less about winning and so much more about playing.

There was an undeveloped parcel of land that was our "park" and home to many of our baseball games. When construction began on houses at the far end of the parcel, our field took on odd dimensions and we had to make "ground rules" to account for the ball landing amongst the bulldozers and backhoes. And after five o'clock, when the construction crews left, we could explore the building lots and pretend to be in prison or in a castle. Everything was grist for our imaginations.

As part of a family that moved around a lot, I heard another phrase from my mother in addition to "go out and play". It was "go out and make some friends". She would say this shortly after we had moved into a new neighborhood. She'd tell me to "go out and play", to which I would reply, "With who? I don't know anyone!" Then she'd tell me to "go out and make some friends". And I would do just that. Believe it or not, I would go to the house next-door to ours and ring the doorbell. If an adult answered the door, I would ask if any kids lived there. If not, I would either ask if they knew where any kids my age lived, or I would simply go to the next house and repeat the procedure. If a kid answered the door or was summoned by the adult who did, I would say, "Hi. I'm Steven Yates. I just moved in. Will you be my friend?" And they would invariably say yes. Sometimes we would become actual friends. Other times we would play together a time or two, usually with other kids and end up being mere acquaintances. The world was just a friendlier place back then.

That's how I met Ernest Garcia, a stocky kid in my third-grade class. He was new to town too, so we became friends at school. He lived down the street from me and he invited me over for dinner. Of course I went over to his house, with my parent's permission. We played ball in his yard until his mother called us in. I met his parents. They didn't speak a word of English. It seemed a little odd, but they were nice and the *arroz con pollo* turned out to be chicken with rice and tasted delicious. Ernest translated for me the few times I spoke to his mom or dad and a few days later, we had him over to our house.

Ernest introduced me to Joey Garcia (no relation) and Isaac Benavides and the three of us were the closest of school friends. Isaac could do a killer Woody Woodpecker imitation and kept the rest of us in stitches. I remember asking Joey and Isaac if they would be my friends. Isaac told me that I had asked too late. We were already friends. I wish the world had stayed as friendly as that.

*****

In Houston, I found a houseful of friends right next-door. The Somers family had four boys. Bobby was my age, 11, then came Timmy, 10, Michael, 8, and Terry, 4. They were practically a baseball or football team all by themselves! I pretty much lived at their house on weekends and in the summer. There were endless games of backyard baseball and football, but also other events. One grown-up neighbor had Estes rockets. He recruited all us boys to be his "field team". We went to a large vacant lot at the end of our street and he shot off these model rockets that went a couple of hundred feet into the air before drifting back to earth via parachutes.

We boys would scramble to try to catch, or at least recover, the rockets.

Digression - Mr. Somers worked for Hunts Foods. One day after we had lived there for a few months, Bobby came over and said I had to come back to his house right away. He wouldn't tell me why. I left and my parents didn't raise an eyebrow. In the Somers living room was a huge man wearing a lumberjack outfit. It was Big John. Hunts' newest product as the time was "Big John's Beans and Fixin's". It was a can of pork and beans that had a smaller can of "fixin's" taped to the top. You were supposed to open both cans and mix them together to make a "home-style" bean dish. Hunts did a huge advertising campaign to introduce the product and Big John was the mascot of the product. And here, in the flesh, was Big John. Of course, after shaking his gigantic hand and getting an autograph, a ten-year-old boy doesn't have a lot to say to an over-sized actor/model, so I went home with the tale to tell my family. - End of digression.

During the summer in Houston, Mrs. Somers or my mom would load all us boys into the car and take us, not to the movies, but to the Astrodome. We were all members of the Astro Buddies Fan Club. For something like five dollars, you got a book of coupons. Some were for discounted tickets, others were for free tickets. Free! We'd get dropped off with some change or maybe nothing in our pockets. We'd head to the Astrohall, flash our Astro Buddies cards, and be admitted to a vast room filled with long tables. We would be served Borden orange drink and ice cream. Then the Astros radio announcer would come out and introduce an actual Astros baseball player! He would do a brief interview and then we would be released into the Eighth Wonder of the World, the

Astrodome. Our free seats were in the "blue level", a stratospheric altitude above the playing field into which had only ever been hit two balls. The seats those balls landed in were decorated. One had a painted toy cannon representing Jim "the Toy Cannon" Wynn, my Astro Buddy. And the other had a painted red rooster for Doug "the Red Rooster" Rader, Bobby Somer's Astro Buddy. We would walk over to those seats and marvel at how far they were from home plate.

The games were usually far from memorable. The Astrodome had deep fences that made for low-scoring games, pitcher's duels that bored the young fans who were eager to see home-runs and offense. To amuse ourselves during the three hour 1-0 snore-fests, we would run all around the the stadium and wait for the computerized score board to put on one of its amazing graphics displays. Although primitive by today's standards, we were agog at the simulated fireworks and animated bull and cowboy.

Sometimes there would be an added event after the game, like a display of military hardware like jeeps, tanks and helicopters, as part of an Army recruiting campaign or a prize bull on display to promote the Houston Livestock Show and Rodeo. We'd stroll up and down looking at whatever was being shown that week. And somehow, miraculously, we'd find my mom or Mrs. Somers and pile into the car and go home. And we were not special in that regard. Literally thousands of Astro Buddies were simply dropped of at a big-city ballpark and turned loose for the day with no adult supervision of any kind. And no one went missing. No one got hurt. No one was kidnapped, murdered, or molested. Parents weren't seen as neglectful. Nobody worried about the liability. It was as normal as going to church or school.

*****

The last place I was told to "go out and play" and "go make new friends" was in New Canaan. Maybe it was the difference between Texas and Connecticut. Maybe it was the difference between 1970 and 1971. But it was different. At least in some ways.

I remember my middle sister and I walking down the street on a hot, bright August morning toward a group of a dozen kids, some on bikes, some just standing around. Some of them had turned to wordlessly watch us approach, giving us no greeting, no smile. When we were among them, we were met mostly with blank stares.

"I'm Steven Yates and this is my sister Michele. We just moved into number five," I offered.

Silence.

I tried again, "So, what do ya'll do around here for fun?"

If I had thought the silence was awkward, the cascade of derisive laughter that answered my question was a hundred times worse.

"YA'LL?!?!?!" came the group reply. "YA'LL?!?!? Where are you from?"

I made a mental note to never say "ya'll" again and to this day I never have without thinking about it and making the conscious decision to do so.

"Houston. We just moved here from Houston. So, do *you guys* play baseball?"

And with that, the tension began to ease as a couple of the guys my age began explaining the ground rules for the street baseball they played in the cul-de-sac. My sister kind of split off and began talking with some of the girls and a couple of rougher-looking kids kind of drifted away from the group.

Over the next few weeks, before school started, I made friends with most of the kids. They seemed to do many of the kinds of things I had done with my friends in Texas, but they were also different in some ways. They often hung out inside, watching TV, or playing board games or cards. They would "go into town", that is, make the mile or so journey on foot or by bike to the little town center. There some of them had an established routine of visiting The Cheese Shoppe for free samples, the sporting goods store to get a drink from the water cooler. It was the kind with the big glass jug on top that would bubble and glug when you filled your little cone-shaped paper cup. Then we'd swing by the library and grocery store (for more free samples). And then we'd head home. It was a way to kill some time without spending any money or getting into any trouble.

Those rougher-looking kids? They were a sign of things to come. Looking back, there were probably equal parts adolescent testosterone and family breakdown that were responsible for the seemingly sudden presence of a whole group, in my neighborhood and at school, of these longer-haired, intentionally sloppily-dressed, young men with practiced vacant stares and slack-jawed, uncaring attitudes, slightly stoned and looking for trouble. Some were bullies. Some were just trying to drop out of the clean-cut America that popular culture in all its forms was telling us was no longer cool. Ironically, in their efforts to rebel and not to conform they simply established another "tribe" with its own strict codes of behavior, dress and belief to which they dutifully conformed.

I found them pretty disturbing. I was afraid of their lack of respect for authority and more personally afraid of being attacked by them as they saw me as definitely not being part of their "cool group". But thanks to the lack of motivation that was part of their code, they never seemed to organize enough to do anything more than express contempt and vague, unfocused menace. Still, at the time, I became aware I had to watch out and try to keep a low profile lest I become a 'target of opportunity'.

Going out to play and making new friends had become a more serious, perhaps more dangerous business. And I could easily write this off as one of the realities of growing up and not part of some larger cultural phenomenon, except that many years later, I had kids of my own. This was twenty years since the last time I was told to "go out and play" and to "make some new friends", but in those years, things had changed. I only have my experience to go by, but I have heard reports from the field that back up my assumptions.

Parents don't just turn their kids loose like they once did. Parents don't trust "the neighborhood" to take care of their precious offspring. Parents want to know where their children are, who they are with, and what they are doing. Allowing an eight-year-old to roam miles from hearth and home with unknown neighborhood kids with no means of contacting them for eight hours or more constitutes neglect or even abuse these days. No reasonable parent assumes that all the kids and adults their child will meet are benevolent or even benign. And why should they? The world has changed. Those rough-looking kids have multiplied. Some of them are parents now and their kids are tough and shrewd and recognize the weak and vulnerable as easy targets. More families have only one parent and that parent goes off to work. And left to their own, not all kids learn the virtues of tolerance and friendliness. Some learn the virtues of toughness, shrewdness, and intimidation.

And so we have the playdate, carefully arranged, vetted play by appointment. And we have heavily-supervised team sports year-round. We have individualized programming (drama, dance, or music) designed to produce well-rounded young people who do well in school so they can get into, and do well in, college. So they can get good jobs and good mates and repeat the cycle. This is the safe way to raise children today. But I do feel bad for these kids who never know the feeling of fearlessly striking out on their own new, daily adventure and returning home from it each evening. I wonder how or where or even if they learn to embrace the unknown and to take that first step outside their comfort zone.

GETTING MY FIRST HUG UPDATE

I am frequently asked by those who have read my first book, how our son is doing. I am pleased to report that he is doing very well indeed, thank God. The degrees that he was pursuing in community college have been achieved, <u>with honors</u>. On May 26, 2016, he was awarded Associates degrees in Multimedia and Broadcast-Cinema. I take enormous pride in his achievement, especially when I think that these are largely "communication degrees". Take that, autism. He is gainfully employed in his field of study. Thank you very much.

Each semester in college with our son followed a similar pattern. He would have three or four classes. We would ask about them and get minimal answers from him. As the semester would proceed, we would ask how he was doing and get a shrug or an "OK". Sometimes he would express concern about one class and say that it was hard or that he didn't think he had done well on a test. We would offer help and suggest that he talk to his professor or the Disabilities Office. And when the semester was over we would wait anxiously for his grades. And then he would nonchalantly mention that he had gotten two A's and a B+, or something similar. It happened over and over to the point where we stopped worrying.

Most of the classes he took were of at least some interest to him. Even in classes that he wasn't particularly keen on, he would persist and do the work and end up doing well. I think perfect attendance, turning in 100% of the homework, and occasionally asking for help indicated to most professors that he was a serious student who was trying. He would also give each professor a letter from the Disabilities Office at the beginning of the semester indicating that he should be given preferential seating, more time on tests, and a study guide. These were the few, small concessions available under the Americans With Disabilities Act. He had to do all the same work and pass all the same tests as every other student. And he did, making the Dean's List numerous times and being invited to join the honors fraternity, Phi Theta Kappa.

At long last he entered his final semester, Spring 2016. He took his final three required classes. Two of them were not a problem. But a few weeks into the semester, we heard, as we had so many times before from him, that he had bombed his first few quizzes in the third class, Intro to Psychology. We gave him the usual advice. Ask for help, extra credit, even a tutor. He came back to us and said he wanted to drop the class. He could "walk" with his graduating class in May, take the Psych class online in the summer, and graduate without ceremony in September. He was at the point of giving up.

My mind drifted back to my own college days. I remembered the temptation to quit all too well. But I also remembered the persistence and ultimate success he had studying for the driver's test seven years before. He told me the deadline for dropping the class was two weeks away. There would be two more quizzes before then. I asked him to let me work with him for two weeks. If he got good results on the two quizzes, would he stick with it? Yes, he said, not really thinking that was possible.

I asked him about the quizzes he had taken and bombed. They were multiple choice and focused almost entirely on the vocabulary of each chapter. I borrowed his textbook and read the next chapter. It was about memory. The thirty or so vocabulary words were highlighted in bold type and defined in the margins. I made a list of them. Then I made a list of just the definitions on one page and a numbered list of just the vocabulary words on another. He had to match the words to the definitions. I gave him the quiz. He got fifty percent correct. We reviewed the ones he missed and I gave him the quiz again the next day. He got sixty percent correct. That's passing. I scrambled the definitions and the words, we reviewed the ones he missed, and I gave him the new quiz.

Eighty-five percent correct! We repeated the process a few more times until he got them all correct!

When quiz time came, he brought home an A! Ninety percent correct! A week later we repeated the process with the next chapter. When quiz time came, he brought back a B. Eighty percent correct! When the deadline for dropping classes arrived, he decided to hang in there. Each week I would prepare a practice quiz for the new chapter. Each week he would struggle at first, then, with repetition, effort, and review, he would improve until he mastered the material. He was passing. Then came the final exam. It was on his birthday! It would actually be two chapter quizzes followed by a final exam on all ten chapters.

Our study time was cut down due to having to study for the final exams in his other two classes. We did what we could. I had to "back-fill" the four or five chapters that he had bombed before we teamed up. There was a lot of material, but some of it was review and he hadn't forgotten much.

Digression - In my mind, I imagined meeting with his psychology teacher. Surely she knew what autism was. For Pete's sake, it was one of the vocabulary words in Chapter 12 Psychological Disorders! I imagined explaining to her how our son learned, how her lectures were mostly lost on him. Lectures can be "just a lot of talking" to our son. He learns best through examples and repetition. And once he learns, he does not forget. But the delivery of the material must be in a form that he can digest. He had succeeded in so many other classes. Scriptwriting. Algebra. Audio Production. TV Production. Advanced Media. Editing Workshop. Digital Imaging. The irony of psychology being a stumbling block was almost too much for me to handle! If there was a teacher of a subject who ought to understand that a bit of special handling of the subject matter might be needed to accommodate a student on the autism spectrum, wouldn't you think it would be the psychology teacher?!? - End of digression.

Moving ahead, I knew that he would simply overpower the material through brute-force memorization. Our son has an amazingly powerful memory and if this teacher was going to evaluate the students in this way, well, then we were going to succeed in this way. And when the grades came back, it was a B-. And more importantly, he had completed his college course work!

And on a warm May afternoon, before a crowd of several hundred including the college professors, deans, administrators, a US Senator, other dignitaries, and fifteen delighted relatives including his mom, his sister, and me, our son received two diplomas, Associates Degrees in Multimedia and Broadcast - Cinema. As I watched him receive those degrees and shake hands with the dean, my mind was flooded with emotion and memories and, to paraphrase Kurt Vonnegut, I became unstuck in time. Suddenly I was back in our basement, sitting on the floor across from our beautiful baby boy, showing him a picture of a red ball and trying to get him to tell me what it was. I blinked and I was in the bleachers of the high school gym watching him sink his first basket in a competitive game. I blinked again and I was in the auditorium watching him play the baritone horn. A moment later I was in our church watching him lead the Great Entrance procession carrying the cross at the head of a line of twenty other altar boys. And the next instant I was in our kitchen with my arms outstretched, overjoyed to finally feel his little arms encircle my neck and squeeze. As my old friend had told me so many years before, "There is nothing wrong with this kid." I feel so privileged to get to see this ongoing miracle and be a part of it. As I saw him graduate and the tears flowed down my cheeks I realized I was getting another hug from my son, one that would never end, that I could take with me wherever I go and enjoy whenever I liked. It was glorious!

*****

And I am proud to further report that a few months prior to graduation, our son applied for and was hired as a Video Technician at a large arena not far from our home. He operates the cameras that provide the images on the big screens for sports, concerts, and other events. He lives with us, but we've already begun talking about the future and he may have his own place before long.

We see the miracle in him continuing every day. His interpersonal communication skills continue to grow in ease and spontaneity. His sense of humor, intelligence and insight are more in evidence each time we converse. And he remains the sweet, caring, sensitive young man he always was. I pray that God continues to guard, guide and protect him, holding us all in His hands forever. Amen.

As for the book *Getting My First Hug*, I am happy with its reception. I've sold a lot of copies and given away many too. I am pleased by the reaction I get from people who are touched by the stories and moved by our family's journey. I am especially happy when people who have someone with special needs in their life tell me that the book has provided them with hope and comfort. Do I wish sales were larger? Of course. But my wise and beautiful wife reminds me that success is measured in many ways and the tears of a mother who has been inspired by my words beats an appearance on the *New York Times* best-seller list any day.

I've done some print interviews, a local TV spot, a few book signings at churches and bookstores. It's actually a lot of work to try to publicize a book. A writer doesn't really think about that when he's writing. And there is a certain amount of privacy that one must give up in exchange for the media exposure to promote a book. Up until now I've been pretty comfortable with that tradeoff. I can certainly see where others might not be. And so I have used very few actual names in this book. I am keen to preserve the privacy of my family and the people whose paths I have crossed over the years. They didn't ask to become part of my story. And they aren't able to provide their side of the story. So the least I can do is give them anonymity.

One of my favorite "reviews" came from the aforementioned old friend who is featured in the book in the chapter called "There's Nothing Wrong With This Kid". He's a hardworking, former-lumberjack from Maine and as tough a guy as you'd care to meet. We got together for lunch a few weeks after I had given him a copy of the book. As he sat down at the table he looked strangely solemn.

"Well, you made me cry twice," he said, finally, chuckling. "I've never had a book do that to me."

In Maine, that is considered "four stars".

The other "review" came from the wonderful actor, director, writer and storyteller Stephen Tobolowsky, with whom I have become friends over the past few years. Stephen writes and tells the most wonderful stories about life, love and show business in his podcast, "The Tobolowsky Files" and in his books, including *The Dangerous Animals Club* and *My*

Adventures With God. The truth is that my style of storytelling is largely inspired by his.

I sent him a copy of *Getting My First Hug* and hoped he would like it. Now Stephen is an actor who has appeared in well over 200 movies and television shows. He works as much or more than any actor in Hollywood. And when I say we are friends, we have exchanged several emails and tweets. And he and his lovely wife, actress Ann Hearn, were gracious enough to share a drink with me after one of his performances in New York one evening. So, I had no idea if or when he might ever actually have the time or the inclination to read my little book.

Last March I caught up with Stephen in Boston at the premiere of his wonderful live concert film *The Primary Instinct*, directed by David Chen. Again, he generously took time to greet my wife and me afterward. He and I took a few pictures and then he asked my wife and me if we would join him back in the now-empty theater. I couldn't imagine what he wanted.

"I read your book, Steven. It's very good. I really liked it," he told me.

I was so happy I almost couldn't believe it. I told him he didn't have to say that.

"No, really. I gave it to Ann. She's reading it now," he said.

Now Stephen is a great actor and a super-nice guy and I wanted to believe that he would enjoy my writing as I have enjoyed his. It was one thing for him to say he liked it, but if he had passed it on to his wife and she was reading it, he must *really* have liked it. I was overjoyed. And then he told me he was writing another book of stories and asked if I would review the pre-publication "galleys". Would I? Absolutely! What an honor!

And that clinched it. He didn't have to tell me about the new book, much less invite me to read and comment. He must *really* think I'm a decent writer! Maybe I am a decent writer. No. Wait. Gosh darn it, I *am* a good writer!

I'll try not to let it go to my head.

*****

www.ingramcontent.com/pod-product-compliance
Lightning Source LLC
Chambersburg PA
CBHW071227290426
44108CB00013B/1315